"Colorful and dramatic. Orly Lobel masterfully draws us in with rich details, urging us to consider the future of innovation and the many ways in which companies employ litigation to achieve market domination."

—Jonathan Zittrain, best-selling author
of *The Future of the Internet*

"Orly Lobel takes the legal campaign that Mattel, the producer of the iconic Barbie, waged against MGA, maker of the upstart Bratz, and spins it into a tale that manages both to fascinate and to illuminate how over-reliance on intellectual property law can damage, rather than aid, innovation."

—Christopher Sprigman, author
of *The Knockoff Economy*

YOU DON'T OWN ME

OTHER WORKS BY ORLY LOBEL

Talent Wants to Be Free

Encyclopedia of Law and Economics (co-editor)

To Janine and David,
Enjoy!

YOU DON'T OWN ME

How *Mattel v. MGA Entertainment*

Exposed Barbie's Dark Side

ORLY LOBEL

W. W. NORTON & COMPANY
Independent Publishers Since 1923
New York • London

For information about permission to reproduce selections from
this book, write to Permissions, W. W. Norton & Company, Inc.,
500 Fifth Avenue, New York, NY 10110

For information about special discounts for bulk purchases,
please contact W. W. Norton Special Sales at
specialsales@wwnorton.com or 800-233-4830

Manufacturing by LSC Communications, Harrisonburg
Book design by Dana Sloan
Production manager: Lauren Abbate

ISBN 978-0-393-25407-5

W. W. Norton & Company, Inc.
500 Fifth Avenue, New York, N.Y. 10110
www.wwnorton.com

W. W. Norton & Company Ltd.
15 Carlisle Street, London W1D 3BS

1 2 3 4 5 6 7 8 9 0

To Danielle, Elinor, Natalie, and all the other leaders of tomorrow who are gutsy, creative, and deliciously competitive.

And to On Amir, I love you.

And another woman has usurped
The place that ought to have been mine

—AKHMATOVA, NORTHERN ELEGIES

There is no point in witnessing the destruction
of a man who is thoroughly virtuous or who is
thoroughly corrupt.

—ARISTOTLE

CONTENTS

AUTHOR'S NOTE

A SUBSTANTIAL PART OF the book is anchored in the *Mattel v.* MGA *Entertainment* litigation papers, which span thousands of pages of testimony, briefs, evidence, and judicial decisions. I also spoke to dozens of sources while researching this book's stories. Some wished to remain anonymous, and some appear front and center, like Judge Alex Kozinski. Mark Lemley, whose productive energies are unrivaled, generously connected me with key people for interviews. I am grateful to the lawyers on both sides of the litigation who candidly shared their experiences, including Patricia Glaser, Annette Hurst, John Keker, Jennifer Keller, Michael Page, and Michael Zeller, and a number of jurors, whose personal accounts of the trial helped me better understand the atmosphere in the courtroom. I have also spoken with independent experts in the toy and entertainment industry. With respect to Mattel and MGA, I requested interviews with senior executives at both companies. At Mattel, I was able to speak to Tim Kilpin, who served as executive Vice-President of the Boys & Girls Global Brands, and then as Mattel's President and Chief Commercial Officer. Bob Eckert, Mattel's then CEO, declined to comment on his time at Mattel. At MGA, I interviewed its founder and CEO, Isaac Larian. Finally, my numerous attempts to reach Carter Bryant, including through his relatives, were unsuccessful. Accordingly, all references to Bryant's background and personal life come from court records and interviews with other parties involved in the litigation. I thank all those who passionately shared their stories of hopes, dreams, losses, and victories with me.

INTRODUCTION

SHE WAS BLONDE AND beautiful—statuesque, with long slender legs, a tiny waist, and a chest so large that Finnish researchers claimed any similarly endowed woman would surely tip over. For years, Carter Bryant dutifully served her. He styled her hair, dressed her in skirts, dresses, and luxurious gowns, adorned her in jewelry, and even applied her makeup. She always looked fabulous. Day after day, week after week, she was unblemished, shiny, and new. And in a three-billion-dollar industry, she dominated over 90 percent market share for five decades. Perhaps that was what Carter despised: her perfection—the absence of a single flaw. She never changed. While people gained weight, their skin wrinkled and sagged, and their hair grayed, Barbie stood perfect and frozen against a changing world.

While she remained ageless and pristine, the world that she had been born into ceased to exist. Everything was raunchier and more perverse. Barbie remained maddeningly clean. A real artist, Carter saw beauty in the broken, the peculiar, the queer, perhaps even the grotesque. Like many creative people trapped in dead-end jobs, he experienced the angst of a servant whose golem had become the master. He dreamed of a new deity. He imagined a new icon that better reflected the modern world, using the beauty of real people. Carter had not intended to assault Barbie's persona, her public image, or those invested in maintaining it. He hadn't even planned to confront his master. He could not have consciously dared to dream of the millions he would make from his rebellion, the millions in ensuing losses, and the decade-long legal battle that would not only change Barbie and the Mattel Corporation, but forever alter both the entire toy industry and the very laws governing creativity and competition. He certainly couldn't have foreseen the incredibly ferocious feud between his overpowering ex-employer and the flamboyant entrepreneur who gambled and risked it all to take a chance on him. Nor did he predict that lawyers would drag both his life partner, Richard Irmen, and his own mother, Jane, to testify on his behalf, asking them to reveal deep-seated intimate details of his life and passions. Most certainly, his dreams would not have included suffering depression and a stroke at the age of forty-one. Carter Bryant only wanted to build his own dream house, away from Barbie.

The story about when exactly Carter Bryant conceived of Bratz, the anti-Barbie doll, the first doll to present a true market challenge to Barbie since her 1959 debut, changes with the teller. The how and when of these dolls with oversized heads and diva-like attitudes is the *sine qua non* at the heart of the billion-dollar lawsuit waged by mega-doll companies Mattel and MGA—the corporation that developed Bratz—for over a decade. According to Carter himself, inspiration hit one afternoon while he was officially on leave from Mattel and living with his parents in Kimberling City, a small town in western Missouri. He traces the precise moment of inspiration to a fateful drive home from the local mall, where he was temporarily working at an Old Navy, when a group of spirited high school girls walked past him. Here was a man who, after spending years in Southern California working on a supposedly teenage doll, suddenly realized Barbie looked nothing like these teenagers. These young schoolgirls shared almost no traits with Barbie, by then in her late forties, yet still sporting a body even a supermodel would envy. At the turn of the century, Carter felt the edgy reality of American youth had little to do with the plastic Barbie, who, despite her unspoken X-rated German past, was so obviously frigid and oh-so-vanilla-white.

In contrast to Barbie's milquetoast façade, the teenage girls Carter spotted coming out of the gates of Kickapoo High School were sassy, hip, and vibrant. They showed midriff and defied typecasting. Unlike Barbie's straight blonde hair, their hairstyles were funky, short, spiked, and colorful. They did not wear pleated skirts and knee-high socks. They wore oversized clothes, baggy jeans—clothes that Carter's bosses at Mattel would have found too shabby, too lowly, and too, well, bratty, for their ice queen. After the serendipitous encounter with the group of teenage girls, he sketched his vision for a new generation of dolls—girl power for the twenty-first century. Little did he know that the sketches would seed both an empire and a billion-dollar lawsuit. And little did we know that the doll wars are, in the words of poet Rabindranath Tagore, where "the whole world meets in a single nest."

It's not all fun and games at the world's most famous toymaker. Mattel appears in court regularly, and from its inception it has sued numerous artists, musicians, competitors, and even its own executives. Play is a sensitive thermostat, and behind the curtains of the cheery toy world we uncover the business strategies presaging cultural shifts and the realities of corporate machinations, backstabbing, and grudges. Indeed, Barbie's very inception can be traced back to international wars over originality and copying. At every turn, Mattel, the aging titan, vigorously attempts to control the image of its iconic best-selling doll, even when the prices paid are deceit, loss, and brutal failure. Although the ultimate battle between Barbie and Bratz began in California, the war is international, from Hong Kong to New York, from Germany to Mexico. The executives leading the charge are near polar opposites in personalities and temperament, yet toying with market shares proves each is susceptible to emotions clashing against rational business decision making. As increasingly is the case among leading brands across all industries, the fights in the toy industry are now focused on controlling existing ideas rather than creating new ones. The battle hymn for market dominance demands that we ask: Does the current hyper-protection of intellectual property promote more innovation or perversely impede it?

Embarrassing internal memos reveal the state of panic at Mattel in the face of competition. The launch of Bratz is described in a document by Mattel executives as a "rival-led Barbie genocide," and the document announces: "This is war and sides must be taken: Barbie stands for good. All others stand for evil." But fighting for Barbie's life ain't cheap, and litigation has taken an enormous toll on both companies. Mattel's estimated legal expenses in its losing battle against Bratz alone has exceeded four hundred million dollars, while MGA, a newcomer to the toy industry, has spent nearly two hundred million dollars defending Bratz. Even more costly, however, is the effect of litigation on the spirit of the companies and their ability to sustain their economic dominance, and no less important, the effect on the personal lives of those partaking in the battle.

Sun-Tzu's timeless truth in *The Art of War* shines light on this story: sometimes you need to lose the battle to win the war. This is a story about how the quest for innovation can lead to ferociously unethical behavior, quashing creativity and innovation itself. It's a story about the risky transitions from ideation to commercialization and what happens when too many cooks claim the inspiration for one invention. It's a story about a savvy yet controversial libertarian judge who has made an incredible impact in taming our contemporary illusions about the law's overreach. It's a story about how passionate people who go against the tide—from attorneys to CEOs, from inventors to artists, from jurors to entrepreneurs—courageously shape our country's ideological, economic, cultural, and legal landscapes. This story is for all those who have ever experienced the creative spark, for all the leaders who are committed to their path and mission, for all employees whose ideas were ever passed off as their boss's, for all entrepreneurs who faced a Goliath who fought dirty, for all parents who ever doubted the choices they make for their children, for all women who feel the unrealistic pressure of femininity, and for all of us grinding through grueling competition in pursuit of fulfillment and success.

• • •

From a young age, while other children were playing with toys for fun, I was learning about the toy world's grip on society. It began when I was nine. My mother asked me to star in some videos. She also asked that I bring some friends along for a strange kind of photo shoot. Fear not! These were not the type of movies that stage moms hope will turn viral and catapult their children into stardom—videos that make viewers cringe and decry the end of childhood. In fact, the videos were quite the opposite, comprising a central part of my mother's groundbreaking research seeking to understand play. My mother is a renowned psychology professor who has published pioneering studies on childhood development. She videotaped me, as a young girl, in research clips designed for experimental studies on the development of gender roles in toddlers, preteens, and teens. In the videos, my friends and I were filmed playing with "girl" toys—Barbie dolls, tiaras, and pretend makeup—and then, in another set of films, with "boy" toys—cars, balls, and Transformers. As part of the experiment, my mother screened these films for groups of children all around the world and asked for their reactions. Among the insights of her research was that, consistently, girls who play with typical boy toys enjoy a boosted social status. Boys, on the other hand, are penalized when they play with traditional girl toys. So, from an early age, I entered the research world and inadvertently became a critic of the toy industry. Rather than just playing with dolls, balls, and everything in between, I began considering how playing with toys shapes our identities, our relationships, our social status, and our future. Despite, or perhaps because of, the numerous hats I have worn over the years—professor, author, researcher, lawyer, military intelligence commander, wife, and mother—I have never stopped studying these ideas. The way we play matters; just as the ways we create, compete, consume, and sell make us who we are.

The toy industry, despite its sweet, innocuous façade, is as ruthless as the most cutthroat businesses in Silicon Valley and on Wall Street. For over a decade, Mattel executives have been in crisis mode: sinking millions of dollars into undercover espionage, counterintelligence operations, and lawsuits. Barbie, their ice queen doll with a veiled German hooker past, was suddenly dethroned by a modern, voluptuous, multiethnic doll that entered the hearts and homes of children across America. What happens if Mattel can prove that the newcomer Bratz—Barbie's greatest competition since making her market premiere—was secretly born in the confines of Mattel's high-security facilities? As Mattel fights against the upstart MGA, maker of Bratz, its own toy empire unravels and its secret history—laced with backstabbing, financial scandals, sexual impropriety, racial tension, ego, and greed—is unearthed. The trials of the industry have fundamentally shaped our markets and society. They've shaped not only childhood play and consumption but also the laws and policies concerning copyright, patents, trade secrets, trademarks, employment contracts, antitrust, product safety, and the scope of fair competition. These trials challenge the right and freedom to leave jobs, compete with incumbent companies, control ideas, and innovate. Ultimately, these battles between toy titans reveal the true colors of contemporary global competition.

Our story begins with genius and creativity and becomes a cautionary tale about how economic wars can slowly morph into a personal vendetta. The twists and turns along the way are a microcosm of litigious America and how the personalities of judges, jurors, and witnesses can make or break court battles. At its core, this is a story about how once-innovative companies can become complacent, opening space for new visionaries to upset the status quo. In my previous book, *Talent Wants to Be Free,* I argued that, whether you look at high-tech, pharma, entertainment, or financial industries, business strategies that imprison talent and attempt to appropriate every creative spark are counterproductive. Today, in the global talent wars, all companies must make decisions about the flow of ideas and knowledge within and outside the organization. Too often, corporate leaders make tactical moves that prove to be detrimental to their success in the long run. Alexander de Tocqueville, a Frenchman observing the nineteenth-century American landscape, famously said, "Scarcely any question arises in the United States which does not become, sooner or later, a subject of judicial debate." To channel Tocqueville in the twenty-first century, when the greatest battleground is on the front of innovation, scarcely an innovative challenge arises that does not sooner or later blossom into litigious action. Intellectual property is the bread and butter of the modern company, and California—home of celebrity and technology—is where the action happens. Be it Apple, Facebook, Twitter, Disney, or Mattel, corporate America's greatest assets are intangible, and the intellectual property wars are steaming hot. Behind the scenes, the fight over innovation raises fundamental questions about corporate leadership, market concentration, consumer behavior, and the psychology of creativity.

The toy wars are also a window into a world where gender, race, sexuality, class, nationality, and childhood all translate into profit in the global consumer market. By the time I reached middle school, I had already developed at least some sense of the toy industry's impact on society. Yet I knew little about the corporate forces that shape the toy market. Like most girls, my body image was inevitably affected by the unrealistic messages blasted by all-pervasive marketing, and I was drawn to fashion and boys from an early age. Truth be told, I was as blonde and slender as could be, but my environment offset the risk of turning into a "plastic" woman myself. From the very beginning, I was raised to resist the Barbie-pink messages of my world. Fortunately, I was also encouraged to challenge the distorted realities of Barbie's world. I was taught to value brains over beauty, and I was lucky enough to have role models who encouraged my aspirations to excel in active military service, law school, and academia, all while becoming a mother of three. Ironically, of all her roles, from Malibu Barbie to CEO Barbie, parent—certainly the most meaningful role for many of us—is one that Barbie has never played.

"Barbie *c'est moi*," exclaimed Andy Warhol's muse, BillyBoy* (who, for no apparent reason other than to be close to a star, spells his name with an asterisk), inspiring the final portrait the pop artist painted before his death: a portrait of Barbie. Barbie has influenced much of western culture for better or worse. She has shaped the world of play for three generations. By Mattel's estimates, 90 percent of American girls aged three to ten own at least one Barbie. And if you collected all the Barbie dolls sold in the first three decades since her creation and placed them leg-to-leg, they would wrap around the Earth four times. But Barbie's reign was destined to end. The legal wars waged over these dolls have led to explosive court battles, federal investigations, public outcry, and overturned lives. After outselling every other doll ever made—with more than a billion dolls sold in over 150 countries—the twenty-first century signals an end to Barbie's reign.

In 2015, for the first time in decades, Mattel was no longer the world's number-one toy company. How did its amazing success eventually spiral into costly, irrational, losing battles in the face of new inventions, entrepreneurs, and innovation? How did its corporate executives fail so spectacularly to keep up with the realities of market competition, the tastes of consumers, and the realities of the global toy industry? How do business practices shift from visionary and ethical into multiple shades of gray?

As a lover of free speech, fair competition, and talent mobility, I welcome with open arms the disruptive shocks rocking consumer industries. *You Don't Own Me* is the result of years of investigation and research into hundreds of internal corporate memos, archives, court records, and financial reports, as well as dozens of conversations with insiders, executives, designers, inventors, entrepreneurs, judges, jurors, and attorneys. The rise and fall of the world's most iconic plaything lays bare the power plays of those who control our contemporary markets. *You Don't Own Me* is a call to arms for all of us who consume and compete in these markets.

PART ONE

CARTER'S ANGELS

1 | INSPIRED

I love LA. I love Hollywood. Everybody's plastic,
but I love plastic. I want to be plastic.

—ANDY WARHOL

IN AUGUST 2000, CARTER BRYANT, a designer at the world's largest toy maker, Mattel, reached into the office trash bin, which the Southern California company labeled *basura* (Spanish for trash for all you non-Southern Californians). Out of the *basura* came a discarded Barbie head, a plastic body, and a pair of Ken doll boots. Carter then went home and put them together, along with a few pieces, clothes and accessories, from his personal collection. MGA, Mattel's nearby competitor, would later refer to this mock-up of recycled trash as *FrankenBratz*. For Carter, reaching into the trash bin that fateful morning meant reclaiming his creativity and ownership over ideas that were continuously discarded at Mattel. In an innovate-or-die industry, dumpster diving is routinely treated as a threat, quite possibly even a federal crime. Corporations claim ownership over any and all tangible and intangible items, even those trashed.

Everyone working at 333 Continental Boulevard in El Segundo, California, was conscious of Mattel's high-security measures. A twenty-four-hour surveillance camera lurked around every corner of the 180,000-square-foot design center. Employees donned color-coded badges that granted access to sensitive areas. Few visitors were allowed into the compound, and, if admitted, guests were required to sign a confidentiality agreement and wear a specially marked badge indicating low clearance. Having visited and consulted for similar high-security companies, I can attest that the badges mean what they say; you cannot wander off, even if just to the restroom or cafeteria, without someone accompanying you. At Mattel, no one may remove property from the building without a pass. In stark contrast to Mattel's thorough surveillance, the company bans guests and employees from bringing in cameras or recording devices. Security personnel make sure that phones aren't used for taking unauthorized pictures. One copywriter at Mattel even recalls being told at a meeting to speak with his face turned away from the window, just in case someone outside with a telescope might read his lips.[1] You would think that they were making weapons of mass destruction rather than plastic toys. If Carter Bryant forgot his badge one morning, he could only enter the office if his supervisor issued a temporary day pass.

The Mattel corporation would later accuse Carter of being a mole: "a double agent of the highest, or lowest, order." The Mattel plant certainly resembled the type of place secret agents might lurk, but Carter, shy and soft spoken, his angelic baby face framed behind wire-rim glasses, his eyes a pale blue, was no James Bond, nor was he the Bond villain. Rather, he seemed closer to a timid and creative young Elton John. Carter, a dreamer, an artist, a designer, an employee turned entrepreneur, and even an occasional songwriter, would become the unlikely hero in the longest, most heated litigation in the doll-eat-doll toy industry.

Carter Bryant was born in 1960s California during a time of economic revival. Americans were finally shaking off the dust from the Great Depression and World War II. As the aerospace industry boomed in California, and the housing market rushed to meet the needs of the new middle class, the very fabric of modern-day popular culture began to unfurl. McDonald's, whose founders were also living in Southern California, became a household name, and halfway through the decade the Big Mac was born. Barbie too had been born in California just a few years earlier. It was a decade that consolidated the state's dominance in entertainment and lifestyle. And yet, the great West was not all prosperity, growth, and innovation; Americans had only recently condemned segregation, and racial tensions remained high. Friction between African Americans and the police collided like tectonic plates running along fault lines beneath a fragile, peaceful surface.

One late summer day in Los Angeles, those tensions became seismic and shook the city to its very core. The riots raged for five days, left thirty-four people dead, and resulted in over 3,400 arrests. This was the City of Angels, the kingdom of Barbie, and the city in which Carter Bryant experienced his first taste of popular culture. La La Land is like that, built on the coexistence of extreme contrasts: impossible beauty, wealth, freedom, and hedonistic living alongside poverty, crime, oppression, and ugliness. Reflecting the same ambivalence toward Los Angeles that would recur throughout his life— attraction and repulsion—Carter and his family moved in and out of California throughout his childhood. When he was only five years old, Carter moved with his parents to Washington State for five years, then to Alaska for three, and back to Southern California. His parents left again for life in the Midwest after Carter graduated from high school. This constant desire to leave California, followed by the irresistible pull back to Los Angeles, shaped Carter's quest for both professional integrity and dazzling commercial success as an adult.

Carter discovered his love of art as a young child. He was making art, he says, "right from the very beginning when I was very, very young." Carter was good at it and drew comics, cartoons, figures, and greeting cards. At twelve years old, *Archie Comics* printed one of his sketches of Archie's girlfriend Veronica in a fringed jacket. Veronica had long, shiny black hair and pouty lips; she was stylish and curvy, while still giving the impression of a sweet teenage child—young Carter already had a type.

Carter's love of art wasn't limited to drawing. He was also passionate about fashion and merged the two worlds early in life. After watching an episode of *I Love Lucy* set in a Hollywood fashion studio, nine-year-old Carter was hooked. The glamorous world of fashion had entered his veins, and all he wanted was to one day be a part of it. He was driven to draw larger-than-life female characters and imagine their beautiful clothes. His mother subscribed to *Vogue* and *Harper's Bazaar*, and Carter eagerly perused the magazines, albeit furtively because these were not the kind of interests expected from a teenage boy in the 1970s. Carter admits, "I was one of those weird kids who liked Barbie as a boy." But unlike some parents who tried to force their son to "man up," Carter's mother was supportive and encouraging. She kept a scrapbook, which over the years grew to hundreds of pages of Carter's drawings of comic characters and fashion sketches. The *Archie Comics'* girls, Betty and Veronica, were prominently featured. The scrapbook also contained dozens of other subjects: drawings of angels, fairies, fashion models, goddesses, and mythological heroines.

As a teenager, Carter was back in California, attending Apple Valley High School in San Bernardino County, where he took advanced art classes and dreamed of a career in design. After graduating, Carter applied to two of the best design schools in the country: Otis College of Art and Design in Los Angeles and Parsons School of Design in New York. Though he was admitted to both, Carter says he chose Otis over the more prestigious Parsons to minimize costs and to stay closer to his family. Looking back, though, perhaps the real reason he chose Otis was that his heart, and the path to his own angels, lay in Los Angeles.

Though not as celebrated as Parsons, Otis College, founded in

1918, is a prominent arts college and one of the finest in California. Otis is particularly acclaimed for its fashion design program. That Otis is housed in downtown Los Angeles means that its students benefit from direct contact with top designers who offer constructive criticism and advice. Vera Wang, Isaac Mizrahi, Todd Oldham, and, my personal favorite, Diane von Furstenberg, are among the designers who support the program by teaching master classes and leading extracurricular events. Carter took hands-on courses, learning to cut fabric, design patterns, and craft accessories. He also took classes in art history to balance practice with theory. He enjoyed learning, but after only one year at Otis he became restless and anxious about the cost of his studies. He decided that life in Los Angeles, while surely not as expensive as New York, was still more than he could afford. He moved back in with his parents in Missouri. His break from Los Angeles would not last long. For Carter, all roads led to California, and Barbie paved his way back to both Los Angeles and fashion. In 1995, less than a year after leaving college to return to the safe nest of his parents' home in the Midwest, Carter applied for a job at Mattel and was called for an interview. His audition and screening test: draw Barbie as a superhero. Drawing a fashionable icon as a spirited immortal? Why, he had been preparing for this kind of work all his life! Carter drew a magnificent cartoon of Barbie flying through the air with her too-good-to-be-true figure defying both gravity and velocity. He got the job. He was hired first as an hourly temp and, a few months later, as a full-time Mattel employee.

If high-fashion design was the dream, designing clothing for fashion dolls was a pragmatic second-best for an aspiring designer. As a person close to him told me,

> *Carter always wanted to be a high-fashion designer since he was a child. He's always reminded me of that character, Dorfmann, from the film* The Flight of the Phoenix—*Dorfmann is an aeronautical engineer who designs toy planes and he insists that it's "exactly the same." But Carter*

didn't want to just color in variations on the same old fashion Mattel had always given Barbie. He wanted to do something different. He hit a wall, though, because Mattel was hostile to change.

Mattel, however, was the only real player in the fashion doll industry and Barbie, with a 90 percent market share, was the only doll worth designing for.

Although designing clothes for Barbie seemed sterile from the start, it is not uncommon for aspiring fashion designers to begin their career designing fashion for dolls. A recent success story of this path is designer Jason Wu, who graduated from Parsons and began his career, much like Carter, as a designer of fashion dolls. Wu's path from dolls to haute couture was meteoric. He rose from the anonymity of doll fashion to designing first lady Michelle Obama's 2009 and 2013 inauguration gowns. Carter had similar aspirations to elevate from serving the plastic tastes of Barbie to covering the flesh-and-blood bodies of real women of all shapes and colors. Equally important, he hoped one day to rise from a rank-and-file creative employee to an independent designer running his own show.

Carter was twenty-six when he started his first round of employment at Mattel, and he was positioned in Mainline Barbie, the part of the business geared for children. His promotion came in the form of a move to Collectible Barbie, the department that made dolls for the adult devotees who continued buying the most expensive version of Mattel's anchor product. Carter was in charge of designing new dresses, planning color schemes, and coordinating the hairstyles of new dolls in the line: for example, Goddess of Beauty Barbie, a limited edition of Barbie wearing "an extraordinary sky-blue crepe gown and a magnificent toga adorned with golden, ancient Greek motifs." Carter was soon bored. Mattel itself was bureaucratic and forced ideas into narrow boxes, determined by people whose understanding of fashion was, Carter felt, subpar. At the very top, Bob Eckert, Mattel's CEO, was a striking example. He knew nothing about fashion or toys. He came from the fast-food world and initially focused most of all on cutting costs.

Carter wanted a footing in the fashion world—the world of *Vogue* and *Harper's Bazaar* that populated his childhood dreams. Instead, he found himself working on what he felt were "widgets and gadgets." He was also tired of constant rejection. Among his many ideas, Carter conceptualized and presented a new Barbie body, more contemporary and realistic, that his bosses refused to let see the light of day. He was seeing too many good ideas shelved under the wheels of bureaucracy—flung into the intellectual *basura*, the trash heap, buried in the graveyard of discarded pitches. But most frustrating was the fact that the ideas that did advance from lab to market were not necessarily good. Mattel was political, risk averse, and stuck in the past.

In May 1998, four years after joining the Barbie team, Carter took some time off. He missed his family and wanted a break from the corporate grind, a break that would give him the space he needed to reclaim his passion. He was in the midst of one of his painful breakups from Richard Irmen, Carter's on-again-off-again boyfriend. Though both inventors, the two could not be more different. According to one of Carter's attorneys, Michael Page, "Carter was a sweet mama's boy who invented angels; Richard this tough guy who invented a knife that could stick into people without breaking—all the police departments were interested." Carter needed some time away from it all. His boss at Mattel, Cassidy Park, also an Otis alum, was sympathetic. She allowed a leave of absence and even offered him freelance work for his time away—another Barbie collection project. He took the freelance work, but much like with the other endless variations of Barbie's wardrobe, he was bored by the assignment. It was just another dreary version of the same ice queen. Carter was pulsing for something edgier. He longed for artistic freedom and the creative spark ignited by his sketchbook. Truth be told, he was also hoping for an adequate reward for those sparks—something beyond a mere monthly salary.

Carter immersed himself in sketching, hoping to reinvent himself in his life away from Mattel. The important thing was that he felt liberated from Mattel's claws and was intent on making his mark in the world of design. He sketched clothing lines, card concepts, and angelic figures. His drawings always returned to girls, and, most often, little angels. Restless and in need of a real job to pay the bills, he rekindled one of his first loves: greeting cards. He designed a series he called Rainy Day Rascals—brightly colored figurines underscoring the power of friendship with phrases like "Whenever I need you, there you are." He applied for an illustrator position at Hallmark, but jobs were scarce and Hallmark never made him an offer.

Mattel would later claim that Carter was using the word *Angel* as a secret code for Bratz, but Carter insists that he had simply been working, quite literally, on angel projects. During his leave, he did some freelance work for Ashton-Drake Galleries, a high-end collectible dolls company, and worked on a wintery angel doll line and a series of illustrations called Southern Brides.

So why did Carter take that seven-month break in 1998, away from Mattel and Southern California, where the grass, real or fake, always seems greener and the girls so pretty? Why would Carter leave the City of Angels to live with his parents and work as a sales clerk at the far-from-haute-couture Old Navy in small-town Kimberling City, Missouri? Was he, as Mattel alleged, scheming to take on the world's number-one toymaker and America's top-selling doll, the very same corporation that gave him his first chance as a designer? Or was he just hoping to resurrect the boy who had sketched angels and made his mother proud?

Carter acknowledges that his leave from Mattel reignited his passion for creative drawing. Far away from Barbie, while continuing freelance and odd jobs, he realized that his desire was to create his own, entirely new line. Bubbling with different ideas, Carter's first instinct wasn't to create a contemporary doll. Rather he went retro and, ironically, created the exact opposite of Bratz in Sabrina, an old-fashioned, transformable fashion doll. Sabrina was imagined as the in-house model that fashion houses used in the 1950s. Carter captioned his sketches of Sabrina, "Every once in a while a girl comes along to steal your heart away. That moment is now." In Carter's blueprint for Sabrina, she had snap-in hairpieces and a removable ponytail. Accompanying Sabrina were a three-piece outfit, hostess pants, a slim skirt, a bolero jacket, a shawl, a sleeveless turtleneck, a clutch purse, and (of course) extra shoes. On one of Sabrina's drawings, Carter wrote, "Sabrina lands a television commercial demonstration, the latest in kitchen appliance technology." Carter mapped the entire scene: Commercial Model Sabrina would come with a kitchen foldout, an accessory pack with kitchen items, and a coffee percolator, blender, and toaster. Sabrina would have a chef's outfit, an apron, oven mitts, head kerchief, and shoes—a far cry from the sassy, midriff-baring doll Carter would later create.

Although Carter looked back in time to create Sabrina, working on the new doll propelled him forward. The imaginative part of his brain shifted into overdrive. As John Steinbeck used to say, "Ideas are like rabbits. You get a couple, learn how to look after them, and pretty soon you have a dozen." Perhaps Carter needed to experience the ultraconservative for his creative pendulum to swing back in full force to the ultramodern. Sabrina's role, while important, was mainly in allowing Carter to design a full, rich concept. The toy industry rests on concepts that represent a universe. Creating a new concept for a doll line means creating her entire world: her personality, hobbies, and history.

Like many an artist, Carter was known to doodle ideas on napkins, on the back of menus, on place mats, or, in his words, on "just anything." If you want to prove in court the moment in which you doodled something, you better have some neatly filed records. As for Carter, sometimes he would pull out the sketches, rip the pages out of the spiral notebook once he was done, and shove them into his large art portfolio. Other times, he would leave the page in the notebook, the same notebook that he would then use for other doodles, or to write up phone messages or shopping lists. He sketched on whatever was available with whatever he could grab. "Whatever's handy. It can be a pen, pencil, marker," Carter recalled, highlighting the triviality of these choices—the artist's mind doesn't succumb to categories or divisions of media or material and isn't dictated by legal evidentiary rules that may arise down the line if a big kahuna corporation decides it owns the artist's creations. When sketching fashion, Carter would begin with pencil, then ink it in, moving in steps from first drafts of looser sketches to tighter drawings; from black and white to color; from skeletal sketches to detailed illustrations. Carter recounts, "That's the way we were taught to illustrate at Otis—to begin on tracing paper, put it onto a light box, and then create your drawing on another board."

Where does inspiration come from? It comes from the world around us, the people we meet, and the images that both consciously and subconsciously penetrate our minds. Looking back at his time away from Mattel, Carter says, "Inspiration can really come from anywhere. It can come from something you see or a magazine, book, people on the street." It can, of course, come from a combination of all these things. Carter explains that creativity takes time and a willingness to experiment. Artistic expression inevitably changes with movement from concept to concrete expression: "A lot of fine-tuning; starts with one thing, develops and just keeps going until I get to where I'm happy with something." For Carter, inspiration struck in Missouri when he saw a group of teenagers leaving Kickapoo High School together. Carter found the real-life Missourian girls irresistibly fresh. As he took out his sketchpad that evening to draw what he had seen, he recalls thinking, "Wouldn't it be cool if there were some characters that accurately represented today's teenager?" As a designer and artist, he had the skill and the will to take what he saw and make something completely new. According to his partner Richard, Carter always slept with a sketchpad at his bedside so he could sketch the most inspiring of his dreams. Seeing these high school teens allowed ideas, which were already deeply planted in Carter's heart, to blossom—ideas he had almost given up on while at Mattel.

In what can only be understood as a snub of Midwestern culture, Mattel executives later asserted in court that it was impossible for a place like Kickapoo High School to inspire anything as hip as Barbie's competitor, Bratz. A decade after Carter saw them, the principal of Kickapoo High School would fly to California to testify before a jury that her teenagers knew how to have fun; that they were tuned into pop culture; that at a school dance in 1998, five seniors at the high school mimicked the Backstreet Boys. To top it off, MGA's attorneys would bring evidence that Kickapoo High School even claimed one of Hollywood's most famous, handsome actors as its alum: Brad Pitt. What other school can make such a claim to fame? And yet, Carter didn't care about any of these superficial details. He just thought the kids at Kickapoo embodied an exciting new energy. So what if they did not grow up in Los Angeles? All the more power to them. Driving by the school, Carter realized a simple truth: even if Hollywood acts as the origin of most pop culture, Californian kids did not monopolize its consumption or its inspiration.

Carter, energized by his serendipitous encounter with the bubbly high school kids of Kickapoo, came home and began feverishly sketching a group of girlfriends. He gave them personalities: they were popular and hip, but neither fancy nor stuck up. They had attitude and self-confidence. They were fearless and strong. Carter drew their hands on their hips to convey "just a bit of defiance," as he jotted down to himself. He first drew a Hispanic girl and named her Lupe. Next came to life an African American girl, Hallidae, and Carter scribbled after her name, "plays drums and spins the turntable, studies French, acting, political science." Jade was Carter's Asian girl, whom he sketched skinnier than her friends. She had attitude but was also "fun and kooky." Carter dreamed of Jade "playing bass and studying classical violin and child psychology." Zoe, the leader of the pack, was a bit sweeter, softer. The magic in Carter's creation was that he made the girls edgy *and* smart. When he sketched his angels he was in the zone, forgetting the constraints of time or space. Hours could pass like a split second. With feverish inspiration, Carter sketched the foundation of his universe, and in the end he wrote above: "Meet the Bratz: They are the cool girls from your school."

Over the next few weeks, Carter continued to breathe life into his four girls. He gave them nicknames: "Meet Zoe aka Angel"; "Meet Lupe aka Princess"; "Meet Hallidae aka Hip-Hop"; "Meet Jade aka Li'l Star." He filled out their individual characters. After getting to know Hallidae a little better, Carter jotted:

Favorite color: Lavender.
Favorite insect: Bee.
Favorite food: Mac 'N Cheese.
If you were a fruit: Nectarine.
Pet: Dalmatian.
Favorite music: Hip hop and reggae.

For Jade, he decided "Favorite color: Pink. Favorite insect: Drag-onfly. Favorite food—nothing." Perhaps in this way he had indeed been inspired by Barbie. Carter too was at fault for being comfort-able with commercializing stereotypes and questionable notions of femininity. Each of his girls had a distinct ethnicity, and the Asian had an eating disorder. But this would all change before the Bratz hit the market—the rigid ethnic lines were Mattel residue that MGA rejected before bringing Carter's dolls to market.

Kickapoo girls ignited the spark, but during those winter months of 1998 Carter drew inspiration from other sources as well, resolved to recast his life away from Barbie. In particular, one issue of *Seven-teen*, a magazine geared toward the teenage market, further filled his mind with girl power images and attitudes. The cover featured Drew

Barrymore, and on the inside was a photo of the Dixie Chicks with "Chicks with Attitude" captioning their strong feminist image. The band, Carter later remembered, had "kind of a gaze" that exhibited an attitude of independence and defiance. They had style and beauty, as well as smart thoughts and opinions. Several years later the Dixie Chicks would launch a political campaign against the war in Iraq and take on serious social issues. These were the kind of girls who would study political science and psychology, mix classic strings with hard rock, and, regardless of the consequences, stay true to themselves.

Perhaps most influential on Carter's initial sketches was a full-page Steve Madden advertisement he spotted while flipping through the issue. The shoe designer's ad *Angel/Devil Girl* featured girls with disproportionate body features, big feet, big heads, pouty lips, and small torsos. "I liked the fact that the proportions were off," Carter said about the Steve Madden ad. He remembers being intrigued by the way one model's hand was clenched into a fist and how her look was exaggerated. This recollection would hurt him as well. In the heat of trial with Mattel over the ownership and inspiration for Bratz, Carter pointed out that the Steve Madden ad had inspired him, hoping to show that his inspiration did not come from work he did at the Barbie department. But in the doll-eat-doll world of litigation over inspiration, the designer for the Madden ad, Bernard "Butch" Belair, immediately launched a lawsuit of his own against Carter, as well as against the two dueling toy companies, MGA and Mattel— not knowing which would eventually prevail in its ownership claims over Bratz—for copying the image.

But in those early days of inspiration, none of these lawsuits were yet on the horizon. Carter was in the creative zone rather than embroiled in defending his creativity against so many who would later want to own it. Carter inhaled inspiration from all the images he encountered. In that same magazine, just a few pages later, a Coca-Cola ad also caught his eye. A girl with a furrowed brow, a full pouty mouth, waving her finger—another girl with an extra dose of attitude, he thought. Then there was Paris Blue, a jeans ad featuring a girl with a big head and big eyes, pouty mouth, the sparkle of a disco ball, and an animated face—a girl who owns the world. It was a critical mass of images together confirming for Carter what he had long felt in his bones: the era of Barbie was reaching its end. 1998 was a year when Japanese Anime found mainstream success in the West; the Spice Girls were hot, before Victoria, aka Posh Spice, morphed into a domesticized Mrs. Beckham; and Angelina Jolie was super-adventurer Lara Croft, before her underwhelming transition into the domesticated Mrs. Smith. It's undeniable that Jolie, with her humongous eyes and almost nonexistent nose, who later married, and eventually divorced, that irresistible Kickapoo alum Brad Pitt, looks a little bit like Carter's fantastic four. Leonardo da Vinci mused that the artist sees what others only glimpse. Carter believes that "different inspirations make an idea come together." The year's inspiration consolidated into one brilliant billion-dollar idea. It was time for Bratz to knock Barbie off the fashion doll pedestal.

Until September 1998, Carter feverishly continued creating his angels. Reinvigorated by the project, he worked constantly and passionately, but he needed to start seeing some actual money from his creations. He set up a website for his greeting cards and continued to send samples of his designs to agencies. He felt that Bratz was not yet ready to be shown to the world, and his search for an agent to represent him as a greeting card artist was fruitless. It seemed that his pursuit of a life away from his nine-to-five cubicle at Mattel, where inspiration was boxed into changing Barbie's scarf color from scarlet to crimson, was going nowhere. After only seven months away from Los Angeles, Carter diffidently returned. Nearing his thirtieth birthday, he felt a need to "get back to something that was actually earning me a steady income."

Right after Christmas 1998, Carter returned to Los Angeles. He got back together with Richard. On New Year's Eve, he showed him the Bratz drawings. For now, it was only Richard and Carter's mother who saw the sketches, and no one else. Although both Mattel and MGA would later refer to Richard not as Carter's life partner or spouse, but as his "roommate" in court proceedings and testimonies, Carter and Richard would share the small fortune. In fact, Richard eventually squandered Carter's money away in frivolous real estate ventures, though their relationship would continue well into the years of stress and pain unleashed by introducing Carter's devilish dolls to the world. For now, returning to Los Angeles required Carter to be practical and realistic. Reluctantly, Carter made the dreaded call to his old supervisor Cassidy Park at Mattel. And as the new year arrived, Carter put aside the drawings and once again began working for Mattel, the company he seemed unable to escape.

2 | BASURA

Twice or thrice had I lov'd thee,
Before I knew thy face or name;
• • •
I bid Love ask, and now
That it assume thy body, I allow,
And fix itself in thy lip, eye, and brow.

—JOHN DONNE, "AIR AND ANGELS"

WHEN CARTER REJOINED MATTEL'S Barbie Division, he shelved his Bratz dreams. Mattel assigned Carter to the Grecian Goddess series of Barbies—another old-style concept they hoped to recycle and refurbish. After that came a Hollywood series, an Alice in Wonderland Barbie, and a Swan Barbie. At Mattel, everyone worked with the Barbie Exposure Gauge: a headless doll with a blue line marked across the chest. Designers had to fit their outfits against the gauge, and if any blue appeared, Mattel refused to use the outfit for their wholesome Barbie. Again, Carter felt suffocated and far from his dreams. His days turned gray far quicker than during his first stint at Mattel. But, hoping to remain in Mattel's good graces, he turned to *Vogue* for inspiration in timeless high fashion and updated his portfolio with attractive gowns for their collectible lines. On his own time, he drew a hatted woman, draped in a cape and holding a leashed dog. He captioned her, "Society Hound Barbie with Greyhound."

Mattel, though bureaucratic and overbearing, did notice Carter's undeniable talent. A new Barbie collector's doll—the Grand Entrance Collection Barbie—paid tribute to Carter as the designer. Cloaked in a light-blue ballroom dress, Grand Entrance Barbie called to mind Disney's Cinderella. The box featured Carter's photograph, and read:

> *Dear Barbie doll collector, I'd like to welcome you to the delightful world of Barbie doll collecting. Designing for Barbie is very much like designing for a high-fashion couture house.*

Down at the bottom, the box featured *About Carter Bryant*:

> *Carter Bryant has been drawing fashions since he was nine years old and always thought it might be fun to design for a Barbie doll someday. Happily for Barbie, that date came five years ago when Mr. Bryant agreed to join the fashion design staff for Barbie doll, and later, Barbie collectibles. His extraordinary natural talent for designing women's fashions combined with his formal training from Otis College of Art and Design has been beautifully captured through many remarkable fashions for the Barbie brand.*

Carter was following in the footsteps of an iconic figure. The first designer named on a Mattel Barbie box was BillyBoy*. BillyBoy* was a young jeweler when, in the mid-1970s, he became known as Barbie's greatest collector. He owned over eleven thousand Barbie dolls and three thousand Ken dolls, and actually designed, as a freelancer semi-celebrity, two dolls for the company—the "Le Nouveau Théâtre de la mode" Barbie in 1984 and the "Feelin' Groovy" Barbie in 1986. Artist Andy Warhol turned BillyBoy* into something of a muse. Toward the end of Warhol's life, he met Billy-Boy*, then just a teenager in New York City. BillyBoy* had consistently balked at Warhol's requests to paint a portrait of him but finally told Warhol, "if you really want to do a painting of me, paint Barbie, because Barbie, *c'est moi!*" paraphrasing Gustave Flaubert's comment about Madame Bovary. Warhol took it quite literally. He painted a portrait of a Barbie doll, provided by BillyBoy*, and named it *Portrait of BillyBoy**. Warhol, who famously painted portraits of Marilyn, Elvis, Jackie, Mickey Mouse, and, of course, cans of Campbell soup, ended his illustrious career with that painting of Barbie. A version of this Warhol painting now proudly hangs in Mattel's headquarters.

After Warhol's death, BillyBoy*, perhaps like Carter Bryant, jaded by the blonde doll queen, gave up his Barbie collection and sold the painting for over one million dollars. When interviewed in 2015, BillyBoy* declared, "If I had a daughter I would not give her Barbie dolls. I wouldn't want my child to be constantly obsessed with getting something and that immense preoccupation with high-heeled shoes and clothes."

Was it the fate of all Barbie's greatest fans to not only move on, but also aggressively reject their once-beloved doll? For Carter, a credit on a Barbie collectible was indeed an honor, but still far from the recognition and creative liberty he craved. Mattel's acknowledgment neither captured Carter's dreams nor paid the bills. Like most inventors and artists working for corporate America, Carter was never paid any royalties for his designs for Mattel. The toy industry, like most other industries, rarely rewards individual inventors. When Carter started working for Mattel, he signed the same standard contract that so many American workers are asked to sign. It assigned to Mattel all his future creativity and innovation with no obligation of Mattel to reward any such innovation beyond Carter's base salary. Carter's contract assigned "all inventions as defined, conceived, or reduced to practice at any time in his employment." The contract defined "inventions" in the broadest possible way: " 'Inventions' includes, but is not limited to all discoveries, improvements, processes, developments, design, know-how, computer data programs, and formulae, whether patentable or unpatentable."

An anomaly of the American legal system is the complete absence of any requirement for businesses to compensate their employed inventors. President and lawyer Abraham Lincoln explained that granting exclusive copyright and patent protections to creators and inventors adds the "fuel of interest to the fire of genius."[1] A look at American patent law, the system that is specifically designed to reward genius with interest, reveals one of its most striking features to be that, unlike other prominent patent systems around the world, it requires no reward for employee-inventors. Meanwhile, other countries in regions ranging from Europe to the Middle East and throughout Asia all require companies to give some type of fair-share reward to the employee-inventor.

Germany, for example, does not allow carte blanche preassignment agreements like the one Carter signed. China, now a high-rate patent nation soon to surpass most of its Western competitors, mandates employers to give the employee-inventor reasonable compensation, including at least 2 percent of any profits obtained from exploiting the invention and at least 10 percent of any licensing profits. The Japanese system similarly guarantees employee-inventors a reward for assigned work, and, recently, the Japanese Supreme Court breathed new life into these compensation standards, when a scientist sued his previous employer, Nichia Chemical, for compensation for his contributions to a commercial blue-light-emitting diode. Initially, the company awarded the employee $200 for his invention—a crumb of a crumb from a lucrative product. A Tokyo district court decided this was not enough and awarded him ¥20 billion ($190 million).

While American companies are under no similar obligation to share profits with the employee-inventor, there are a few smart companies that have, under their own initiative, put into place reward systems for their workforce. Qualcomm, for example, the San Diego-based wireless telecommunications research and development company, as well as the largest chip supplier in the world, gives its employees a significant reward for any patents. Hewlett-Packard's "right of first refusal" program is another example. When an HP employee develops an idea on his or her own time and volition, HP requires disclosure and the right to market the invention, but grants the employee a share of the profits. Mattel, however, offered Carter nothing for his innovations. For the most part, at least for its creative designers (as opposed to its top executives), it used sticks more than carrots to prevent employees from leaving. This occurred despite California, relative to other states, boasting a long-standing aversion to the over-control of human capital. California, unlike all other states, bans noncompete agreements. But California companies still enjoy the same intellectual property laws and similar contract laws that allow employers to require the preassignment of innovations and the signing of strict confidentiality agreements by their employees. Mattel was known to intimidate its employees who sought to leave by threatening to invoke these generic agreements.

Within this strict contractual confine, under which more and more American workers find themselves today, Carter saw his year away from Mattel as an opportunity to reclaim his love for design and his independence. Although he was a dreamer, Carter was not naïve—he remembered his contract with Mattel and, in fact, knew quite a bit about copyright, having registered thirteen songs between 1986 and 1992 with the US Copyright Office. He understood the power of intellectual property, and he was cautious of the dangers of going against his Mattel contract.

When he returned to Mattel, in between dreary new assignments—Barbie in a gold top, Barbie in a crimson gown, Barbie every day and all day—Carter went to Jacqueline Ramona Prince, the secretary of the vice president of Barbie Collectibles. Prince was a certified notary and Carter asked her, simply and matter-of-factly, to notarize some drawings. Prince notarized Carter's original Bratz drawings on August 26, 1999. Carter signed the bottom of the drawing and added "1998" to refer to the months of leave away from both Southern California and Mattel.

Before he worked at Mattel, Carter once described the "poor man's copyright" to his father, explaining how the only way to prove you created something is to mail it to yourself. Carter was only partly right about the poor man's copyright. Under American copyright law, while registering your work with the Copyright Office is useful, the creator automatically owns the rights to the creative material once his or her idea is expressed in a tangible form—such as a song, sketch, novel, poem, or photograph. At the same time, mailing something to yourself does not prove you're its creator. The poor man's copyright is traditionally used by authors, who mail copies of their manuscripts to themselves without opening them to establish a date of creation. But this method is, of course, flawed, as anyone can pre-send an envelope, get it stamped, and then, even years later, put the work inside and seal the envelope (unless the stamp is interlocked with the seal). Similarly, asking a notary to recognize and date your artwork can help ascertain a timeline of ownership, but it does not establish the original date of the work's creation. At the very best, these methods prove you possessed it as of a certain date. Still, Carter considered the implications of copyright law and as he sought out a notary among his Mattel coworkers, he was attempting a defense if things with Mattel took a nasty turn. In the back of his mind, he knew that Mattel would not let him go without a fight.

Upon his return to Mattel in early 1999, human resources asked him the standard question, "Have you or any relative of yours, by blood or marriage, acted for any Mattel competitor in any capacity?" He responded that yes, he had freelanced design and artwork for Ashton-Drake, the high-end collectible doll company. But Bratz—his dream girls scrawled onto the sketches in his drawer—remained unmentioned. Carter had a vision and a goal, but transforming dreams into reality meant getting help. He was afraid of giving up his stable job at Mattel and of striking out on his own again, but he also couldn't stand the thought of handing over a blockbuster idea to his boss. Beyond the question of who would benefit from these ideas, Carter questioned whether his bosses would see the potential behind his creative designs. The company constantly dismissed ideas and shelved plenty of lines. The creative *basura* was overflowing. Mattel's *basura* would be Bratz's fate as well, Carter intuited. He thought Mattel's world was too small for both Barbie and Bratz. Barbie's very existence depended on a complete lack of rivalry.

At home at night and on weekends, Carter began to color the drawings. "I felt that whatever I did on my own free time was my idea, I owned it," he later explained. MGA's attorneys would later dub this line of reasoning the "weekend and nights defense." Carter knew that anything he designed for Barbie belonged to Mattel, but no one could say that this new line of dolls—dolls who were everything Barbie wasn't—was somehow "related" to Mattel's flagship toy. Using a light box, Carter transferred the black-and-white images sketched in 1998 to an illustration board and heavier stock of paper, and then used markers and colored pencils to finish them off. He breathed life into the original, thin sketches, and they slowly emerged in rich details and vivid tones. As Carter gathered the courage to reveal his creations to others, he began describing the girls as dolls rather than kids. He was, as we would say in the business world, shifting his mindset from ideation to commercialization. He believed his next set of drawings would be ready for the toy market, and on them jotted: "Four best friends with totally transformable looks. Simply pop off their hair and shoes and trade for a new look. Each doll comes with two pop-off wigs and two pairs of shoes, plus two hip fashions."

Carter sent the drawings to Alaska Momma, an agency representing artists. He hoped they could help him find an investor. The agency failed to spot the potential and passed on the venture. Carter was discouraged and, as with previous setbacks, returned to Barbie's cold embrace. He reluctantly focused on daily work at the cubicle, again shelving his creations. It was almost another entire year before he resumed searching for a champion for Bratz. In early 2000, while he and Richard were moving to a new house, Carter stumbled upon his sketches again. They were dusty and neglected but, he thought, still fresh and still cool. This time, Carter resolved to bring the dolls to market, no matter the rejection, stalling, or setbacks.

Carter called an old friend, Veronica Marlow, a former Mattel coworker who left to start her own fashion doll design-consulting firm. She marketed herself as an independent expert able to identify the zeitgeist of the industry. Carter asked to meet Veronica in person, already wary to offer details over the phone. They agreed to meet in the Mattel parking lot, and during that brief, clandestine meeting, Carter revealed his designs. Veronica was instantly impressed, and enthusiastically promised to show them to others in the industry. Carter finally had his champion—a connected insider with enough industry credibility to make something happen. Veronica made good on her promise, and she soon called Carter to let him know MGA, an up-and-coming toy company based in Van Nuys, aka "the Valley," just miles away from the hulking Mattel compound, was interested in meeting with him.

In August 2000, Veronica introduced Carter to two MGA executives, Paula Garcia, another former Mattel colleague who was now an MGA product manager, and Victoria O'Connor, MGA's director of licensing. Like Carter, Garcia had spent several years working for the

Barbie conglomerate, and had signed the standard innovation assignment agreement that Mattel demanded from all employees. Garcia
denies that she knew Carter when they were both at Mattel. Still, all
agree that Garcia was eager to move forward once she saw Carter's
work. At MGA, she had proven herself indispensable in handling
the company's development and the production of its leading lines.

Garcia's job upon coming to MGA was to oversee ongoing projects. MGA had several dolls on the market: My Dream Baby, Hoppity
Bouncy Baby, and Prayer Angel. Those dolls were launched before
she had arrived at MGA, and they were doing fine. Although none
of these lines had achieved doll stardom, they had given MGA, and
Isaac Larian, MGA's founder and CEO, a taste of the doll market.
MGA expected Garcia to infuse new life into these doll lines, and
she feverishly worked to fulfill that expectation. She jumped into
quality control, traveling to Hong Kong to oversee production. Constant mechanical challenges consumed most of her time, but she
knew that these dolls were not what would make MGA great. Using
these early months to train herself, she recalls thinking, "When I
just have a second, I would really love to do really cool fashion dolls
for older girls."

Garcia recognized the opportunity she had been waiting for at her
first meeting with Carter: "I thought they were incredible." She loved
how Carter played with disproportion—a head blown-up to half the
doll's body size, and the unrealistic dimensions of the eyes and mouth.
Though she didn't believe Carter invented the wheel, and recognized
that "certainly within the world, there were dolls that were created with
a big head and big feet," she still believed Carter had created something truly special: "It was unique in the combination of multiethnic
and the snap-on shoes, and there were a lot of things that made it—in
combination, made it unique. Paris Blues were doing things. Steve
Madden were doing things. There were a lot of disproportioned trends
in art." But the Bratz were special in how they came together, and
Garcia told Carter after his pitch that she would urge Isaac Larian to

produce the dolls and persuade him that the idea was a goldmine. A second critical meeting was set for a few weeks later, on September 1, and Garcia promised Carter that Larian would attend.

Carter wanted to bring a model of one of the dolls to this crucial meeting, so he did a little *"basura* diving." He searched Mattel's waste bin for scraps and constructed a mock-up doll from bits and pieces of discarded Barbies. He then went home, raided his private doll collection, and took boots off Ken, Barbie's on-again-off-again metrosexual boyfriend. *FrankenBratz* was blonde like her archrival, but she looked funky in a short skirt and oversized boots. Invigorated by the upcoming second meeting with MGA, Carter asked another friend, Elise Cloonan, to prepare a little Bratz logo, with an angelic halo hanging over the letter R. It was a trademark of sorts—Carter was legally marking his territory, although the timing of the logo creation, while Carter was a Mattel employee, would prove detrimental. Armed with the prototype, polished drawings, and a fresh logo, Carter took a day off from work to meet Isaac Larian.

At first, Larian did not embrace Carter's ideas. In fact, Larian, who is anything but subtle, recalls that his first impression was that the doll looked "ugly and weird." But just as it appeared Franken-Bratz would be sent back to the *basura*, Larian's daughter Jasmin interrupted the meeting. Challenging her father's business instincts, she thought the doll was "cute," and the light in the young girl's eyes sparked her father's interest. Today, Jasmin is grown up and works side by side with her father. She has an office at MGA where she runs a women's accessories business and acts as a creative director for Bratz. Larian says about his daughter's career at MGA, "The one thing I don't like about it is that I can't control her now. She has her own money."[2] Jasmin still vividly remembers the moment she sat at her father's meeting when Carter pitched Bratz:

> I was 12 years old. Barbie had all the shelf space—90 percent market
> share at the time—so they were looking for something to come out and

kind of rival that. There was nothing diverse on the market at that time. It was just this blonde, blue-eyed girl. A designer came to my dad with some drawings [of Bratz dolls]. I was in the meeting, and I was obsessed with them. My dad thought they looked like aliens. He was like, "Why do they have such big heads and feet that come off?" but I was like, "These are so cool! I need these!" And so, that's it. He made them.[3]

Still today, Jasmin speaks in a Valley girl accent, and she herself looks a bit like a Bratz girl. She says that the clothes MGA eventually gave Bratz were also much more "her" than anything Mattel was offering: "Barbie is more Rodeo Drive. We're more streetwear Melrose: mix and match, make your own clothes."[4]

Larian gave Bratz the green light within thirty minutes of Carter's initial pitch. He prides himself on making decisions based on "instinct and gut feeling," though in the case of Bratz, it seemed his gut had led him astray until his daughter Jasmin serendipitously changed his mind. Less than two weeks after the meeting, Larian offered the quiet creator of Bratz the recognition and money he had craved for so long. Negotiations were quick, and a deal was struck. Bratz would be the flagship of his company. "This is going to be big!" Carter excitedly said as he made his pitch to MGA. Larian, the confident decision maker, responded, "We are going to risk and spend millions making this brand happen." Larian knew Carter was a doll designer at Mattel but would later claim as proof of no conflict with Carter's obligations to Mattel that, "the inventor has a roommate, Richard, who witnessed Carter designing and developing the Bratz line at his free time outside Mattel on weekends or evenings."

Within weeks, an agreement was drafted. Carter was getting his dream: he would become an independent inventor-consultant, not a salaried employee. He was promised a 3 percent royalty on everything coming out of the Bratz doll line (though not on other Bratz-branded products, such as movies, clothing, or backpacks). He would also receive $5,500 a month for providing design services to the MGA

Bratz production team for the next six months. On September 18, Carter signed the agreement. The contract had a clause in which Carter agreed to return his 3 percent of the royalty if MGA was ever sued and lost ownership of Bratz. It isn't clear how much of this indemnification clause Carter actually read and recognized as significant—as attorneys well know, clients rarely concern themselves with the fine print until things go south. In the years to come, Carter received royalties from dozens of evolving Bratz lines: Little Bratz, Bratz Boyz, Walking Bratz, Talking Bratz, Pixiez, Bratz Mom, Baby Bratz, Bratz Big Sister, Bratz Fashion Show, Bratz Star Singers, Bratz Movie Stars, and Bratz Ice Champions. Most of these lines had little or nothing to do with the original pitch. Still, each later version, iteration, and transformation Bratz underwent was conceptually grounded in the prototype Frankendoll that Carter had presented to Larian on September 1, 2000. That fateful meeting marked the evolution of Carter's idea into the toy industry's next big hit. His 3 percent would net him thirty-five million dollars within ten years of the line's launch.

Could the anti-Barbie revolution really begin with an insider, who still showed up to work every day, badge intact, to dutifully plan the ice queen's next look? Could such a potent rival to the reigning doll be born from the same mind who remained devoted to preserving Barbie's flawless image? It seemed so, though, like all of us, Carter just needed a little help from his friends.

Once Carter signed on as an independent consultant with MGA with a stake in the new doll line, he put all his energy toward turning the Bratz dolls into a full-fledged product line. Problem was, he was still officially a Mattel employee. It would take Carter another month to quit his day job. Immediately after signing the contract with MGA, Carter worked closely with Paula Garcia, who immersed herself in turning their acquisition into that gold she had promised Larian. She intended to stay true to Carter's vision, but, at the same time, she had her own ideas for the dolls. Looking back, Garcia credits her ideas as invaluable to the Bratz line. She recalls that some of the material in Carter's portfolio "was wonderful. However, there were a lot of challenges."

Although MGA would soon transform Carter from creative genius to unmentionable ghost, and hail Larian as the father of Bratz, Garcia and Larian wanted Carter nearby during those first, heated days of October 2000, when excitement crackled through the MGA offices.

Larian personally e-mailed Carter on October 5, 2000:

Carter, now that we have the agreement in place, we need you and Paula to focus 200 percent on getting this done. Think different. Think the fashion. Think and design the accessories. Think about the commercial. Think about the New York showroom presentation. Think about all of the royalty you are going to make. . . . Carter, this is your big break in business life. . . . You need to put 16 hours a day, starting now, on this and nothing else. That's the only way it will happen.

The same day Carter e-mailed Larian back:

Hi, Isaac. I just want to thank you for your message earlier, and mostly I want to thank you for this incredible opportunity and for believing in me enough to make this happen. I have a great story line for a commercial which I will work up a bit for you all to see, as well as a great song in mind for it. I also have a lot of great ideas for the entire line, and this is going to be big. Thanks again. Carter.

Larian replied:

Carter, I believe you are very creative and the line, if done with focus and strategic thought, will be huge. Please arrange to meet with Paula ASAP and work on this full time.

Carter was specific in his vision. He insisted, for example, that Bratz would look her best with hollow Saran hair fiber. His choices, however, were expensive, and it was Garcia's job to ensure costs didn't spiral out of control. She found a cheaper alternative, but Carter persisted. He convinced her that the right hair—luxurious hair—would make a huge difference. In fact, Carter was so insistent in his belief that he independently sought out a vendor who could produce that hair at a reasonable cost, and Garcia eventually gave in.

Garcia, however, had final approval, and many choices to make. The MGA Hong Kong manufacturing office was filled with engineers who finalized the production plans, and while in Hong Kong, Garcia navigated through the dozens of technical, complex, minute decisions, including component costs, packaging, fabric yields, and grams of hair. Each choice was a tiny step toward creating the Bratz doll they envisioned. But like hair, shoes can make or break a look, and Garcia happily let Carter lead that decision. Carter knew shoes. Coming full circle, some of Carter's earliest inspiration for Bratz came from Steve Madden ads for shoes. Now with the financial and institutional backing of Larian and Garcia, Carter pushed his idea of strap-type shoes, with a snap-on feature at the ankle that meant different feet, with different shoes, could be mounted on the doll. The skin tone of the doll's lower leg would match the exposed areas of the feet. MGA was onboard. On February 24, 2003, MGA filed a patent application to the United States Patent and Trademark Office for the removable feet feature, called "Doll with Aesthetic Changeable Footwear." The application named its inventor as none other than Isaac Larian.

But before hair and shoes, the first and most critical step was to create the actual sculpt of the doll. Garcia called Carter's drawings "unique and exciting and amazing," but knew the dolls would be difficult to sculpt. Carter had drawn one-dimensional characters. There were no designs from the back. Translating from one to three dimensions was always complicated and rarely perfect upon the first attempt. The project required another artist—someone who could transform Carter's drawings into actual dolls. During his time at Mattel, Carter had built a network of trusted colleagues, all of whom were talented and creative in their own way. These friends knew the doll business intimately. Soon after Carter signed his contract with MGA and before he quit his job at Mattel, he helped MGA hire Margaret Leahy, a former Mattel colleague, who had taken a permanent maternity leave and was now a stay-at-home mom freelancing in the doll industry. Her husband was still a Mattel employee. Carter asked Margaret to prepare sculpts for Bratz, guiding her through changes and revisions, asking her to sculpt and re-sculpt. Carter specified which features to fine tune. His emphasis: "Head bigger, waist smaller!" Along with his drawings, Carter gave her a copy of the Madden *Angel/Devil* ad, which had appeared in the 1999 *Seventeen* magazine, and Leahy hung the image on the wall of her workspace. All doll sculptors start with control drawings, but Leahy didn't think these were very controlled controls. In her words, "Every project is different. In some projects, you are very, very, very controlled about the references you give to your sculptor. Sometimes the sculpting process is more fluid . . . sometimes, like with sculpting, the controls are less controlled, which means that you allow your artist, in this case, a sculptor, to create from their instincts." Indeed, Garcia and Carter were not too happy with Leahy's interpretation.

Garcia decided to hire another experienced sculptor and try again. An engineer by training, Mercedeh Ward assured MGA that she could do better. Garcia, Ward, and Carter agreed: the girls needed to look younger. The preliminary sculpts were discarded, and they began again until both Garcia and Carter were satisfied. Ward took the initial skeletal sculpts and turned them into a doll. Garcia felt Carter's Lupe was too stereotypically Hispanic, and her look too suggestive of her ethnicity, with shaved and redrawn eyebrows in an extreme arch. In fact, Larian, too, insists that loosening the stereo-types was his own contribution to the evolution of Carter's vision. Carter, perhaps having served Barbie for so long, was thinking in ethnic boxes. Each girl had a distinctive ethnicity in his original sketches—an Asian, a White, a Hispanic. But Larian pushed to make the girls simply multiethnic, rather than defined along rigid and archaic race lines. He says that MGA made a conscious decision to not define Bratz by race or ethnicity, so consumers can choose dolls that reflects their own fashion, style, or appearance. Larian explains that "We didn't want somebody to say, 'this is an African American doll,' or 'this is a Brazilian doll,' or have any religious or any race attached to it." He confesses that this insight had a lot to do with his own background of coming to America as an immigrant.

As for their sex appeal, to Garcia, all four girls seemed too sexy. Their hips, waist, and upper thighs seemed disproportionate in all the wrong ways. Their "va-va-voom" voluptuous body was inappropriately suggestive for the target market. She wanted a sweeter, younger, and more human-looking face. As the drawings were recast into three-dimensional sculptures, Paula demanded a more believable figure, a more flat-chested bosom—again a complete divergence from Bratz's nemesis, and Carter's longtime mistress, Barbie.

In order to make a stunning debut, a girl needs not only the right curves, but she also needs to put on her best face. Carter turned to a face painter expert, a Mattel coworker. Although neither of them uttered the new doll's name, the game of the doll-sized thrones had been set in motion. A code name was needed. According to Mattel's accusations, Bratz became "Angel," which allowed Carter and his friends at Mattel to operate undercover as double agents, nominally on the Mattel payroll but, in effect, working for the competitor. Carter denies that he used the name Angel as code, contending instead it was simply a nickname for Zoe, one of his original four Bratz girls.

Fueled by MGA's growing enthusiasm for Bratz's impending entry into the world, Carter more boldly approached his fellow workers. He needed more people working faster. He told more friends about his personal project and sought their advice and energy. A second face painter and a hair designer entered Carter's circle of helpers. Unaware of his pitch to Mattel's rival, MGA, they were simply happy to help a creative friend. Garcia also hired an independent contractor to style and root the doll's hair. As the team worked on the girls, their looks changed. Eyes softened. Skin shades were rendered lighter. Heads were made slightly smaller. The girls looked younger and slightly less sexual. Jade's hairstyle was redesigned from tight pin curls to a long ponytail. MGA decided it could not produce the dolls with changeable hair, which Carter had wanted. Nor would the original names remain as Carter had planned. Lupe became Yasmin, using the Persian version of Larian's daughter Jasmin's name. Hallidae became Sasha. Zoe became Cloe.

Now it was time to design fashion to match the divas. A small squad of seamstresses began moonlighting for MGA while continuing business as usual at Mattel. Veronica Marlow, who introduced Carter to MGA, helped Carter coordinate the seamstresses. Marlow approached several experienced sample makers, all longtime Mattel employees. They were, for the most part, Mexican American women who worked at the very bottom of the Mattel food chain. They earned little as seamstresses and they often had to supplement their day job by moonlighting work out of their home garages in the seedier parts of Los Angeles. They had received odd jobs from Marlow in the past. This time too, without asking questions about the ultimate beneficiary of their work, they took on sample-making jobs for the first clothing line for Bratz. According to Mattel, they were paid using false social security numbers to cover MGA's tracks. Larian had offered to permanently hire Marlow as an MGA employee. However, while Marlow thanked Larian for his very generous offer, Garcia explained to Larian that if Marlow goes "to work for MGA, she will no longer be able to offer work with her team of pattern and sample makers. They have secure day jobs with an outlook of many more years of stability that they are unwilling to leave. They only moonlight for Marlow." She empathically explained, "These older ladies are

comfortable with the way things are. They don't want to change. We
pay them very generously because they are risking their day jobs, even
a nice retirement, to work for us. If they were ever discovered, they
certainly would be painfully humiliated and fired." Those at MGA
wanted to know how they got any work done under those worrisome
nightly conditions. Marlow bragged about the seamstresses, respond-
ing in an e-mail: "Maybe it's just that they are so talented, they have
more than 100 years total of doll-making experience between them.
They are extremely fast and accurate." Years later, the possibility of
being painfully humiliated and fired materialized. When Mattel discovered the seamstresses' contributions during those early days of the
Bratz line development, the company fired them.

Larian oversaw the marketing and strategy behind the launch,
and Carter continued to hone his vision. For Carter, inspiration most
often came from the unconventional, unique aspects of our society.
Although he visited toy stores to observe the most current crop of
dolls, most of his inspiration came from places outside the toy world.
He enjoyed trips to stores like Hot Topic, which specialized in rock
music and pop culture. He brought thongs and metal belts back to
MGA, hoping to implement them into the designs.

It was only on October 19, 2000, that Carter resigned his job at
Mattel once and for all, after the frenetic preparations at MGA to
bring Bratz to market had already begun, although long before they
were complete. Not mentioning Bratz or MGA, Carter told his supervisors he was planning to take another break from Los Angeles, to
spend time with family and find new directions. Carter told his boss,
Ivy Ross, a newcomer to the Barbie department, that his decision was
a lifestyle change. He enthusiastically described the opportunity to
go back to the Midwest, where he could rest and draw at home, with
a dog at his side. "He painted this very idyllic relaxed lifestyle," Ross
later recalled. She remembers him saying, "All I can tell you is I'm not
going to the competition." While California, unlike most other states,
does not allow an employer to restrict its employees with noncompeti-

tion agreements, it still allows the strong enforcement of trade secret law against former employees as well as intellectual property assignments like the contract Carter signed. In most large corporations, exit interviews are designed to remind quitting employees of their post-employment obligations. In fact, most attorneys recommend companies adopt this practice to defend their intellectual property, trade secrets, and proprietary information. Indeed, had Carter said he was leaving for a competitor, Ross would have had security escort him out that morning. Instead, Carter was allowed to give a two-week notice and have continued access. Carter concedes that he misled his boss, but he denies the white lie was designed to cover up unlawful behavior. Larian swears Carter also misled him and his staff at MGA by not telling them he was taking his time quitting Mattel. Mattel claims that hiding his tracks showed Carter knew that his deal with MGA was in breach of his contract and the duty of loyalty that American law deems inherent in any employment relationship—a duty to not compete with one's employer while working for it. But Carter insists it was an innocuous omission, explaining, "I just didn't want to burn my bridge with Mattel if things didn't work out with MGA."

Mattel executives would later accuse Carter of inciting a coup. Was this any different than the legally accepted, dog-eat-dog world of the Silicon Valley, with entire teams planning their departure and co-opting the company operation? Mattel's lawyers would later urge a jury to agree that, during the critical months Carter spent designing his prototype in the summer of 2000, Mattel's fashion doll department effectively became MGA's design department.

3 | SUGAR DADDY

"Who is that?"
"Nobody. The author."

—MARC NORMAN AND TOM STOPPARD,

SHAKESPEARE IN LOVE

IN ORDER TO SOAR, Bratz, like the finest of all archetypal heroes, had to write off her father. In a matter of months, Bratz disowned Carter Bryant for Isaac Larian, a very different father figure who adores publicity, seeks out conflict, and enjoys provoking Mattel. Reigning supreme over his private toy kingdom, Larian's very identity is inextricably intertwined with MGA's success. Was Larian's uncontainable ego the reason Carter went unmentioned whenever a reporter asked about MGA's overnight sensation? Or was it instead business savvy and caution that held Larian's tongue? Did he anticipate the fallout if Mattel found out?

With his boyish, goofy smile, and eccentric elegance, Isaac Larian likes to describe himself as a big kid. In his late fifties, with graying hair, he remains youthful and continues to credit the against-all-odds success of MGA to his ability to channel his inner child and to his devotion to his own children. But when he describes the toy business at large, he transforms from an excited child into a grown man set on winning a game of money and markets. "I love the toy business because it has such sex appeal," he confesses.[1] He claims that the toy business is "like getting hooked on drugs." And he immediately adds, "Don't think anybody at Mattel would put it quite that way."[2] His love of play and the ease with which he straddles the dueling worlds of naïveté and cynicism that together define the toy industry have helped him excel in a crowded, cutthroat market. Larian feeds his image of an outsider to the industry. He describes an industry that is entrenched and political, risk averse and unimaginative. He believes he can maintain his edge better by remaining a privately held company unaccountable to the stock market and shareholders. Although his corporation remains private, Larian himself is vocal and his persona is very public. He accepts interviews frequently and emphasizes how the effort of one immigrant family built MGA up from nothing to the country's top privately held toy company. He is the industry's *enfant terrible* and underdog, and he relates his success as the embodiment of the American dream.

Born in Tehran to a poor, Jewish family of seven, Larian knew he had to leave Iran for the land of opportunity. Larian's personal journey to the United States began in 1971 as a seventeen-year-old boy clutching a one-way ticket to Los Angeles:

> *I had $750 in my pocket, and a big American dream. My first job was washing dishes in a coffee shop in Lawndale and I was getting $1.65 an hour working from 11 at night to seven in the morning. Then I went to school during the day and I worked throughout college until I obtained a civil engineering degree. I was planning on going back to Iran and become a civil engineer but we had a little thing called the revolution.*[3]

Larian washed dishes at a Los Angeles coffee shop and waited tables at the landmark Theme Building restaurant above the LAX Airport. The modern, mid-century building was a giant white egg perched high above the airport's bustle, and it rotated excruciatingly slowly, providing diners with a 360-degree view of Los Angeles. It was there, waiting tables at night, slowly spinning above travelers, that Larian dreamed of one day conquering this City of Angels. The view from atop can be misleading. One day a business is bubbling with clientele, the next it can topple and succumb to competition. Like so many L.A. businesses, the iconic LAX rotating restaurant permanently closed its doors for business in 2014. But while Larian's first employer was on the decline, his remarkable path took him from waiter to the founding CEO of one of the world's most successful multinational toy companies.

Even if Hollywood rags to riches stories often seem serendipitous, Larian's meteoric rise is not simply a matter of luck. He worked hard during those first years, studying at California State University Los Angeles and graduating in 1978 with a degree in civil engineering. At night he braved the infamous L.A. traffic to wait tables across town. The following year, 1979, the year Larian planned to return home, marked the start of the Iranian revolution. The moderate Pahlavi dynasty was overthrown and replaced by an Islamic Republic under Ayatollah Ruhollah Khomeini. Larian, a Persian Jew, lost any chance of returning to build a safe home in Iran. The United States government granted him religious asylum that same year, and he was naturalized as an American citizen. An entrepreneur at heart, Larian shelved his engineering degree and founded a company selling brass giftware and electronics from the back of his truck. He also prides himself on bringing over the entire Larian clan, overcoming the political upheavals, and providing them all with a comfortable life: "I arranged for my parents to leave through Afghanistan and Pakistan on camels and cars with my little sister, and then they went to Austria, and then they came to the USA as refugees." Eventually, he says, he gave them all a comfortable life. "My mother receives a salary at the company. My mother is seventy years old, and she cooks and brings food for the children to the office and other employees." He named his father the chairman of the company "out of respect for him."

In 1984, Larian married a woman who shares his immigrant beginnings. Angela Larian is a Jewish-Iranian woman who was born in Tehran and moved to the United States as a teenager in 1978. Isaac and Angela built a home in Los Angeles, and had three children, Jason, Jasmin, and Cameron. Over the course of their marriage, the couple watched their family grow and their business boom into a toy empire. Larian's kids are his inspiration and pride, and he designated only the best toys to share their names. Both Jasmin and Cameron are the namesakes of Bratz dolls. Through three decades of marriage and over a decade of court battles, Angela never once wavered. She stood beside her husband through every battle, of which there would be plenty.

It's undeniable that Isaac Larian's success was born from conflict. Countering his gregarious nature and familial devotion is an ability to eviscerate even those closest to him. Isaac originally partnered with his brother Farhad back in 1979, after being granted asylum. Farhad Larian (Fred, as he calls himself now) was his older brother's business partner for over twenty years. Together they started an import company called Surprise Gift Wagon. They operated in the gray market of parallel importing: importing consumer electronics that were sold cheaper in Asia and selling them here in the United States for a lower price than the official distributor offered. While working in that business Isaac was introduced to the American legal system: he fought companies like Yamaha and Panasonic when they tried to shut down his gray import business, and his legal battles helped clarify US national customs regulations on parallel importing: only if there are real physical and material differences between the unauthorized imported goods and those sold by the authorized distributor can the brand owner then prevent unauthorized importation. Larian learned then what he firmly believes to this day—that big companies use litigation simply to drive out the competition and that the American legal system is rigged against the small guy. He tells me that "it takes someone bold and perhaps stupid like me to actually fight a corporation in court all the way to the end." He believes that, like patients these days, who must become even more knowledgeable about their disease than their physicians, as a litigant, you can't let the lawyers just handle your case. As a young immigrant entrepreneur, he got into the practice of reading every single court document, memorandum, and motion, and helping his attorneys win in court.

In 1987, the Larian brothers realized the potential in the emerging market for video games and shifted their focus. They called their new company Micro Games of America (which Larian would later change into the initials MGA) and began distributing handheld Nintendo games. But that wasn't exactly what Larian was looking for as an entrepreneur. He was tired of working for the Japanese, merely making money as a distributor, and wanted to start something truly American. MGA began making and selling toys. The first doll, a singing bouncy baby, sold a million units in its first year. Larian was encouraged and set his sight even higher. He says that he would fly every year to Bentonville, Arkansas, to the Walmart headquarters to pitch new toys. But he didn't get much traction:

> *Eventually, I begged the Walmart buyer, "Throw me a bone, buy something from me." The buyer told me Micro Games of America didn't really sound like a toy company. I changed our name to MGA. Then he took me to one of the Walmart big box retail stores and showed me something that blew my mind. The vast shelves in the toy department that held Barbie, ninety-eight square feet of Barbie boxes, it was something else. Barbie completely controlled the market. The Walmart buyer told me, "Bring me something that can compete with her, and then we'll talk." I said, "Write that down on your business card and I will see you back here soon."*

Larian did not want to make it just as a distributor or a licensee, but instead as a brand owner in his own right. He also didn't really want a business partner, even if his partner was his own brother.

The relationship between Isaac and Farhad became tense. Craving control, Isaac opted to aggressively buy out his brother so he could run the company solo. In Genesis, the Bible tells the story of Jacob buying his brother Esau's birthright for the meager price of red lentil stew. Similarly, the biblical Isaac won over the love of his father at the expense of his older half-brother, Ishmael. The intensity and flux of brotherly love and rivalry have not diminished with time. The brothers had been constantly arguing over MGA's operation since the early 1990s. Slowly, Isaac, who was the president of the company, assumed full control of product development, sales, and finance. Bit by bit, he removed his brother from the company's day-to-day operations. Then, in 2000, Isaac pushed Farhad to let him buy his share of the company, failing to mention that MGA was about to release Bratz. Oblivious to the company's hidden potential, Farhad sold Isaac his 45 percent ownership interest in MGA for just nine million dollars. The Bratz line would bring in three billion dollars in sales just a few years later.

Both Larians agree that their problems started long before the partnership ended. The brothers had argued about running MGA for years. As Farhad was increasingly phased out of the company, Isaac tried to dissuade him from going to the New York Toy Fair, which they regularly attended. When Farhad showed up anyway, Isaac was inexplicably (at least to Farhad) furious. Farhad also alleged that his brother excluded him from important meetings and, worse, gave him misleading financial statements to demonstrate the company's poor performance. Isaac painted the company as failing and offered his brother the once-in-a-lifetime chance to jump ship with money in the bank. On September 28, 2000, just ten days after the Bratz deal was completed, Farhad signed away his ownership of MGA for the proverbial lentil soup. The dissolution quickly eroded into a public feud when Farhad sued Isaac, claiming Isaac had lied about the company's profits and defrauded Farhad out of his rightful share. Farhad claimed Isaac knew Bratz would become the company's top seller, and by omitting this small fact, effectively cut his own brother out of millions, if not billions, of dollars. Farhad collected and produced dozens of documents revealing that MGA began developing Bratz prior to the dissolution of the brothers' partnership.

Amid their public face-off, Farhad attacked Isaac's romantic underdog story about his self-made success. In contrast to Isaac's tale of a hardworking immigrant armed only with his dreams who later saves his extended family and elevates all to riches, Farhad insists it was their wealthy parents in Iran who funded the brothers' toy and electronics startup. Isaac denied this repeatedly during the trial. Though their lawsuit was about one man inducing his business partner to sign an agreement while allegedly hiding material information in order to buy him out cheaply, it was also a story of two brothers who could not agree on the legend the older brother narrated about his life.

The brothers eventually settled out of court, with Farhad agreeing to stay out of the family business. When Mattel attempted to use the brothers' feud as evidence of Larian's deceitful character, Isaac testified that Farhad regretted his action: "Before the case was over, he got up, over the objection of his attorney, dropped the case, and he apologized to me." But Farhad says he dropped the case out of respect for his parents, and that he still refuses to speak to his brother. He describes Isaac as greedy and conceited: "Isaac once told me he wants to see how many people show up for his funeral. It goes hand in hand with his greed."[4]

Still, blood runs thicker than water, and when Farhad heard that Mattel was suing MGA, he e-mailed Isaac to ask how he could help. Mattel claims that help meant destroying ten boxes of documents Farhad had collected for his own lawsuit just a few years earlier. The brothers' dispute was merely a prelude to the decade-long litigation that would ensue between MGA and its great competitor. A small legal battle between brothers was nothing compared to a full-fledged war with gargantuan Mattel.

Larian likes to cultivate his reputation as the newcomer. He mastered the English language but never lost his heavy Persian accent. He mastered the world of business but never shed his identity as an outsider. Even after being twice named Entrepreneur of the Year by Ernst and Young in 2004 and 2007, Larian continues to make a point of first of all apologizing for his accent, one way of accentuating his immigrant roots. He knows that Americans love a good Cinderella story and enjoys playing up his own tale. In trial, his lawyers would tell the jury, "He came here for the same reasons that the United States has been a magnet for so many immigrants over so many years, for education, for opportunity and for freedom of religion."

As his business grew, one of Larian's public mantras became: "*The dream is more important than the money.*" Yet his showy life stands in stark contrast to that platitude. His corner office and conference room display the prized toys that have made him the owner of the country's largest privately held company. Alongside these toys are framed dollar bills from bets won from those who doubted his vision. Written on one of these framed one hundred dollar bills are the words "I was wrong"—a permanent concession from an executive who bet against one of MGA's successful lines.[5]

Larian shrewdly links his humble start as an outsider to his willingness to challenge the seemingly undefeatable Barbie empire: "When you come here without having money you become very resilient and you become driven." The memory of hard times, at least in Larian's narrative, remains the vivid center of his story, even after he made millions, moved to Beverly Hills, and toppled the big boys down the road. "I came to this country washing dishes," Larian would stress during his trials, "and I am not going to let Mattel walk all over me." When you remain an outsider, you see the benefits of knocking down the cathedral. Larian is no stranger to litigation with the giants, not only Mattel, not only with his own brother, not only with most of his own attorneys, but also with McDonald's over the licensing of Bratz for Happy Meals and with LucasFilm over the licensing of video games. "I am not just going to get pushed around by these big bullies," he has declared.[6] From the start, Larian and MGA presented their problems with Mattel as "a case about how the world's biggest toy company tried to crush a small but successful competitor after it could not beat it in the marketplace." The media ate it up. "Score one for the little guy," wrote the *Los Angeles Times* after one of MGA's court-room victories.[7] In Larian's eyes, Mattel is an anachronistic, lumbering behemoth, and as for Barbie, it was time for fresh plastic blood.

When I first tried to interview Isaac Larian, I hit a wall. MGA's communications department wrote me that MGA is a privately owned company and therefore is under no obligation to talk about its affairs. I was considering alternative ways to contact him when one day out of the blue I received the following e-mail from him:

> *Dear Orly, I understand that you are writing a book about [Mattel/ MGA] and have talked to some of the lawyers and jurors in this case. Mattel's stated goal (since they aren't able to compete and innovate) was to "litigate MGA to death." Mattel has a history of using litigation to stifle innovation. . . . This time they faced a persistent Iranian Jewish immigrant who stood up to them and prevailed. I would be happy to discuss further detail as I was personally involved from day 1 in this case.*
>
>

Thanks & Best Regards,

Isaac Larian CEO MGA Entertainment

His e-mail signature ended with the mantra "Fortune Favors the Bold." This is his favorite maxim, which he has also placed in strategic spots on MGA's walls, such as in the corporate boardroom where I interviewed him. Boldness is at the heart of Larian's persona. Nevertheless, along with his loudly defiant nature, Larian has a soft side, which he is confident enough to display. He weeps in public, writes poetry, enjoys fashion and, well, loves his dolls.

The love of dolls and creative energy were perhaps the only traits shared by Carter Bryant and Isaac Larian, otherwise polar opposites

in their personalities. Carter envisioned Bratz as the modern iteration of girl power and imbued his angels with street smarts, hobbies,
and intellect. Larian hoped that Bratz would become a fashion-
forward icon relevant to girls as old as sixteen and that it would
expand into a lifestyle phenomenon. Each in his own way hoped
that Bratz would be the anti-Barbie: defiant and current. And yet
Bratz would not escape feminist scrutiny and psychological critique.
In 2007, an American Psychological Association (APA) Task Force
on the Sexualization of Girls criticized Bratz's miniskirts, fishnet
stockings, and feather boas as overly sexualized. It decried the dolls'
"objectified sexuality" as harmful to the young and adolescent girls
who constitute the doll market. When asked to respond to these
accusations of over-sexualizing the doll, Larian stated: "I have seen
a few pages and I have to tell you it's a bunch of garbage. The people
who have written this are irresponsible. We're talking about plastic
toys for God's sake. If plastic toys are setting up the morality of this
world then we are all in big trouble."[8]

For Larian, all business is personal, and the personal is good
for business:

> A hundred years from now what's important to me is the difference I make
> in the life of a child—not how much money I have or how many cars
> I own. I am very involved with many children's causes. I have proudly
> coached my kids through soccer and basketball. So the accusation that
> Bratz promotes sex is negative publicity that has been put out by people
> who have a different agenda.[9]

Within three years of their launch, Bratz sales grew from ninety-
seven million dollars in 2001 to one billion dollars by the end of
2003. With expanding global retail sales, the brand hit almost three
billion dollars in sales the following year. By 2006, MGA had sold over
one hundred million Bratz dolls. Barbie, as one business magazine
reported, was losing her groove.

As the Bratz dolls' popularity continued to rise, Larian began creating their birth story. Beyond posing with the dolls and crediting different members of the Larian family for the dolls' inspiration, Larian had trouble recollecting exactly when they were created. At one point, he was quoted as saying that they were born in September 2000. His licensing director, Victoria O'Connor, warned him in an internal e-mail, "Don't you think we should say Bratz was born in October when a certain person was no longer with their company?" Larian affirmed, "Good point. Thanks."

As Larian's boisterous personality consumed Bratz, Carter, the hardworking creator, began to disappear. MGA's internal memos warned workers to keep his identity secret. "Make no references," they were instructed. And so no one at MGA dared to mention the name Carter Bryant. The bigger a hit that Bratz became, the more he faded—and was happy to fade—from MGA's memory. Carter later claimed he just wanted his anonymity to avoid fame. He wanted to retreat and be left alone. "I am just a very private person," he said. In March of 2002, Carter wrote Paula Garcia: "David Dees wrote something to the fan club or something like that and mentioned that I created Bratz. I know that by now everyone knows that I created them, but I do not want my name mentioned to the fan club or anything else. I just want to be anonymous." Larian was furious to hear about Carter's exposure: "Why are we telling people this information about where the dolls come from anyway? I don't want to see anything said or told or written about Bratz without my written approval ever again." Larian scolded his employees, warning against "legal grief," and declaring, "There must be no mention about Mattel or any of their properties, Carter, any MGA Bratz arts, etc."

At the Toy of the Year award ceremony in 2002, Larian told the press that MGA developed the concept of Bratz by conducting marketing research into what girls really want. In 2003, on a radio show, Larian explained that he came up with Bratz as his daughter outgrew Barbie. He explained that he adopted the name Bratz because he wanted something catchy and short. He also noted how the spelling with a Z rather than an S kept pace with cooler, modern trends. Bratz's almost instantaneous success brought MGA more media attention than Larian ever dreamed, and the toy tycoon seized every opportunity to tout his products.

Ever the family man, in 2004, the *San Fernando Valley Business Journal* quoted Larian crediting the doll's invention to yet another person, this time to his teenage son Jason. When confronted with these different versions as to who came up with the doll, Larian would later claim he was misquoted. On the stand, accused of purposely lying about the inventorship of Bratz by naming his own son the inventor, Larian insisted that he would never have said such a thing. He says he described to the journalist his eldest son's creativity and how he came up with the idea of another popular toy, the Commandobot, a robot that was the first robot toy to work on voice recognition. But he refutes ever saying that Jason invented Bratz: "If you see him, you will know that he will not have anything to do with dolls or creating—[or even] looking at them. My wife is laughing back there," he said winking at her from the witness stand. Larian has attributed successful business ideas to each of his children, and has also described his youngest child, Cameron, as having come up with several of MGA's best-selling products: "We were on a family ski vacation, and he said, 'Dad, you should do a Bratz winter break.' So we did it, and it sold wonderfully."

Was Larian purposely misleading the media to cover up the tracks to Carter Bryant, and thus Mattel? Was Larian different from any other CEO taking fame and credit for his company's hit product? Was Steve Jobs the one who sat in the trenches with the dozens of engineers who worked on the iPhone and the iPad? Did Ruth Handler, founder of Mattel, in fact create Barbie as proclaimed? Can we simply assume that most people at the top of their organizations want all the glory and downplay the contributions of the designers and engineers? Behind every president are creative departments, and often a story of an independent inventor, either in the trenches of the company or on the outside. In the better case scenario, the independent inventor receives acknowledgment. Often, though, independent inventors find themselves in a situation where they pitch an idea to a toy company, the company says it passes, and then develops the idea without rewarding the inventor. Inventors report that more often than not they make a decision to forgo any legal claims because to survive in the business as an independent, you don't want to be labeled a "Sue Happy": someone who is willing to take on the titans by filing a lawsuit.

At Mattel, former president Neil Friedman was credited as the father of Tickle Me Elmo, another overnight sensation. In Friedman's public profiles, you see him smiling from ear to ear, proudly holding the wiggling Sesame Street plush toy, similar to how Larian likes to pose with Bratz. Friedman's quotes also echo Larian's: "the job keeps him a kid at heart."[10] Elmomania began in earnest when the unprecedented demand put the toy in short supply and crazed consumers fought in stores over them to the point of injury and police intervention. A secondary market emerged with scalpers selling the toy for hundreds, even thousands, of dollars.

Yet, despite its creative personnel and strong leadership, Mattel did not originate the idea behind Tickle Me Elmo. In fact, the idea started as Tickle the Chimp, invented by toy designers Ron Dubren and Greg Hyman in 1992, who presented their invention to Tyco Preschool, a subdivision of Mattel. At the time, Tyco did not have rights to make *Sesame Street* licensed dolls, so at first the company cast the invention as a *Looney Tunes* Tickle Me Tasmanian Devil, or "Taz." These plans were derailed when, before launch, Tyco lost the rights to Looney Toons. Luckily, it acquired the rights to Sesame Street around the same time that Taz was swapped for Elmo. Despite the precursors, behind-the-scenes metamorphoses, and outside inspiration, it is Neil Friedman who grants interviews and gets credit for the smile that Tickle Me Elmo brought to everyone's face.

Isaac Larian posed with his Bratz dolls whenever he had the chance. He explained to the market that Bratz was the "Anti-Barbie": "Bratz are everything Barbie is not. Who can identify with a six-foot-two blonde? The Bratz exist in a changing world. Children today are exposed to change at a very fast pace, so the Bratz change too." Bratz wasn't quite the overnight success that Tickle Me Elmo was in the United States, but their first launch in Spain in 2001 was an instant hit. In the United States, Bratz took some time to succeed commercially. Larian takes pride in the fact that the retailers had no choice but to purchase Bratz as a group of dolls, multiethnic and diverse. With Barbie, a retailer could buy only white Barbies for their stock. Walmart bought the entire group of first generation Bratz, although it placed the dolls in a poor spot in the toy displays. Toys "R" Us, the other big retailer of the industry, canceled the six million dollar order for the dolls in the first year Bratz came out, explaining that sales were low; customers coldly turned from the new girls on the block.

However, Larian remained confident his girls would catch on like fire. He borrowed money by mortgaging his house to aggressively invest more in building the Bratz brand and marketing the dolls. Larian cleverly turned MGA from a toy company into a licensing empire. Unlike most companies, which wait until their brands are successful before licensing products, MGA prefers licensing at launch. That strategy has proven to be genius. It not only provides more revenue streams early on but, more importantly, it serves as a cross-marketing technique. If you see Bratz everywhere—on T-shirts, backpacks, notebooks—you will want a Bratz doll. MGA granted hundreds of Bratz licenses in Europe, Australia, and South America. Bratz appeared in books, on board games, clothing, shoes, dental products, bicycles, electronics, makeup, luggage, school supplies, party favors, and even a karaoke machine. Larian had personally overseen the packaging, marketing, and commercials for each Bratz product. Ultimately, actual production was outsourced to China.

Despite the Bratz dolls' slow beginning, by the end of 2001, sales soared. Bratz was getting orders by the tens of millions. By 2002, Bratz began collecting toy awards from around the world. MGA capitalized on their success by adding new products to their main line. More Bratz were born: Ciara, Dana, Diona, Felicia, Fianna. Soon, everywhere you looked, a new Bratz popped up: the Bratz Flower-Girlz Cloe, the Bratz on Ice doll Yasmin, Bratz Boyz, Lil' Bratz, Bratz Lil' Angelz, Bratz Petz, Bratz Babyz, Itsy Bitsy Bratz. Slumber Party Sasha, Bratz Girlfriendz Nite out Cloe, Bratz Funk 'N' Glow Jade, Bratz Wild Wild West, Bratz Cowgirl Stable, Bratz Spring Break Pool, Bratz Babyz Ponyz Buggy Blitz, Bratz Los Angeles, Bratz Girlz Rock. In 2005, MGA teamed with Fox for a short-lived TV series featuring Bratz, which found popularity in Britain but fell flat in America. Most recently, MGA created an entire division focused on developing a new Bratz series for television.

Larian became the champion of the Bratz revolution. Just a year after their release, Bratz dolls were awarded the People's Choice for Toy of the Year Award at the 2002 Toy Fair. Larian says he and his family were sitting in the back at the award ceremony, while the industry awards all went to Barbie. He got so frustrated that he was ready to leave in the middle and went to the restroom. Then the People's Choice award was presented and he was called back to the banquet. That was a memorable moment for Bratz—she was on a roll: she then won Family Fun Magazine Toy of the Year award and, for two consecutive years, won awards from the Toy Industry Association. In 2003, MGA was named Supplier of the Year by Walmart, as well as Vendor of the Year by both Toys "R" Us and Target. Toys "R" Us even created a boutique-within-a-store for Bratz. *Buzz* magazine hailed Bratz as having "spunk without being trashy." MGA quickly developed other Bratz products and expanded the toy line. Five Bratz boys joined the girls: Cade, Dylan, Eitan, Cameron, and Koby. In the WASPish world of Mattel, Barbie was center stage, Ken was her arm candy, and there were one or two friends or sidekicks trotted out during the holidays. Bratz was a clan, a tribe. With Bratz, you hang— you don't schedule a play date. You don't say "let's do lunch" and then never call. You knock on the door and stay for dinner.

Like dog owners and their dogs, doll executives and their dolls come to resemble each other over time. Larian could easily be describing himself when he outlines the dolls' bratty personality. If Bratz was the anti-Barbie, Larian was the anti-Eckert. CEO of his archrival Mattel, Robert Eckert was laconic and exuded an air of superiority, much like the ice queen he served. Mattel executives would affirm Barbie's lasting depth, values, and character, and dismiss the passing trends served by "those other dolls." And in 2004, in the face of Bratz's unceasing rise in the market, Mattel sued MGA for developing an idea of their former employee, claiming that Mattel owned Bratz.

Perhaps Larian's position was similar to Mark Zuckerberg's defiant stance against the handsome Winklevoss twins, Olympic champions no less, when Zuckerberg started Facebook on his own. The Winklevoss twins, fellow Harvard students, sued, claiming he stole the idea for Facebook from them. The Winklevoss twins had hired Zuckerberg to program their idea for a social network. In the movie *The Social Network*, the fictionalized story of Facebook's dazzling success, Zuckerberg (played by the excellent Jesse Eisenberg) coldly delivers the movie's best line: "If you guys were the inventors of Facebook, you would have invented Facebook." The American business woman Mary Kay Ash liked to say that ideas are a dime a dozen; people who implement them are priceless. Defending himself against Mattel's litigation, Larian could have just as succinctly said, "If you were the inventors of Bratz, you would have invented Bratz."

Larian was determined to fight the giants all the way through. He wanted to be seen and heard rather than silenced by his enemies. His statements showed a willingness to engage and win, but underlying his bravado was a very real wish to be liked, respected, admired, and honored.

Larian had built a billion-dollar empire, grown from a seed planted in the mind of a competitor's employee, in his own image. What could possibly go wrong?

PART TWO

REWIND:
BUILDING TOYLAND
UPON EGO, SECRETS,
AND LIES

4 | ONCE UPON A TIME, BARBIE WAS A GERMAN HOOKER

History doesn't repeat itself, but it does rhyme.

—MARK TWAIN

BARBIE HAS BEEN AS American as apple pie since her birth back in 1959. At least, that is what Mattel wants people to believe. The truth is that history repeats, or at least, as Twain would say, rhymes, either straight up or with a twist. Barbie, similar to Bratz, was an amalgamation of ideas—and the kitchen was crowded with too many cooks bitterly fighting to claim and own her.

American icons are often uncomfortable when faced with their Old World origins. The Walt Disney Corporation made Snow White and Sleeping Beauty appear all-American, and it owns the wholesome images that are inextricably attached to their names. Yet these beloved princesses are rooted in the German tales of the Brothers Grimm. The Disney versions are sweetened—that is, Americanized—versions that omit the scary scenes and the explicit physical violence and, always, add a happily-ever-after ending. In the Brothers Grimm version of "Cinderella," for example, one of Cinderella's evil stepsisters cuts off her toes, and the other stepsister cuts off her heel, so they can fit into the tiny glass slipper. When the sisters attend Cinderella's wedding, their eyes are pecked out by birds. In *The Little Mermaid*, based on Hans Christian Andersen's story, the Disney movie leaves out the price the mermaid pays for having legs: every single step she takes will feel like she is walking on sharp shards of glass. Beyond that, the prince ends up marrying another woman, and the mermaid throws herself into the sea and turns into sea foam. In the Brothers Grimm's version of Snow White and the Seven Dwarfs, the stepmother, the Evil Queen, asks the hunter to bring her back Snow White's lungs and liver. The hunter cannot kill Snow White, so he brings back a boar's lungs and liver instead, which the queen voraciously eats, believing them to be Snow White's. When eventually the prince rescues Snow White and they wed, the Evil Queen is invited to the wedding and is forced to wear burning-hot iron shoes and dance until she drops dead.

Just as Walt Disney obscured the violent and tragic German heritage of his princesses, Mattel purposely blurred Barbie's humble start in Germany. Building and expanding on culture is the essence of humanity, and yet many of these conglomerates, all of whom borrowed and remixed preexisting conditions, later policed and banned any further reimaginings. As always, a lawsuit uncovers the truth, awakens the dead, makes us face our own history, and, most of all, clarifies our values and beliefs.

An American in Switzerland

In 1956, during a family trip to Switzerland, American businesswoman Ruth Handler came across a German doll called Bild Lilli. Lilli was a popular doll in postwar Germany. Before Lilli was produced as a doll, she was born in the mind of the German cartoonist

Reinhard Beuthien in 1952. Beuthien had a vision for a sassy new comic-strip character and, like Carter Bryant many decades later, he sketched away until he got Lilli just right. At first, he drew her as a cute baby. Alas, his boss at the daily newspaper, *Bild Zeitung*, was not impressed. He directed Beuthien to keep the baby doll face but add long blonde hair and a voluptuous grown woman's body. From this combination emerged the ultimate woman-child fantasy.

As a cartoon character, Lilli was also about sex. In every comic strip, Lilli declared her preference for rich older men. In one scene, Lilli says, "I could do without balding old men but my budget couldn't!" In another cartoon, Lilli is splayed naked with only a newspaper covering part of her body. She explains to her friend, "we had a fight and he took back all the gifts." When a policeman cites Lilli at the beach for wearing a two-piece swimsuit, she offers a sultry response: "Which piece do you want me to take off?" When a friend asks Lilli how best to marry a rich guy, Lilli generously hands out practical advice: the best strategy is to marry someone who will drop dead soon after the wedding.

In 1955, three years after her creation, when Lilli's drool-enticing curves transcended the two-dimensional page, her plastic visage was deemed unfit for toy stores. Instead, Lilli the doll was marketed as an adult toy and sold at tobacco and liquor stores. Quite bluntly, both her two- and three-dimensional forms were designed for sex-hungry, postwar German men. After the defeat and in a decade of shame and ruin, these German men bought Lilli for girlfriends and mistresses in lieu of flowers, or as a suggestive gift. Her promotional brochures had such phrases as "Gentlemen prefer Lilli. Whether more or less naked, Lilli is always discreet."

Lilli's transition from plaything bought by grown men into a toy for young American girls happened almost accidentally. On her Swiss vacation, Ruth Handler, a cofounder of the new toy company Mattel, eagerly bought several Lillis: one for her daughter Barbara, and the rest for Mattel.

Handler was another Horatio Alger's rags to riches hero. She, the youngest of ten children, was born in 1916 to a Jewish-Polish family in Colorado. Her father, a blacksmith, emigrated from anti-Semitic Poland, finding work in Denver and sending for his wife and children two years later. Life in Colorado was certainly better than in Poland but the Moskowiczs were extremely poor, and the older siblings worked instead of going to school. When Ruth was still an infant, her parents put her in the care of her older, married sister Sarah because Ruth's mother had to undergo surgery. Once Ruth's parents returned home to their routine, they never brought Ruth back, and she was effectively raised by Sarah, her sister turned surrogate mother. Ruth said later, "It has been suggested to me once or twice that this supposed 'rejection' by my mother may have been what spurred me to become the kind of person who always has to prove herself. This seems like utter nonsense to me." Nonsense or not, the doll she claims to have invented would never become a mother. Rather, Barbie was destined to live the early dreams of Hertopia: a self-realized woman on her own.

Ruth—petite and busty, a chain smoker with a sharp mind and a hot temper—had bigger dreams than what she saw in Colorado. Before she turned twenty, Ruth left her home of shared rooms and cold winters far behind. She followed her dreams west and made a new home in Los Angeles. Here in Southern California, like so many entertainers and entrepreneurs, she made her mark. Fortunately, she would not have to do it all alone. Elliot Handler, her high school sweetheart, whom she had met at a Jewish youth dance in 1929, followed her west. Elliot was an aspiring artist, and was also from a poor, immigrant family. She was the pragmatic doer; he the romantic dreamer. The Handlers married in 1938. Their daughter Barbara was born in 1941, and their son Kenneth followed in 1944 (the dolls Barbie and Ken were born later). New to California, the Handlers founded Mattel in 1945 with a friend, Harold

Matson. They named the company Mattel; Matt-El a blend of the names Matson and Elliot (but notably, not the name Ruth, the driving force among the three). The two men designed knickknacks for sale—costume jewelry, picture frames, toys—found cheap manufacturers to produce their designs, and Ruth sold the products during her lunch hours and after her day job. Ironically, it was the very practice that created Mattel—entrepreneurial moonlighting during weekends and nights—that Mattel would later deny its own employees. The three founders had their offices in a single-car garage, and their guiding principle was "follow the money." They were on the lookout for new materials and new designs, and were happy to hop from one business line to another depending on where they could find buyers. Their largest order came when Elliot and Harold Matson designed a realistic-looking miniature piano, of which 300,000 were ordered. Unfortunately, the young entrepreneurs realized too late that they mispriced the piano and lost a dime on each one they produced.[1]

Ruth Handler had a better head for business than either of her two partners. She walked confidently into meetings, closed tough sales, and thrived on adrenaline. She even learned to drive a truck to make deliveries as needed. Despite the piano-pricing blunder, she saw potential in the plastic toys, and Mattel focused in. As often happens, friction followed success. In 1955, Matson left the company, bought out by the Handlers for fifteen thousand dollars, and never enjoyed the emerging toy giant's future fortune. The Handlers' explanation for dissolving the partnership was that their friend Matson just could not keep up with them. Matson, however, recounted a darker story of Ruth's cutthroat ambition, culminating in his ejection from the company he cofounded and built. His story certainly parallels that of Isaac Larian's brother: corporate dominance often comes at the expense of others. Now Ruth and Elliot solely owned Mattel and would make it the world's largest toy company.

Guns and Dolls

When Ruth Handler saw Lilli in the beautiful lake town of Lucerne, Switzerland, she immediately recognized the European bombshell's potential. As a child, Handler herself did not like dolls. In her childhood, her young adult life, and later, in her career, Handler shirked the stereotypical, often misogynistic ideals of a woman, choosing instead to focus on entrepreneurship, salesmanship, and leadership. She was one of the few businesswomen of the mid-twentieth century to found and lead a Fortune 500 company. And yet, though undoubtedly a trailblazer, Handler also emphatically denied she was a feminist. She disliked the word *feminism* and disassociated herself with the women's rights movement of her time. Ironically, Handler would only assume the mantle of feminism at her lowest moment. After her conviction for securities fraud, she wrote in her biography that she was targeted and zealously prosecuted because she was a woman—a famous woman—with the nerve to climb to the top.

Ruth Handler wanted all the glory. Throughout her life, she made it perfectly clear that she alone was "the inventor of Barbie." She wanted the original Bild Lilli forgotten, and she fought hard to keep others from claiming their stake in the birth of Barbie. Handler's official story of how she *invented* Barbie, much like Isaac Larian's narrative fifty years later, was rooted in inspiration from her daughter. Handler told the story dozens of times: her daughter Barbara liked playing with dolls, but preferred adult-looking figures with a sense of fashion. Handler watched her daughter and her friends cut out paper dolls because no plastic, three-dimensional dolls on the market catered to their taste. Handler thus got the idea to fill that hole in the market.

Once back from Europe, with Lilli safely stowed in her bag, Handler confided in a recent Mattel hire, an engineer-turned-toy-designer named Jack Ryan. Ryan was a former weapons engineer who helped develop the government's Hawk and Sparrow III missile systems. The Handlers, with an eye for talent, needed someone technologically savvy to bring their dreamed-up toys to life, and positioned Ryan as Mattel's chief designer. Though he was first hired to design a miniature rocket capable of shooting up to two hundred feet, he proved indispensable and struck a rather unique deal in manufacturing: he stayed on as an independent consultant rather than in-house employee. Ryan was even promised a share of each patent and a royalty from each sale of his inventions. Today's autocratic Mattel would likely kick anyone asking for a similar deal out the door, but Ryan was shrewd, and these were the days when Mattel was small, adventurous, and understood the need for hungry talent to build the toy empire. Ryan leveraged the value he brought to negotiate a profit percentage from the toys he would develop. Even more unique, and almost non-existent in today's invention landscape, the Handlers agreed that he would own the patents filed in his name. Some of his patents would never be assigned to Mattel.

Handler wanted Ryan to recreate a new, Americanized Lilli—less German streetwalker more Californian movie star; a bit less Marlene Dietrich, a bit more Marilyn Monroe. Curiously, the first adjustment Ryan made was shrinking her "bee-stung" lips, the very lips which came back decades later as a central feature in Bratz's design. Ryan also rid her breasts of nipples, though he kept her breast size intact, and widened her eyes for a more innocent look. Other than that, Barbie remained the spitting image of her German ancestor. The filed-down nipples and molded-over vagina were a faux answer to Lady Macbeth's call to "unsex me here." Lilli-turned-Barbie would remain a sex symbol, with Ryan's own lifestyle of sexual exhibition further fueling her sexual legend.

Lilli's transformation into Barbie spanned three continents and took three years. Ryan flew to Japan in 1957 to oversee Mattel's manufacturing, and brought along German Lilli. As they did with their other toys, Mattel contracted a Tokyo-based manufacturer to cast the first doll. Barbie finally made her debut at the American Toy

Fair in New York City on March 9, 1959, her official birthday. Mattel introduced Barbie to the world with a story. Barbie's full fictionalized character was Barbara Millicent Roberts hailing from the fictional Willows, Wisconsin. Barbie was a hybrid Midwesterner and Southern Californian, adopting the life path of her "creator" Ruth Handler, and foreshadowing the story of Carter Bryant and his "imitations." Barbie's birthday suit—her first outfit—was a strapless, zebra-striped one-piece bathing suit and stiletto heels. Although Mattel wanted to conceal Barbie's European origins and present her as all-American, it thought it was very American to borrow from European fashion. In fact, Charlotte Johnson, Barbie's first clothing designer, frequently traveled to Europe to see the trends from the most celebrated designers—Christian Dior, Givenchy, Yves Saint Laurent, and Chanel.

Right from the very start, Jack Ryan tried to wrest credit for Barbie's invention from Ruth Handler. He was thirsty for Hollywood-style fame, and he found it by dubbing himself Barbie's inventor. He told anyone willing to listen that, long before Barbie arrived, he urged Mattel to create a realistic, feminine form for a doll because girls, as he understood them, did not want to play with dolls "with a dopey figure." While Ruth Handler always explained that Barbie was named after her daughter Barbara, Ryan claimed Barbie was named after a different Barbara: his wife. One of them, anyway; Ryan eventually had five.

Regardless of the wife du jour, Ryan crafted a Hollywood lifestyle pursuing hedonistic pleasure; he sat atop a throne in his Bel Air mansion-turned-sex castle, spending each night with a different woman. Ryan spent most of his adult life building his dream house and filling it with human Barbies. He bought the five-acre, eighteen-bathroom, seven-kitchen estate of silent actor Warner Baxter in Bel Air, and he transformed the mansion into something befitting "Hugh Hefner out of Kubla Khan."[2] He held hundreds of parties, with jugglers, fortune-tellers, handwriting analysts, calypso musicians, go-go dancers, rhyming minstrels, harpsichordists, and guests upon drunken guests—all of whom were strangers in the night. Ryan had a notorious passion for orgies, drugs, and prostitutes. He found new partners faster than Mattel introduced new toys. Starlets bounced on his daughter's trampoline and offered martinis to her pony, geese, and ducks who roamed the grounds, while his daughter and his estranged wife hid in a separate wing.

One of Ryan's wives was his Bel Air neighbor, actress Zsa Zsa Gabor. In 1975, *People* magazine ran a story about their marriage. Ryan was Zsa Zsa's sixth husband, out of nine. Gabor divorced Ryan after less than a year of marriage, telling the press she could not cope with Ryan's dungeon, which she called the torture chamber, decorated with black fox fur. Many Mattel women employees who worked under Ryan's supervision visited this furry dungeon. Ryan was the first—though sadly not the last—to try modeling his lovers after his fantasy-girl Barbie, urging partners to undergo surgery to better resemble plastic perfection. The most famous of Ryan's Mattel employee playmates (or inmates to his notorious home dungeon) was Gwen Florea, the first voice of talking Barbie.

To paraphrase Weird Al Yankovic, if money can't buy happiness, perhaps it can rent some glory. Both Handler and Ryan wanted to go down in history as the inventor of Barbie. The vicious fight between Ruth Handler and Jack Ryan over Barbie's inventorship persisted until each of their bitter ends. After two decades of collaboration with Mattel, Ryan sued the company and the Handlers for cutting his royalties and pushing him out of the company. In 1980, after years of disputes and days before the trial was about to start, Mattel settled with Ryan for $7.5 million. Despite this legal victory, Ryan spent his final years wrestling with his own mental demons. In 1991, he shot himself in his bathroom after writing "I love you" on the mirror with his fifth wife's lipstick.

Ryan was far from the sole blemish on Mattel's corporate record. Ownership over Barbie was contested from her launch. The secret truth that Mattel hoped to conceal was that Barbie was merely a metamorphosis of the German doll Lilli. Neither Handler nor Ryan paused to consider whether copying Lilli was legal. Mattel would later become one of the most litigious companies in the industry, suing for any kind of perceived intellectual property infringement. Just as the most jealous lovers are often also the most unfaithful, Mattel's beginnings are unmistakably tainted by an intellectual property dispute.

The German company Greiner & Hausser held a patent and the copyright for Lilli. For the brief period when Lilli was manufactured and sold, G&H sold about 130,000 Lilli dolls. When it designed and launched Barbie in 1959, Mattel neither offered G&H royalties nor sought permission to use its design. In 1960, Rolf Hausser, then the managing director of G&H, received a US patent for a doll hip joint. That same year, still producing and selling the German Lilli, G&H agreed to license Lilli, her image, persona, and patents, to the American toy company Louis Marx, then a hugely successful toy manufacturer based in New York known, among other things, for introducing the yo-yo in 1928. After World War II, Marx was the world's largest toy manufacturer. In 1955, Louis Marx himself was featured on the cover of *Time* magazine as "The Toy King." He had single-handedly introduced mass toy manufacturing to the United States in the 1930s, and by the 1950s, forged an empire. (In the nineteenth century, Germany dominated the toy industry. The way American companies gained more market share domestically was through the formation of the American Toy Industry Association, which lobbied Congress for a high tariff on imports.)

The agreement struck between the German G&H and the American Marx granted exclusive Lilli production in the United States, Canada, Hong Kong, and Great Britain. In 1961, with the contractual permission of G&H, Marx used the "Bild Lilli Hong Kong" head mold to launch an American fashion doll, Miss Seventeen. (Last year, I found a vintage 1960s Miss Seventeen on eBay. She has auburn hair and painted facial features with high, arching eyebrows, red lips, nail polish, and toenail polish. She wears high heels and is wearing a full-length wedding gown lined in satin with an overlay of tulle and floral lace with tiny beads attached. On her back she has been branded, like cattle: "U.S. Patent # 2925684 / British Patent # 804566 / Made in Hong Kong.") Though Miss Seventeen briefly gave Barbie a run for her money, she never really took off. Miss Seventeen came too late and Barbie, boosted by Mattel's bold vision and marketing strategies, was guaranteed dominance in girl's toys for decades.

In 1961, two years after Mattel introduced Barbie, the German G&H and the American Marx jointly filed suit against Mattel in California.[3] The complaint accused Mattel of stealing the hip-joint patent and infringing their copyright, calling Barbie "a direct take-off and copy of" Lilli. The lawsuit alleged that "the Lilli doll was logically copied one to one and, in the process, modified only very slightly; *et voilà*, Barbie was created." It also argued that Mattel falsely represented itself to the world as the doll's originator. The lawsuit specifically alleged that Mattel had copied the form, posture, and facial expression of Lilli. Marx called Barbie a fraud and hoax, and claimed she misrepresented herself as an original American. Mattel retaliated by asserting unfair competition claims, much like MGA's counterattack years later, claiming that G&H and Marx were "campaigning and harassing Mattel's customers and potential customers." The Handlers also launched a countersuit against Marx for copying the mechanics of its Thunderburp cap gun, which Jack Ryan had invented. Mattel even marshaled a fleet of evidence to convince the court that Barbie was not Lilli, but rather was inspired by nineteenth-century American wooden dolls.

Mattel's defense and counterattack ultimately paid off. In 1963, G&H and Mattel settled G&H's patent infringement claim with a two thousand dollar per year license agreement, and they stipulated to the dismissal of G&H's copyright claim in exchange for the dismissal of Mattel's counterclaims. After settling the case, the German toy company entered into an agreement with Mattel. In 1964, five years after Barbie was launched in the United States, Mattel purchased G&H's Bild Lilli copyright and all its German and US patent rights for the meager lump sum of twenty-one thousand dollars. Mattel agreed not to use the names "Bild Lilli" or "Lilli," and G&H agreed not to produce any more dolls. Mattel reaped billions of dollars over the following decades, becoming the largest toy maker in the world, while in 1980 the New York-based Marx, once the world's largest toy company, was forced to declare bankruptcy. Following close behind their co-plaintiff, G&H declared bankruptcy in 1983, signaling the beginning of Mattel's almost total domination of the toy market. Mattel was then, and perhaps is still, too big to fail. In 2000, G&H made one final attempt to chase claims against Barbie. Rolf Gausser's wife revived the company for the sole purpose of pursuing a new lawsuit against Mattel. It filed suit in California, and this time the lawsuit alleged fraud, claiming Mattel made material misrepresentations during the 1964 negotiations, downplaying Barbie sales, which induced the German company to accept a flat fee, instead of insisting on a per-doll royalty. G&H again claimed that plagiarism of its Lilli began at the 1959 New York toy show, and that $1.7 million in copyright and patent infringement took place between 1959 and 1964. The court shot down G&H's final plea and dismissed the 2000 lawsuit for being too similar to the one that had been settled forty years earlier and was now well beyond the statute of limitations.

In 1963, the same year that G&H originally settled with Mattel, Ruth Handler was officially named president of Mattel. By then, thanks largely to Handler's undeniable marketing talent, Mattel was the largest toy company in the world. But the 1970s marked the end of Handler's reign. Ruth, along with her husband Elliot, was forced out amid an extensive Securities and Exchange Commission investigation of financial improprieties. In 1975, shadowed by mounting allegations of fraud, she resigned her position as CEO. In 1978, at the age of sixty-one, she was convicted of inflating Mattel stock market price, padding the books, falsifying financial statements, and profiting from the sale of her own overvalued stock. After repeated denials and refusals to settle, Handler pled *nolo contendere*—no contest. The judge who sentenced her, Judge Robert Takasugi, called her actions "disgraceful" and "parasitic." Handler was sentenced to a suspended prison term and ordered to perform 2,500 hours of community service, the largest number of hours ever ordered at that point. Although the community service was extensive, she was free to choose what type of service to perform, and founded the Foundation for P.E.O.P.L.E. (Program for Ex-Offenders on Probation for Learning Experience). Her foundation provided white-collar probationers with an opportunity to train young, disadvantaged men. Over the years, Handler continued to proclaim her innocence, and she described her resignation from Mattel as "heartbreaking" and the aftermath of the SEC investigation as "a very demeaning humiliating experience."

Extending over two hundred pages, the SEC report describes a pervasive fraud orchestrated from the very top, with all roads leading to the Handlers. In the late 1960s, despite Barbie's meteoric success, Mattel faced serious losses. Ruth Handler's unstoppable ambition brought dazzling new acquisitions. Mattel grew too quickly and acquired too much. To top it off, a fire ruined one of Mattel's factories, burning thousands of completed toys. In 1972, Mattel's stock was in decline, and the company was not turning enough profit. The SEC report describes how Mattel executives concocted a plan to falsify profit reports by listing customer orders as earnings, then secretly calling those customers and offering to cancel those orders. An astounding 80 percent of these orders were successfully canceled, all while Mattel undercontributed to the employees' profit-sharing plans, and either cut down or failed to pay inventor royalties, including Jack Ryan's. For example, in 1971, $14 million of purported sales were invoiced but never actually made. In one instance, a single sale of $4.8 million was recorded twice in Mattel's published financial statements. And, amid these financial improprieties, Mattel went on a shopping spree. It acquired the Ringling Bros. and Barnum & Bailey Circus, and purchased a book publisher, an audio company, and a pet supply company. All of these companies were sold off at a loss when the SEC charges became public. Five shareholder class action suits were filed, and eventually settled for $30 million—the largest securities fraud settlement of its era.

In 1970, a few years prior to her rapid decline and criminal conviction, Ruth Handler faced an even more challenging foe than the SEC when she was diagnosed with breast cancer.

Late in her life, after years of battling cancer, and in exile from Mattel, Handler founded a company producing breast prostheses called Ruthton. The silicon breasts were named *Nearly Me*. She told a reporter in the early 1980s, "When I conceived Barbie, I believed it was important to a little girl's self-esteem to play with a doll that has breasts. Now I find it even more important to return that self-esteem to women who have lost theirs."[4] She promoted her new breast prostheses using the same, aggressive self-promotion with which she led Mattel. A *New York Times* article described how she would frequently open her own blouse during interviews about the product, asking the reporters to feel her breasts and identify which one was real and which one fake.[5]

For years after their legal condemnation, Ruth and Elliot Handler were *persona non grata* at Mattel. Only near the turn of the century did the company's new leadership feel enough time passed that it could reassociate with its old CEO without shame. When, in 2002, the year Ruth Handler died, Barbie's hands and feet became the tiniest ever cemented at the Egyptian Theatre along the world-famous Hollywood Boulevard, Barbara Handler, Barbie's namesake, was given the honor of placing the plastic limbs in the wet cement in memory of her late mother. Six years later, in April 2008, Mattel hosted Elliot Handler's ninetieth birthday party at its headquarters in El Segundo, California.

The tradition of naming their dolls after family members continued throughout the Handler era at Mattel. When Barbara married Allan Segal, Mattel introduced Allan, Ken's buddy. Baby Cheryl, one of Mattel's first talking dolls, released in 1965, was named after the Handlers' first grandchild. Todd, Barbie's younger brother in the doll line, was named for their grandson. The real Handler kids were not particularly happy about their unsolicited claims to fame. In 1989, Ken Handler told *People* magazine, "Ken is Malibu. He goes to the beach and surfs. I was the kind of kid who played piano and went to movies with subtitles. All the girls thought I was a jerk." About Barbie he said, "Barbie should care about more than going to the beach and having a good time. She should care about poverty and suffering in the world." Stacey, Ken's daughter, would later publish a book of troubled poetry about her own suffering called, *The Body Burden: Living in the Shadow of Barbie*, in which she reveals a lifelong struggle with her body image and low self-esteem. The poems are pubescent, and mostly just sad: "If only losing my fat could help me lose my pain / now I am obsessive vain and insane."[6]

At the end of the Handler era, still bleeding from its founder's criminal conviction, shareholder class actions, mounting financial losses, and public shame, Mattel's future was far from certain. In 1984, financier Michael Milken, known as the Junk Bond King, ventured to save Barbie. To say that Michael Robert Milken is a controversial figure is an understatement. To his critics, he is the iconic big bad wolf of Wall Street, a convicted criminal representing the era of pure greed immortalized by the 1980s. Like Ruth, he was convicted of securities fraud and eventually turned to medical philanthropy having been banned from working on Wall Street. Others view Milken's actions as transformative, propelling economic growth in the country to levels never seen before. One thing is undebatable: Milken was a risk taker, and when he saw Mattel was in trouble, he stepped in to revive the company. Milken personally invested $2 million and mobilized other banks and venture capitalists, altogether providing

Mattel with $231 million, the lifeline that allowed the company's survival. In an interview with Barbara Walters, Milken explained he saved Mattel because "I believed in Barbie. There's more Barbie dolls in this country than there are people."

Despite the legal scandal, the Handlers left their mark on the toy industry and consumer markets at large. For better or worse, Mattel under Ruth Handler's leadership became a model for other companies in product innovation, branding, licensing, and marketing. Handler not only pioneered in bringing a fashion doll to the kids' consumer market, but she also was ahead of her time in understanding how to create a comprehensive lifestyle brand, how to develop advertisement campaigns in new media, and most of all, how to use psychology to direct consumer choice.

5 | THE PSYCHOLOGIST WHO SOLD SEX

A particularly beautiful woman is a source of terror.

—CARL JUNG

ARE YOU A BBP—a Barbie Buying Parent? For many of us, this deceptively simple question opens up a Pandora's box of parental anxiety. Would Betty Friedan buy her daughter a Barbie? Would Sheryl Sandberg, while urging her daughters to *Lean In?* Would Amy Chua, the Tiger Mom? Would the Obamas allow Sasha and Malia to play with her? Toys matter. As psychologist Jean Piaget said, play is the work of children. Play is vital to their physical, emotional, and social development. Toys shape the way children understand the world and interact with it. With Barbie, Mattel revolutionized the toy industry in more ways than one. First and foremost, it changed the way toys were sold, consumed, and played with.

After her transition from German Lilli to naturalized American Barbie, the ice queen became an instant hit. A few years after her debut, the *Saturday Evening Post* hailed Barbie as "the hottest toy to come along since the balloon."[1]

Barbie sold over three hundred thousand units in her first year alone, three million by 1961, and more than one billion over the next four decades. Without as much as a blip, Barbie reigned as the number-one-selling girls' toy in the world throughout the twentieth century. By the 1990s, Barbie and her long line of products were sold across 150 countries, with annual worldwide wholesale revenues in excess of two billion dollars. What was the secret of her success? How was she marketed? How did Barbie inspire such a mass following? How did she, in a pre-Internet era, go viral?

Barbie was the first mass-manufactured adult-looking doll for girls. Before Barbie, dolls were all modeled after babies. Girls played make-believe as mommies, nurturing their baby dolls, feeding them, bathing them, walking them in their mini stroller, and tucking them into bed. Barbie forever transformed the very core of how these girls, and boys as well, interacted with dolls. For the first time, girls were imagining themselves *as the doll*, not the caretaker. They dressed Barbie in high fashion, made up a busy social life, and dreamed about growing up to be her. Barbie guided these girls to adulthood. Boys like Carter Bryant, who says he was "one of those strange kids" for liking Barbie, were not strange at all, and in fact could also now find an outlet for their imagination and dreams.

Humans have always had a complex relationship with dolls. Of course, nowadays we associate dolls with childhood, and dolls often represent that fleeting innocence. Dolls spark language development, imagination, and socialization. Playing with dolls opens up a new world for kids: it can be therapeutic and calming, creative and escapist. That may be why, even though we now understand dolls as gendered and marketed primarily—if not exclusively—to girls, dolls appeal to girls and boys alike. Psychology research indicates, for example, that preschool boys are equally interested in dolls.

Homo sapiens have long used dolls for these purposes, though not only humans play with dolls. My primatologist colleagues are finding wonderful examples of young chimps and orangutans playing with sticks and leaves as dolls, nurturing the stick, rocking the leaf, and even putting their organically made dolls to bed. One study by Harvard researchers shows that female primates carried the sticks like dolls until they had offspring of their own, and that young males did this as well, though less frequently. These young male primates seemed to prefer playing with the sticks as toy weapons.[2]

Dolls existed in ancient Egypt and ancient Rome to enhance fertility, to assume worry, and to unload sin. At the same time, dolls appear in the darker moments of our history. In many cultures, dolls function as stand-ins for humans in rituals of a more unsavory nature: voodoo, sacrifice, and, yes, sex. This is unsurprising. If dolls are mini representations of us, they can and do assume the entire spectrum of human emotions and behaviors, in both children and adults alike. This is perhaps why, for some people, dolls are frightening—just seeing one elevates their heart rate, induces panic, breathlessness, nausea, and at times, crying and anger. Psychologists have given it a clinical term, *pediophobia*, the well-documented fear of dolls. Why is pediophobia such a real phenomenon? Why is Chucky scary? Sigmund Freud theorized that children fantasize about dolls coming to life while playing with them. Freud explained that it is then natural to fear anything that we can imagine potentially coming to life.

Psychologist Ernst Jentsch studied the uncanny feelings triggered by the uncertainty of whether an object resembling a living being is actually alive.[3] As Alice remarked upon arrival to Wonderland, "you have no idea how confusing it is, all the things being alive." The Japanese roboticist Masahiro Mori integrated Freud's and Jentsch's studies, developing what he termed the uncanny valley hypothesis.[4] When an object, such as a talking doll, becomes more human-like, it is easier for others to empathize with it (or shall we say her/him?). At the same time, an uncomfortable, perceptible gap separates it from real humans, hence the uncanny valley.

Ironically, in a sad case of life imitates art, Barbie has inspired an inverted uncanny valley. Futurist writer Jamais Cascio imagines an upturned uncanny valley effect when humans modify themselves. Transhuman individuals, according to Cascio, are likely to elicit revulsion. One immediate such reality is women and girls made to be doll-like. For example, in 2015, a young couple, Anastasia Reskoss, twenty, and Quentin Dehar, twenty-three, morphed into Barbie and Ken through an alarming number of plastic surgeries, including nose jobs, cheek fillers, butt and pectoral implants, breast augmentation, ear reshaping, eye-bag removal, Botox injections, and veneers, costing them hundreds of thousands of dollars.[5] Sadly, Anastasia is one of many women who have over the years gone to extreme measures, including the removal of ribs, to transform themselves into living Barbies. Anastasia chillingly explained: "We want to spend the rest of our lives together morphing into the dolls we love. My parents bought me all the Barbies I wanted." She said, "At one point I had over 100 and I loved them all, they are so beautiful."

It would not be a stretch to say that Mattel shrewdly understood Barbie's ability to transplant the complex interactions between adults and dolls seen in other cultures into what, until then, was the very simple, naïve world in which children played. Before Barbie, the two worlds were clearly delineated. Children embraced the nurturing behaviors they knew and saw in their parents, while adults embraced the therapeutic, escapist, and subversive usage of dolls—the voodoo rituals, pseudo-sacrifices, and all shades of sex play. Ruth Handler and Jack Ryan, each in their own way, understood that an adult doll opened the door for youngsters to the "world of grown-ups" like no baby doll could. From the beginning, Mattel positioned Barbie as a real person, not a doll. Barbara Millicent Roberts had a story and a life. She had careers and prospects. She had family, friends, a boyfriend, then a husband, and then an ex-husband. Barbie got fan mail; in the 1960s, she was getting more fan mail than Elizabeth Taylor and Audrey Hepburn combined—and now she has a Facebook page and a Twitter account, #YouCanBeAnything.

At first, Mattel's revolutionary vision viscerally repulsed the toy stores. Retailers were reluctant to sell Barbie. Sears—Mattel's biggest buyer—refused to purchase the doll because of her overly sexual nature. The ban would not last long. In the commercial world, the customer, the driving force of the market, is always right. Within one decade, Mattel shed its humble beginnings as a picture frame and dollhouse furniture company and evolved into one of the largest toy companies in the world. In large part, Barbie carried Mattel through the second half of the twentieth century. Not even Hot Wheels could keep pace with Barbie's high sales. In 1993, Mattel acquired Fisher-Price, Inc., and in 1997, it bought Tyco Toys. Despite these megalithic acquisitions, Barbie remained Mattel's best-selling toy. From the moment Barbie hit toy stores, kids voted with their feet and parents with their wallets, and once Mattel hooked the child-consumer, retailers followed suit.

Barbie not only represented a shift in the way children related to dolls, but also, more broadly, she represented a paradigmatic shift in consumption. Ruth Handler was a risk taker, and that adventurous attitude extended to Mattel's marketing and merchandising techniques. Barbie signified the beginning of an era of consumers influenced by celebrity, fashion, and pop culture. In the postwar affluence of the 1950s, the victorious American people wanted to feel as glamorous and flawless as their leaders. While German Lilli was joking about catching a wealthy old man to buy her clothes, American Barbie never had to think about scarcity. America's victory went hand in hand with its freedom and adherence to unflinching capitalism—the nation was commercial and privileged, dominant and exceptional. The rest of the world could only look over and imitate. They too would drink the consumer Kool-Aid soon enough.

Early on, Mattel hired the most controversial and expensive marketing consultant available. Dr. Ernest Dichter was a Jewish Austrian immigrant turned American marketing guru. He was also the nemesis of mid-century feminists. Trained in psychology, Dichter's notorious reputation was based on his sinister manipulation of human desire, most often sex, to sell products, and on capitalizing on the wider misery of housewives to sell even more. To some, he is known as the father of motivational research. To others, he is the inventor of the focus group. Before Dichter, businesses had marketing departments and psychologists had clinics—Dichter merged those worlds. He applied Freudian psychoanalysis to selling, forever shaping America's consumption fetishism: a desire to own stuff, which has yet to subside.

His methods were scientific. He pioneered the focus group, a term he coined, which is to this day a keystone of marketing. Dichter also referred to those focus groups as living laboratories. Dichter's focus groups were similar to the experimental research that my mother and other psychologists employed in university labs to better understand child development and human behavior, but Dichter experimented to increase corporate profit. Children and adults were asked to watch television programs, view advertisements, play with new toys, or use new products, all while his team of psychologists watched and filmed them behind one-directional screens, studying their reactions, their facial expressions, their movements. As they observed the pathological patterns of human urges and desires, Dichter's small army of psychologists turned Freud's insight on emotion, subconscious fears, and hidden desires into sales opportunities. More than that, as he then inserted the insights from the focus groups in marketing campaigns, Dichter offered consumers moral license to buy hedonistically—consumption became a way of life. He was a true believer, and he described consumerism as the only alternative to the specters of communism and totalitarianism destroying the Old World from which he originated and fled.[6]

In the 1950s, Dichter transformed products beyond their mundane functions. Soap was about sensuality, not personal hygiene. Tobacco relieved stress, symbolized virility, and was a reward for a good day at the office. On smoking and health concerns, Dichter wrote, "Efforts to reduce the amount of smoking signify a willingness to sacrifice pleasure in order to assuage their feeling of guilt. Guilt feelings may cause harmful physical effects not at all caused by the cigarettes used, which may be extremely mild. Such guilt feelings alone may be the real cause of the injurious consequences."

Rather than a lethal habit, tobacco smoking, he said, was "comparable to sucking at the nipples of a gigantic world breast." One campaign displayed a man smoking next to his date, captioned "smoking rounds out other forms of enjoyment." Illicit sex then, along with tobacco, was another reward for a good day at the office. Lipstick too was a phallic play on that desire, and subconsciously hinted to women—and men buying makeup for women—an invitation to fellatio. Dichter marketed cars to trigger men's fantasies of a mistress. In his autobiography *Getting Motivated*, Dichter wrote about his own understanding wife who seemingly accepted his middle-aged escapades. "I did not tell her directly," he wrote, "but my body or its most expressive part did." His autobiography includes explicit, exhibitionist, accounts of his life at his marketing empire, the Institute of Motivational Research in New York:

> *One day, I could not perform. We both searched for the reason. I guessed. I had a very sexy secretary who would get next to me behind the desk and "play," while being hidden from any sudden visitors. We also developed a technique, which I highly recommend, of asking her to bend over the desk to hand me my dictations or other office material. Since she wore very low-cut blouses, a very comfortable opportunity for a "reach-in" if not a full "love-in," was created. After a few days of these various "hors d'oeuvres" we became interested in the main dish, the consummation of which took place on top of a very uncomfortable desk in an unoccupied conference room.*[7]

How did such a questionable character rise to the level of national marketing guru who ultimately shaped American consumption for decades to come? Dichter was born to a poor Jewish family in Vienna in 1907. He narrowly escaped the horrors of the Holocaust by moving to New York in 1938. He was already married, and, as he recalled, had only one hundred dollars in his pocket. In those days, and in Dichter's eyes, a heavy accent was an impediment to the American dream, and he spent hours at lessons to lose his Austrian accent. As an ad man, he especially knew how to market himself. So a year after he came to America, and though he had landed a job with a traditional market research firm, he sent letters directly to corporations offering his psychological expertise in transforming their business. Ivory Soap was the first to take a chance, hiring him directly as a consultant. Dichter told Ivory that soap has *gestalt*, an organized whole that is more than the sum of its parts—in other words, personality. This was radical: Dichter convinced top brands that products had a "soul." Things are bought because they reflect ourselves: "Soaps could be old or young, flirty or conservative."[8] Food could be progressive or traditional, feminine or masculine. In Dichter's campaigns, baking, for example, was not simply about cake. Baking became an expression of femininity, fertility, and love. In 1963, in her acclaimed *The Feminine Mystique*, Betty Friedan indignantly wrote that Dichter is "paid approximately a million dollars a year for his professional services in manipulating the emotions of American women to serve the needs of business." He was, according to Friedan, exploiting women's insecurities to keep them baking with Betty Crocker and Aunt Jemima.

Dichter even changed how banking services were marketed. He hypothesized that Americans preferred borrowing money from loan sharks, payday lenders, and other sketchy institutions at an irrationally high interest rate, rather than from an established bank. This was, in his view, precisely because banks were respectable institutions, transforming bankers into judgmental father figures. Shady lenders were preferred because of their seditious nature. They were closer in kind to those who needed money, and they lacked the moral authority to judge financial failure. Dichter recommended that banks reframe loans to overdraft and credit. In other words, beginning in the 1950s, Dichter helped banks create and market new, magical offerings through checking accounts, as well as debit and credit cards, which took the moral judgment and the face-to-face interactions away from requesting a loan. Be it Barbie dolls or credit cards—seduction by plastic was Dichter's specialty.

Dichter's ideology and methodology thrived. Consumerism, as Dichter explained it, was a substitute for European nobility and lineage. Nobility for the masses, if you will, and like opium and religion, his teachings spread like fire. He quickly opened up a dozen more offices for his marketing firm outside of New York, and eventually around the world. Industry leaders queued for Dichter's advice "like desperate patients for a miracle medical doctor."[9]

Naturally, Mattel wanted in on some Dichter action. Dichter conducted controlled studies for Mattel of kids playing with toys, dolls, and guns. In return, like Ruth Handler and Jack Ryan before him, Dichter too wanted to claim Barbie as his own. Dichter told interviewers that Barbie was actually born in his focus groups. "What they (kids that is) wanted was someone sexy looking, someone that they wanted to grow up to be like. Long legs, big breasts, glamorous," he said in a mid-1950s interview.[10] In *Cosmopolitan*, he published an article titled "Why Men Like, Love and Fondle Breasts."[11] He wrote he discovered that to a man, "embracing a woman's breast with the hand creates a feeling of mastery. A man who is anxious and insecure is apt to be attracted to women with large, opulent breasts; their largeness seems to provide him with the extra reassurance he needs." Looking back on his life as the man who used sex to sell iconic American products, from soap to cars to cigars to hot dogs to toys, Dichter asks the readers of his autobiography whether he is "as devilish as some think I am." Dichter, the man who sold Barbie's sex appeal to children, answers his own question this way:

> I consider working for a company almost like an interesting game. I make no secret of the fact that I obviously don't care whether Lever Bros. has a larger share of the market than Procter & Gamble. . . . I find the

solution and produce the sale increases. I have acted as a discoverer, as
a general on the battlefield of free enterprise. If my candidate gets elected,
I have a feeling of power.

If Buddhists are correct and desire and attachment are the roots of all suffering, Dichter was a world-class sadist. His methods helped manufacture and sustain the endless desire to consume that still grips our world. In preparation for Barbie's launch, Dichter interviewed 191 girls and forty-five mothers. While the girls were excited about Barbie, Dichter detected deep-seated resistance among the mothers to expose their girls to this new doll. Dichter recognized that mothers needed a reason to reconcile their instinctual hesitation about the sexual, overcooked nature of Barbie with their daughters' attraction to the doll—a logic to the farcical madness of little girls playing with a fully grown, busty blonde. This was Dichter's greatest talent: turning consumer weakness into corporate advantage. He recommended positioning Barbie as a role model. She would help daughters become more poised, well dressed, properly groomed, and feminine. Barbie, with all her sexuality, would guide girls down the path of refinement. Playing with her, and imagining themselves as her, would prepare them for an elegant future.

Even the most feminist mothers could buy into this goal because, well, if you cannot beat them, join them. The underlying message was this: if your daughter was going to succeed in a culture that values good looks in women, and in which Barbie ties her own achievements and appeal to sexuality and appearance, then as a mother it would be irresponsible to overlook this key to success. Rather, one should prepare her daughter to thrive in this world because the reality, even if unfortunate, is that businesswomen, politicians, and other high-powered women are rated according to their looks. The same remains true to this day. In 2016, Jacyln Wong of the University of Chicago and Andrew Penner of the University of California at Irvine used data from a long-running national study of more than fourteen thousand people to analyze the association between attractiveness and income.[12] Like past studies, the 2016 study finds both men and women benefit from appearance; better looks meant higher salaries. But the key difference between men and women involved grooming—applying makeup, styling hair, and selecting clothing. For men, grooming did not make much of a difference, but for women, grooming is more important than being naturally attractive: "In fact, less attractive but more well-groomed women earned significantly more, on average, than attractive or very attractive women who weren't considered well-groomed."

Dichter understood that a mother is a mother. She wants the best for her child, no matter her politics. Mothers recognize the challenges their daughters would face finding work—they will need to compete with men plugged into an old boys' network, run up against biases and stereotyping, balance work and family life without much institutional support, and all the while the world requires them to look good and be groomed. It almost seems irresponsible for a mother to ignore these realities and not sensitize their daughters to the daunting, never-ending societal and corporate demands: "Women are never the right age. We are too young, we're too old. We are too thin, we're too fat. We wear too much makeup, we don't wear enough. We are too flashy in our dress, we don't take enough care. There isn't a thing we can do that is right."[13] Except for Barbie: she is always perfect, ageless, and childless.

While Barbie has always been pregnant with meaning and conflict, she herself has never carried a child. She is not a mother, and this lacuna was an intentional vision Ruth Handler and Ernst Dichter had for her. The only pregnant doll in Barbie's world ever produced by Mattel is teenage Midge, Barbie's cousin. Preggie Midge was introduced in 2002, sporting a husband, child, and a removable baby bump attached to Midge with a magnet. After an outcry by parents who claimed the doll encouraged teenage pregnancy, Walmart pulled it off the shelves just weeks before the holiday season.

When they came on the market, Barbie dolls were targeted toward girls aged nine to twelve. Girls were becoming teenagers, and they wanted to play with fashion, but they also still played with dolls. Those preteen years were a force in marketing. Generation after generation, girls seemed to mature faster. What Mattel didn't predict was the snowball effect it induced: older girls did not want to play with the same doll as their little sister. In the 1980s, Mattel witnessed a decline in the older girls demographic—the more it sold to younger kids aged six to nine, the less it was selling to its target nine to twelve demographic. This induced acceleration of adulthood would later prove detrimental to Mattel. But as long as Barbie enjoyed a monopoly over the entire fashion doll market, things were looking good, regardless of which age group sought Barbie's company.

Dichter helped Mattel understand that Barbie needed a complete persona. With elaborate story lines relating to endless accessories and Barbie brand products, Mattel was a pioneer of the ideas of a lifestyle brand and the experience economy that have become so central to today's strongest brands. Everything surrounding Barbie, from her style to her friends, from her car to her dream house, should tell a story of American luxury and success. And thus, Mattel gained doubly. It could convince parents to buy their daughters a Barbie despite their initial instincts, and along the way make tons of money from merchandising multiple story lines. Indeed, merchandising is a crude evolution of the Dichterian marketing methods, which imbue products with a soul. Merchandising uses a brand or an image from one product or service to sell other products in an endless virtuous (or vicious, depending on your footing in the consumer market) circle. A brand name, logo, or character is licensed to manufacturers of other items. As merchandising grows, the importance of intellectual property—the ownership of the trademark of the brand or logo and the copyright of the images, characters, and storyline sold—grows as well. Merchandising is the most lucrative part of the fashion doll industry; the company sells the doll to get children hooked, but actually turns a larger profit from all the related accessories—clothes, shoes, jewelry, bags, movies, books, stationery, cars, and homes. Ken is also a type of accessory, as are all of Barbie's friends. None serve a primary or autonomous purpose, but instead exist only in relation to Barbie.

Beyond embracing Dichter's devilish breakthroughs in using living laboratories as ground zero for advertisements and product development, Mattel was a marketing pioneer in other ways. Mattel was the first corporation to target commercials directly at children, rather than parents. In 1955, the Happiest Place on Earth opened in Anaheim, California: Disneyland (the "Florida Project" that became Disneyworld opened much later, in 1971). That same year Walt Disney was developing a variety TV show for kids, *The Mickey Mouse Club*. An opportunity presented itself, and Mattel jumped onboard.

The Handlers made a deal with ABC and the Disney Channel, investing nearly their entire profit from Mattel at the time, five hundred thousand dollars, into sponsoring the new, year-long show. The undertaking was nothing short of a radical gamble. At a time when TV marketing was still in diapers and marketing to children was virtually nonexistent, the Handlers were willing to invest all of Mattel's worth on these advertisements. The first Mattel commercial came out just before the holidays and advertised the Burp Gun. It was a rapid-fire gun and, except for the fact it belched out smoke when fired, rather than bullets, it was the spitting image of a real gun. A little boy named Billy ran around the house with his toy machine gun, imagining an African hunting trip. Another commercial featured a little boy with his automatic gun chasing a burglar who had entered his house. Each commercial ended with the voice-over slogan: "You can tell it's Mattel—It's Swell!" Come Christmas and Hanukkah, little boys around the country were begging for the Burp Gun. It sold out by Christmas Eve, with Mattel scrambling to repair a defective unit left behind for shipment to the White House as a special order for President Eisenhower's grandchild.

Directly marketing toys during kids' programming dramatically changed, or more specifically, expanded, consumption patterns. Kids now found out about toys from television, and could make demands beyond their parents—to grandparents and aunts and uncles. They could play parents against each other and, from that angle, Mattel was aware that rising divorce rates were good for the toy business. Asking for new toys was no longer a seasonal phenomenon. The market grew into a year-round business. Commercials took the form of stories. Now parents had to break through these pseudo-realities and tell children not to believe everything seen and heard in a commercial. In the first Barbie commercial a woman sang: "Someday, I'm gonna be 'xactly like you / Til then I know just what I'll do / Barbie, beautiful Barbie, I'll make believe that I am you."[14]

With Dichter's marketing genius and Handler's business savvy, Barbie became the icon of the me generation. By the 1980s, Mattel reported that Barbie reached 100 percent name recognition among mothers.[15] Ella King Torrey, a Yale University scholar who studied the rise of Barbie, described her as a cultural artifact of America's incredible consumerism.

An even more aggressive form of marketing emerged from the focus group method. Mattel contracted with the Girls Intelligence Agency (GIA), a Los Angeles market research firm that became infamous for orchestrating girls' slumber parties. The agency recruits girls, popular and cute, as young as eight years old. The girls get free products, have a sponsored slumber party, and report back to the agency about how the toys were received. The idea is not only to collect market intelligence but also to actually advertise through the parties and let the endorsement of "cool girls" (also named in the industry "alpha pups") create additional guerilla buzz. The agency promises that five hundred sponsored slumber parties can eventually reach six hundred thousand girls nationwide. Predating social media and YouTube, the corporate sponsored slumber parties were the original viral marketing.

The more Barbie went viral, the more the moral license that Dichter gave consumers—the license to focus away from her sexual nature and toward her image as a refined woman—began breaking down. Critics pierced through the rhetoric. They saw Barbie nakedly, despite attempts by the Handlers, Ryan, and Dichter to subdue her blatant sexuality, as, underneath it all, a plastic blonde bombshell aggressively marketed to little girls. The first set of critiques was directed, of course, at body image. When Lilli became Barbie, her body moved further toward anatomic impossibility. As a real-live adult woman her measurements would be 36-18-38. A group of Finnish researchers at the University Central Hospital in Helsinki calculated that if Barbie were a real woman, she would literally tip over due to the disproportionate weight of her breasts compared to the slenderness of her waist and limbs. According to their figures, she falls squarely within the weight criteria for anorexia and lacks the 17 percent to 22 percent body fat required for a woman to menstruate. Dr. Carole Lieberman, a Beverly Hills-based psychiatrist, once said that Barbie should be sold with a warning label, calling the doll the most destructive force on a woman's self-image ever produced. Several psychological studies have supported these allegations. For example, a 2005 study in the United Kingdom confirmed what mothers across the world feared: that girls tended to have heightened body dissatisfaction after playing with or being exposed to Barbie. Another British study finds that many girls go through a stage of hatred toward their Barbie, including punishing their dolls with decapitation and placing them in the oven. In the research, girls of seven to eleven years old were especially prone to burning their dolls, breaking their dolls' body parts, and cutting their hair off. Child-on-doll mutilation appears almost as a rite of passage in the secret life of girls.

In a 1977 interview with the *New York Times*, Ruth Handler explained why she gave Barbie those famous breasts: "Every little girl needed a doll through which to project herself into her dream of her future. If she was going to do role-playing of what she would be like when she was 16 or 17, it was a little stupid to play with a doll that had a flat chest. So I gave it beautiful breasts."[16] The focus on breasts has always been controversial. In 1975, Mattel launched Growing Up Skipper, a version of Barbie's little sister, which, if you twisted her left arm, you would witness the sprouting of her breasts and the narrowing of her waist ("2 Dolls in 1 for Twice as Much Fun.") The National Organization for Women accused Mattel once again of emphasizing breasts over brains and demanded that if Growing Up Skipper was to stay on the market, Mattel had an obligation to produce an equivalent boy doll, which grows his penis when his arm is twisted. Needless to say, Growing Up Ken whose penis hardens with the twist of his left arm, never came to market.

Ruth Handler insisted, however, that Barbie was so much more than her breasts. She was about a woman's choices, claiming, "My whole philosophy was that through the doll, the little girl could be anything she wanted to be."[17] Sex-positive feminists of the 1950s and '60s could get onboard with Handler's idea of women's choice, but the next generation was less receptive. The critique of Barbie's sexualized body accelerated. Women in the 1970s decried, for example, that even Barbie's feet were sexualized. Her heels are in a constant flex-point, arched to wear high heels, never flats—the Barbie *foint*, as it is now referred to by dance and yoga instructors—the excruciating ballet position of an unnatural semiflexed point.

Over the decades, Mattel introduced subtle changes into Barbie's body. An important year was 1971, when Malibu Barbie ditched the coy sideways glance and became the first doll that looked straight ahead. Barbie was growing more independent, and the message was one of confidence and autonomy. By then, Barbie had epitomized Southern Californian glamour: forever young, sun-kissed skin, and gym-toned body. In the mid-1980s, Barbie's heyday, Mattel launched the slogan campaign "We Girls Can Do Anything, right, Barbie?" The ad shows a girl greeting her mom, who comes home from a day in the office wearing a business suit and carrying a briefcase. Another ad scene shows an athletic girl running in a field, taking off her sports cap after a game—long hair releases from under the cap, and the girl rushes to her Barbie doll. The campaign perfected the combination of visions that each of Barbie's cooks had for her: Ruth Handler's idea of women as independent and career-oriented, Jack Ryan's idea of women's and girls' sexuality, and Ernst Dichter's understanding of the mother's need to see her girl successful but feminine and groomed. Mattel reached dominance in the girls' toy market by presenting a fully balanced image of modern women: they take on jobs and play in a man's world but they retain their traditional femininity and sexuality.

But as Barbie tried to reconcile modernity with conventional notions of sexuality, she and her product line were further attacked for becoming increasingly sexualized. One Australian report used *Barbie Magazine* as a lead example of what it termed *corporate pedophilia*.[18] As a law professor, having investigated actual pedophilia cases, I cringe at the analogy. It is surely overblown and unfairly dilutes the most appalling crimes, a bit like freely applying the term *Nazi* to people or settings (think Seinfeld's Soup Nazi). At the same time, the sexualization and distortion of body image in the world's leading girls' toys was undeniable. Child advocacy groups became tremendously critical when the Girl Scouts partnered with Barbie in a joint public relations campaign. "Holding Barbie, the quintessential fashion doll, up as a role model for Girl Scouts simultaneously sexualizes young girls, idealizes an impossible body type, and undermines the Girl Scouts' vital mission," wrote Susan Linn, director of Campaign for a Commercial-Free Childhood, one of the groups leading the charge.

Race critics have also been vocal about Barbie. Since the 1970s, advocates for racial equality and justice pointed out the obvious: Barbie was unmistakably vanilla-white. If dolls represent humanity in all its beauty and ugliness, Barbie was another link in a chain of racially controversial dolls. Parents and psychologists repeatedly raised the concern that, while children relate better to a doll of their own ethnicity, Barbie's market dominance meant that children of color were often left to play with the white queen of dolls. It was not until 1967 that the first black Barbie friend came on the market. She came to be known by the media as Colored Francie. In the midst of the civil rights movement, three years after the passage of the Civil Rights Act of 1964, which banned discrimination based on race, color, religion, sex, or national origin in employment by schools and public accommodations, and two years after the Selma to Montgomery marches in Alabama, the name *Colored Francie* was controversial, to say the least. The country was moving forward, and such terminology was stuck in the dark ages. Predictably, the market did not react well to Colored Francie, and she was quickly discontinued. Not a company to give up easily, the following year, Mattel released Christie. Then, in the 1980s, Barbie herself was infused with different skin complexions. By pouring darker colors into Barbie's original mold, Mattel executives believed they successfully checked the ethnicity box. And yet the African American Barbies had long straight hair, light skin, and Barbie's perfectly unreal figure.

Despite Mattel's effort to diversify its leading doll, critics continued to point out that black Barbies were merely "dye-dipped" white Barbies—dolls "modified only by a dash of color and a change of costume." Moreover, compared to Bratz, where the multiethnic girls are all presented equally, critics decry how groups of multiethnic Barbies are presented on the toy store shelves and in Mattel commercials hierarchically, with "white Barbie at the front, top, or center."[19]

The critics got louder, but over the years, Mattel has been remarkably tone deaf when reacting to controversy—often, in trying to take one step forward, it takes two steps back. As an example, in 1994, Mattel partnered with Nabisco to create an Oreo Barbie—a Barbie doll that carried an Oreo shaped purse and donned Oreo logos on her clothes. As it had done since the 1980s, Mattel produced the doll in the dominant, top-selling Caucasian version, as well as an African American counterpart. Predictably, an African American Barbie named Oreo did not sit well with the public. The derogatory nickname Oreo can be used to describe someone who "looks black on the outside but is white on the inside," which, paired with Black Barbie, caused controversy and outrage. Again, Mattel stopped production.

With regard to body image, Mattel willingly fueled some of Barbie's controversy. During the swinging '60s, the decade after Barbie took over the doll market, Twiggy became the world's first supermodel. Twiggy had a skinny, anorexic look and was sometimes called "Sticks." In 1967, Twiggy also became the first Barbie doll ever released by Mattel based on a real person. Slumber Party Barbie, in 1965, came equipped with a scale—stuck at 110 pounds—and a book called "How to Lose Weight." The book's first rule: "Don't eat!"

The conflict over body image has yet to fade. In 2009, as Barbie celebrated her fiftieth birthday with huge bashes around the world, controversy about Barbie's negative influence on girls' body image reached new heights. A West Virginia legislature introduced a bill to ban the sale of Barbie dolls in the state:

ARTICLE 25. BARBIE DOLLS.

§47-25-1. Unlawful sale of Barbie dolls.

It shall be unlawful in the state to sell "Barbie" dolls and other similar dolls that promote or influence girls to place an undue importance on physical beauty to the detriment of their intellectual and emotional development.

Thankfully, the bill, with its attack on people making their own choices as to which toys they buy, did not pass. But the unhappiness about Barbie's body, and Mattel's unresponsiveness, continued well into the first decade of the twenty-first century. With growing discontent centered on Barbie's unattainable perfection and her exclusive hold on the market, entrepreneurs attempted to disrupt the fashion doll with competing products every few years. The creators of those alternatives normally followed the script: *We read the studies about the damage to body image caused by Barbie so we launched a new doll.* Small entrepreneurs introduced such dolls as Lottie, modeled after the average nine-year-old girl's body and, most recently, Lammily, created by using proportions of the average nineteen-year-old woman as indicated by the Centers for Disease Control. But, until Bratz came on the market, this competition never put even a minor dent in Barbie's sales. Mattel executives passively observed their humble competitors but could not imagine a world where Barbie did not dominate. Lulled into a false sense of security, when Mattel finally took action to freshen up its brand, it was incremental and slow, minute and mundane. Too little, and too late, in the 1990s, Mattel introduced a mild redesign that shrunk Barbie's breasts and widened her midsection. It would not be until 2016 that Mattel would give Barbie an entirely new body, complete with a slightly more realistic twenty-four-inch waist and thirty-six-inch hips.

Still, the most poignant critique of Barbie has surrounded her choices and preferences—her soul, to use Dichter's original marketing parlance—rather than her body. In a memorable and critically acclaimed *Simpsons* episode called "Lisa vs. Malibu Stacy," Lisa Simpson takes on Mattel. Lisa purchases the new talking Malibu Stacy doll (standing in for Malibu Barbie, as perhaps the *Simpsons* producers were unwilling to deal with a Mattel trademark lawsuit; they would have won their defense of fair use, but the pain of litigation extends beyond the question of who wins). Lisa is dismayed when sexist phrases come out of sweet Stacy's mouth: "Don't ask me, I'm just a girl." "I wish they taught shopping at school." "Let's buy makeup so the boys will like us." "Thinking gives you wrinkles." Lisa takes action. She sets out to find Malibu Stacy's creator, Stacy Lovell (voiced by the wonderful Kathleen Turner) and challenges Lovell to create a less sexist doll. Lovell, who had long since been ousted from her company, is initially dismissive, uttering her memorable line, "Not now, I'm too drunk." But finally, Lovell agrees to work with Lisa and creates Lisa Lionheart: a doll with the wisdom of writer Gertrude Stein, the wit of cartoonist Cathy Guisewite, the tenacity of journalist Nina Totenberg, the common sense of suffragist and abolitionist Elizabeth Cady Stanton, the down-to-earth good looks of first lady and human rights activist Eleanor Roosevelt, and the voice of Lisa herself. At Malibu Stacy headquarters, executives have an emergency meeting about the threat posed by Lisa Lionheart. For a brief moment, Lisa Lionheart seems poised for success, but Malibu Stacy proves undefeatable. The corporation introduces a line of Malibu Stacy dolls with new hats. Lisa tells the eager crowd of girls that, "it's just the same doll with a stupid cheap hat," but largely to no avail. Barbie, or Malibu Stacy (who perhaps coincidentally shares the same name with Handler's granddaughter, Ken's daughter, who eventually wrote the sad book of poems about growing up in Barbie's shadow), marches on in the hearts of little girls everywhere. Lisa Simpson has been fighting windmills. She had answered the question no girl was asking.

A talking Barbie that only speaks sexist phrases was not born within the *Simpsons* writers' imagination. In 1992, Mattel introduced the Teen Talk Barbie line of talking dolls, which spouted lines like: "Will we ever have enough clothes?"; "I love shopping!"; "Wanna have a pizza party?"; and, wait for it, "Math class is tough!" This last phrase was heavily criticized by feminists and was featured prominently in an official report by the American Association of University Women, "How Schools and Corporate America Shortchange Girls." Just months after Teen Talk Barbie hit the shelves, Mattel CEO Jill Barad issued a statement: "We didn't fully consider the potentially negative implications of this phrase," and announced that the doll would no longer say the phrase. The company offered to replace the dolls that said the line. Once again, Mattel demonstrated its inability to proactively predict social temperature, and instead it remained reactive to yet another scandal. It also didn't seem to learn much from the controversy. When Mattel introduced a Barbie laptop loaded with design software and no other educational programs, a feminist magazine reviewed: "We knew Barbie was dumb, but her maker Mattel, is making her even dumber." In a 2014 Mattel-licensed book called *Barbie: I Can Be a Computer Engineer,* published by Random House, Barbie designs a game but needs a boy to come program it. Next, Barbie inadvertently infects her computer with a virus, and has her friend fix that too. "I'm only creating the design ideas," Barbie says, laughing. "I'll need Steven and Brian's help to turn it into a real game!" In the end, after the two guys program her game, Barbie victoriously declares: "I guess I can be an engineer!" Among the Amazon reviews by upset parents about the book's message, one parent suggests it be called "I Can Manipulate Boys Into Programming While I Sit Back and Take Credit."

"Lisa vs. Malibu Stacy" also features a scene pulled from real life. In the episode, one girl's Malibu Stacy doll says "My Spidey Sense is tingling! Anyone call for a web-slinger?" The reference is to the Barbie Liberation Organization's (BLO, deliberately parodying the acronym of the PLO) guerrilla action that swapped talking Barbie and G.I. Joe voice boxes. BLO began operations in 1993 and was composed of performance artists hailing from New York City and expanding into California. Led by a University of California student in San Diego, the group included artists as well as parents. They walked into stores, took Teen Talk Barbies and Talking G.I. Joes, switched their voice boxes, and returned them to their shelves. Barbie now said, "Eat lead, Cobra!" while G.I. Joe eagerly exclaimed in falsetto, "Let's go shopping!" The goal of the guerilla stint was disruption—of gender roles, of stereotypes, and of big corporations setting the standards of consumption and play.

Featured prominently in Mattel's marketing is a quote purportedly from Ruth Handler that her "whole philosophy of Barbie was that, through the doll, the girl could be anything she wanted to be." I've heard this line uttered many times by all the Mattel people I've talked to. Building on that story, Mattel has released a long line of career-minded Barbies, most recently as part of the "I can be . . ." line. Barbie has been a businesswoman, professional surfer, class president, and astronaut. Back in 2012, before Hillary Clinton's candidacy, Barbie even ran for the "Pink House" as the B Party's presidential candidate. But despite this pretense of empowerment, feminists remained unconvinced that Mattel cared about Barbie's careers apart from fashion modeling. In 2014, psychologists Aurora Sherman and Eileen Zurbriggen designed a lab experiment in which girls aged four to seven played with either a "fashion" Barbie, "doctor" Barbie, or—for the control group—Mrs. Potato Head. They then showed the girls pictures of different professions that are either traditionally female-dominated—teacher, nurse, flight attendant, or male-dominated—doctor, police officer, or construction worker. The researchers asked the girls whether they thought they could have the career in the picture and whether a boy could have that career. While girls overall thought boys had more career options than girls, the girls who played with Mrs. Potato Head reported more career options than the girls who played with either fashion or doctor Barbie.

One of my favorite authors, Anna Quindlen, has a particularly contentious relationship with Barbie. She writes, "My theory is that to get rid of Barbie you'd have to drive a silver stake through her plastic heart." Quindlen further compares Barbie to Dracula: "she appears in guises that mask her essential nature: Surgeon, Astronaut, UNICEF Ambassador." She also never ages and her physique is unreal. Quindlen described a conversation where her daughter asked, "Mama, why can't I have Barbie?" She responded, "Because I hate Barbie. She gives little girls the message that the only thing that's important is being tall and thin and having a big chest and lots of clothes. She's a terrible role model." Her daughter's comeback: "Oh, Mama, don't be silly. She's just a toy." Feminists constantly protest Mattel's responses to these critiques, and demand that the corporation just "quit fronting and abandon the pretense" that Barbie has anything empowering to offer young girls. Instead, critics decry that "Barbie sends our girls one message, and it's this: 'You can *do* anything and you can *be* anything—as long as you look like *this*: very tall, very thin, very Caucasian, and very beautiful.' "[20]

Did decades of criticism catch up to America's golden girl? Or was it the competition? As Carter Bryant grew restless with Barbie's perfection, Barbie herself began to struggle with her own self-image. She was aging, she was being bashed by the media, and she was about to divorce Ken. Was it avoidable? Mattel tried making over her image, but each adjustment seemed superficial, and it was difficult to avoid the new truth: Barbie was losing her edge.

6 | THE COLDEST MEN IN THE ROOM

If you don't have a competitive advantage, don't compete.

—JACK WELCH

It doesn't make sense to hire smart people and then tell them what to do; we hire smart people so they can tell us what to do.

—STEVE JOBS

WE REACT TO BEING BITTEN. We spend a lot less time thinking about what might bite us next. Barbie has meant something special to girls, and oftentimes to boys, all around the world. As the company's most lucrative brand, she has meant the world to Mattel. Throughout the second half of the twentieth century, Mattel execs relied on her reign over the market. Barbie's loyal servants anthropomorphized their plastic doll in corporate statements and stories—grown men were as involved in the make-believe as their young consumers. Barbie was a diva-celebrity who needed around the clock PR to help manage her image, which was in need of serious rejuvenation. When she entered the twenty-first century, the *New York Times* wrote that Mattel's efforts to revitalize her image smacked of "a desperate publicist trying to revive the moribund career of a Hollywood star . . . Mattel is pulling out all the stops to put her back on her feet."[1] Channeling Dichter's vision for Barbie at her birth, Mattel executives repeatedly told their employees to think of Barbie as human—inspiring not only fashion and fun, but also friendship and dreams. In marketing campaigns, Barbie is always talked about as a real person, not a plastic doll. Inside Mattel's boardroom, Barbie is flesh and blood and so, naturally, any attack on her is bound to get bloody.

Decline and Divorce

Hindsight is 20/20, but could Mattel have predicted the rapid decline of its top moneymaker? Every major brand, be it Apple, Walmart, Nike, or Facebook, attracts disapproval. So do leading celebrities, politicians, and industry leaders face amplified feedback. If Barbie was the subject of criticism, why could it not just be a sign of her success—a symptom of her invincible popularity? In 2015, the ever-illustrious Madonna surprised rapper Drake, much younger than she, with a long, steamy kiss during his Coachella set. To some, the kiss was "disgusting." These online haters flooded the web with offensive comments. Madonna reacted by posting on Instagram, "If you don't like me and still watch everything I do, bitch, you're a *fan*." While Mattel would never dare respond to its critics using such crude language, the company's reaction to any Barbie criticism was similar in attitude: haters—whether feminist commentators, journalists, parents, or aspiring competitors—are simply a symptom of the greater picture. Everyone everywhere is a Barbie fan, whether they like her or not.

And indeed, for decades, despite the controversy she attracted, or perhaps in part because of it—after all, it is better to be hated than ignored—she dominated the market. As Barbie entered the 1990s, she was so popular that two Barbie dolls were sold somewhere in the world every single second. Her annual sales soared to nearly two billion dollars.

But despite Barbie's success, Ruth Handler's forced departure in 1975 had marked the end of an era for Mattel. While Handler expanded Mattel too quickly and without regard for securities law, the company was edgy and fluid under her leadership. Without Handler's unrestrained ambition, Mattel relaxed and relied on Barbie's success as if it would never end. Mattel switched from inventing new products to accessorizing and protecting existing toy lines. Over the next thirty years, Barbie would wear a hundred different hats, but still consumers eventually began to crave something beyond the same old doll playing new, yet always similar, roles.

Indeed, after five decades of market dominance, Barbie was facing death by a thousand cuts. Three generations of parents and children spent decades simultaneously embracing and criticizing Barbie, but by the turn of the century, the doll queen's popularity was in decline. Behind the scenes, Carter Bryant was getting tired of her, and young girls were too.

Suddenly, in the mid-1990s, for the first time since her dazzling transformation from Lilli into Barbie, sales started to sag. Barbie's infallible mythos began to wrinkle: she was having a midlife crisis. It wasn't all due to her inconsistent messages, but it was certainly happening well before Bratz entered the scene. As the world around Barbie changed, so did the girls to whom she was sold. For years, Barbie had been marketed to preteens, or *tweens*, girls from nine to twelve, but the world of play is dynamic and shifting. The toy industry thrives on novelty—when truly competitive, it is an innovate-or-die market—and a new generation of girls were no longer interested in playing with Barbie.

From a marketing perspective, tweens are viewed as having more market potential than other kids age groups because they are three markets in one. Tweens spend money of their own, from gift cards, the tooth fairy, and allowances; they direct the spending of their parents, and they also are a future market—they soon become teenagers who will continue with the consumption patterns and tastes they acquired as tweens. However, the age group for Barbie shifted slowly downward until she became a toy for toddlers and preschool girls. The irony of course is that the phenomenon of kids acting older at a younger age has, in large part, been driven by the toy industry and Mattel's dominance therein. Parents have spent years decrying the fact that Barbie dragged children into adulthood, and sexualized girls, much too early. And yet, as explained by an internal Mattel memo, the company's leadership missed this critical shift:

> *In 2001, the Barbie brand was in a critical stage of its life cycle. The impact of media, TV, music and other external factors were pushing girls to mature faster than ever. Barbie sales were seeming younger. Older girls, 8 to 10, after playing with Barbie since they were 3, were seeking a variety of alternative play opportunities. They were aspiring to become teenagers and be associated with things that represented that stage in a girl's life. As a brand, Barbie did not appear to have evolved with the times or with the consumer.*

In other words, girls were maturing quickly, and Barbie was aging ungracefully. By 1999, the year Carter returned to Mattel from his sabbatical in Missouri, Barbie's sales were in free fall.[2]

The toy business is about storytelling. A successful toy brand is a rich ecosystem, which lives in other consumer products and has staying power. Fads come and go, but a true franchise is the golden goose of the toy industry. And yet Mattel had not introduced a truly new product in twenty years, nor did it know how to bring the Barbie franchise into the twenty-first century.

The last major brand that Mattel had successfully introduced to the market was not even within the "pink-shelf" space—the girls' toy market. It was Masters of the Universe, which was a response to Mattel's slow reactions to changing tastes in the boy's toy market. And even that was rooted in mistake. In 1976, Mattel's CEO Ray Wagner, Ruth Handler's successor, was approached by George Lucas. The filmmaker offered a partnership: Mattel would produce the action figures and other toy products for a new film—*Star Wars*—that he was about to launch. The first *Star Wars* movie, as fans remember well, came out in 1977. But Wagner blithely passed over the opportunity, not seeing the immense potential of the franchise. Upon seeing the commercial success of the original *Star Wars* trilogy over the next few years as well as of all related merchandise, Mattel scrambled. It attempted to launch several toy lines, each a flop. None even made a dent in the action figure market. Then a lead designer for Mattel came up with a simple idea: He-Man—a parallel to Barbie's impossible ideal of female beauty—a massively bulked up action figure—a caricature of masculinity. Masters of the Universe was created around the conflict between He-Man, aka Prince Adam, and the evil Skeletor on the planet Eternia, a hybrid medieval sword and sorcery and sci-fi technology world, with a vast number of supporting characters. Before He-Man and Masters of the Universe, male heroes were rather normal looking, but since then, "if Barbie's responsible for Pam Anderson and Victoria's Secret models, then He-Man deserves at least some of the credit—or blame—for Brad Pitt in *Troy*."[3]

Masters of the Universe enjoyed great success in the years initially following its 1981 release. But its release was tainted with lawsuits and its success was short-lived, due mainly to Mattel's poor marketing decisions. Immediately after the brand took off, Mattel filed suit against a small toy competitor, which launched an action figure series, Warlords, designed to compete with Masters of the Universe. Mattel claimed copyright and trademark infringement but the court, comparing the two groups of heroes, found very little similarity between the copyrightable and trademarked elements of each. After Mattel lost its case, it was back in court. This time, it was Mattel who faced suit brought by the creators of Conan the Barbarian, claiming that He-Man was simply Conan disguised with a blond wig. As the judge described in the case, the lawsuit pit "Conan of Cimmeria, the Barbarian, against He-Man of Eternia, a Master of the Universe, two warriors who have been fighting for five years on anomalous terrain: the courtroom, instead of the battlefield." And, at the end of all that fighting, the case was dismissed; as the court ruled, no one deserves a copyright over hunky men.

In 1980, before filing their lawsuit, the rights holders of Conan the Barbarian negotiated the character's toy rights with Mattel, but eventually Mattel passed on developing Conan character toys and instead launched its own series, Masters of the Universe. The court dismissed the lawsuit, finding that all bulky masculine action figures were basically the same anyway—no one deserves a copyright over the idea of male hunks: "The Court has read comics starring characters named 'Atlas'; 'Beowulf, Dragon Slayer'; 'Hercules'; 'John Carter, Warlord of Mars'; 'Tarzan, Lord of the Jungle'; and 'Tor, the Caveman.' All of the protagonists are square-jawed and broad-shouldered. All are inordinately strong, and all wear scraps of cloth that reveal every distended muscle. In the vernacular, they are all 'hunks.' "

Regardless of Mattel's hunk du jour, Barbie remained the company's perennial brand and for another twenty years, no one at the corporation created a major new franchise. Mattel barely even developed Barbie's existing franchise. The dolls introduced along with Barbie were sidekicks: accessories meant to flesh out her world. Barbie's partner, Ken, named after the Handler's son, was introduced in 1961, and epitomized the proper role of any supporting characters in the Barbie Show. Like Barbie, Ken was aggressively desexualized, though his anatomical correctness was less of a priority. Mattel may have filed off Lilli's nipples in transforming her into Barbie, but her breasts remained disproportionately huge. Ken sadly got little more than a suggestive nod. To her credit, Ruth and other female designers at Mattel had wanted to give him a more realistic and bigger bulge, but the male executives were reluctant. The result was a compromise, a respectable *bump*, as it was called in the company, but nothing to write home about. Over the years, Ken and his bump remained the passenger in Barbie's pink corvette until 2004, when Mattel announced Barbie's and Ken's divorce, the same year it filed its lawsuit against MGA.

The courtroom saga and the divorce were both attempts to revive Barbie. With Barbie newly single, the company hoped to revitalize her image and match the edginess of her unexpected rival, Bratz. However, fans saw the divorce as the forgone conclusion to a loveless, mismatched relationship. Mattel's reimaginings and thin expansions of the Barbie franchise were, at best, mired in mistakes and over-reactions, and Ken's character was a prime example. In 1993, Mattel introduced Earring Magic Ken, who donned an ear piercing, faux-fur vest, and lavender mesh shirt. Sexuality rumors swirled. In 1994, Exhibitions International produced an art show telling the story of Barbie's evolution as a cultural icon. Mattel, though initially supportive to the point of funding the exhibit, pulled out its support in outrage when it discovered the exhibit included an exploration of Ken's homoerotic vibe. That same year, Mattel refused a request from gay men's lifestyle magazine *Genre* to shoot two Ken dolls in a photo spread about first dates. Rather than taking their chances with a copyright lawsuit, by that time Mattel's modus operandi, the magazine's editors opted to white out the figures, leaving only traces of their outlines. Copyright intimidation and homophobia seemed to unite under Mattel's corporate umbrella at the time.

Carter Bryant, who was openly gay, could not have been happy with Mattel's conservative managerial decisions that suppressed fan explorations of sexual identity; after all, his prototype FrankenBratz doll consisted partly of a Barbie body wearing Ken's boots. He was also disillusioned by the glass ceiling he hit after returning to Mattel and rejoining the Barbie division. Mattel's corporate culture is infamously stifling, with an established hierarchy overpowering the mammoth corporation: there were workers and there were bosses. When Carter worked at Mattel, his annual salary was fifty-eight thousand dollars. Ivy Ross, his boss and the head of his division, made closer to four hundred thousand dollars. Mattel's plutocracy ensured the reigning elite never felt pressured to think outside the box. The announcement of Barbie's and Ken's separation was one of many calculated publicity stunts, but the divorce reflected the end of an era. Critics and fans alike were losing interest, pointing to Barbie's unimaginative plateau.

Isaac Larian was among the most vocal about why Barbie should call it quits. At first, when MGA launched Bratz, Larian simply described Barbie as "horrible." He criticized her lack of detail and the doll's poorly executed design. But soon enough, Larian shifted to mocking Barbie specifically for her age. "It is time for Barbie to retire," he said, "I mean, even Michael Jordan retired." Larian's favorite provocation was to analogize Barbie's decline to that of Mike Tyson: both (pathetically) didn't know when to retire. Barbie started to look like the ultimate desperate housewife. Midlife crises in Toyland, similar to the real world, meant that in her mid-forties, Barbie was discontent with her longtime spouse, wanted to continue flaunting her perfect body, and anxiously hoped to regain her popularity. But real change was something that had not happened at Mattel for decades.

Cannibals Need Not Apply

Mattel's failure to reward their most creative employees certainly explains part of Mattel's lack of innovation, but why couldn't the company even capitalize on its own success? Why was Masters of the Universe, a boy's doll line, the last new franchise the world's largest toy company introduced in over twenty years? In internal Mattel memos, a surprising term is repeated: *cannibalization*. As the dominant manufacturer of the industry, having reached a quasi-monopoly position in the toy market, Mattel's executives constantly worried that any new product it put out would compete with the company's own products. The talented Nora Ephron used to say, "Writers are cannibals." She meant that creative people take from the ideas and world around them, and transform those ideas into their art. But at Mattel, not only was the company ferociously averse to anyone outside the corporation reusing or remixing the images of Barbie, but the company was also averse to competing with itself.

This aversion is not entirely irrational. Nobel laureate economist Kenneth Arrow explained that competition spurs innovation. Arrow showed that once a company receives a near-monopoly status, say, dominating the fashion doll industry for three generations, it has far fewer incentives to undertake the risks of improving and innovating. A company that maintains a dominant market position will measure the costs of innovation research against the profits that the company already receives through its current product line. The "Arrow effect" predicts that under such continuous market dominance, innovation will only lead the monopolist to replace its own market share, leading to only marginal gains over current profits.[4] In other words, another doll would compete with Barbie, cannibalizing her, and Mattel would be trading the dollars it garnered from the new doll with losses on Barbie—not the best motivator for market innovation. In contrast, when a competitor, an upstart perhaps, enters the market, it calculates far greater profits from innovative improvements because, initially, its profit baseline is set much lower. MGA, for example, until Bratz, did not have a truly successful doll on the market. MGA therefore had far more incentives, according to the Arrow effect, for drastic innovation. It was far more likely to launch a new product, which a larger corporate behemoth might not consider worth its while.

Most significantly, the Arrow effect explains why industries stagnate when too concentrated or, conversely, why companies need competitors to be motivated to innovate. For markets to be competitive, some regulation, for example antitrust law, which promotes market competition by regulating anticompetitive practices—monopolies, cartels, price fixing—must be in place. But where does intellectual property protection fit in? Ironically, intellectual property used to be a branch of antitrust law because it was understood that monopolies over inventions and expressions can have the effect of limiting the competition. Over the decades, this wisdom has been forgotten, and nowadays intellectual property often serves to drive out competition and concentrate markets.

Mattel, having held the position of number-one toy company in the world for decades (until it was unseated by Lego in 2015), has been extremely reluctant to introduce new toys, fearing that any new product would cannibalize its top sellers. Insiders describe the atmosphere at Mattel as the cult of Barbie. As one insider to Mattel told me, "if you wanted to do something different, you were dismissed as violating the 'pure rules of Barbie.' All that was expected of you was to come up with multiple versions of the same dress." In the corporate boardroom, it was safer in the short term to focus on previous successes. Mattel's story is not unlike other great industry leaders that started out with revolutionary creative sparks and then became, in a sense, too big to innovate.

The CEO Who Came from Cheese

CEO Robert Eckert arrived at Mattel in the midst of Barbie's sales crisis and just as Carter was preparing for his final farewell from the company. In May 2000, Eckert ended a twenty-three-year term as CEO of Kraft Foods and seemingly seamlessly took the reins at Mattel.[5] A Chicago-born career executive, he was a newcomer to the toy industry, but approached his new position at Mattel like he approached any other job, focusing on cost cutting, efficiency in sales, and bottom-line profits. In 2002, Eckert was named as one of *BusinessWeek*'s "Top Twenty-Five Managers of the Year," describing him as "a voracious cost-cutter." When Eckert came to Mattel he looked for deadweight: spending to eliminate and people to terminate. He closed Mattel's last manufacturing plant within the United States, sharing his predecessors' position that *Made in the USA* is a wasteful anachronism. According to *BusinessWeek*, under Eckert's leadership "Mattel delivered strong growth, improved operating margins, and generated over $8.2 billion of cash flow." *Fortune* magazine gave Eckert a far more backhanded compliment, writing, "blandness becomes him." At the executive level, Eckert replaced some major personnel, including Adrienne Fontanella, the president of the Girl's Unit (though Fontanella walked away with an almost ten-million-dollar severance package). In the rank and file, depending on who's counting, Eckert fired between 10 percent to 15 percent of Mattel's workforce.

Eckert himself took pride in being an underpaid CEO—his cash salary was just over one million per year—and he declined to raise his salary the entire time he worked for Mattel.[6] And yet, before we applaud his scruples too loudly, note that the bulk of his annual pay consisted of stock options valued in the millions. To replace Fontanella, Eckert appointed the head of the boys' toys division, Matt Bousquette, to become the president of a newly consolidated division Eckert created, Mattel Brands unit, combining the girls and boys. Bousquette was the first man to be put in charge of Barbie for a long time, and he issued a statement that he planned to take Barbie off her pedestal.

Eckert was the polar opposite of Isaac Larian in both background and temperament. Eckert's voice flattened to monotony; his style impassive and utterly unremarkable. He came from the food industry to the toy industry and rumor had it that he was planning to use Mattel as a stepping stone on his way back to fast food. The whispers suggested he was being groomed as the next McDonald's CEO. In one of many snarky remarks Larian made about Mattel's leadership, he shot, "Mattel's boss comes from the cheese industry. They do not see that selling cheese and toys are very different." And while Larian came off as a man with something to prove—a man who needs to pick, and win, fights—Eckert embodied an air of over-confidence, a man who believes in his natural and secure place in corporate America.

Part of an old boys' network of Fortune 500 professional CEOs, Eckert frankly admits that lucrative executive gigs only go to members of an exclusive society. When asked what it is like to become a CEO, Eckert flatly replies, sans gusto or cogitation,

> It's like a lot of things in life. It's like getting into a tough school. This is a club that's hard to get into. If you're a Fortune 500 C.E.O., there are only 500 people in that club. But once you get into the club, it's not that special. It's not intimidating. It's not the toughest job I've had, but it's the toughest job to get. Once you're in the job and you're comfortable in the job, it's just like any other job. You do the best you can.[7]

It's like any other job, except you have to first "get it." When contemplating the kind of people he wanted surrounding him within the corporate hierarchy, Eckert states simply, "I'm looking for fit, personality, values. Is this the kind of person we want around here?" Fit, personality, values—the trio word combo reminds me all too well of a contemporary body of research which reveals how concepts like "organizational fit" used in today's recruitment practices operate as code for hiring people just like you.

Eckert's predecessor at Mattel did not, in fact, come from Eckert's professional CEO old boys' club. Jill Barad started her career after college as a beauty consultant for a cosmetics company. She had dreamed of being an actress and actually landed a small role in a film called *Crazy Joe*. She also married a Hollywood executive, Thomas

Barad, and moved to Los Angeles, where she took a job at an ad agency. When she applied to Mattel, she pitched her idea to sell cosmetics to children. Mattel brought her in, and she rose in the ranks, becoming Mattel's CEO in the 1980s, the second woman after Ruth Handler to reach the top of the company. Times had not changed much since Handler's generation, and when Barad became CEO, she was one of only three female CEOs of Fortune 500 companies. However, as sales began to dwindle in the late 1990s, and following a gravely miscalculated $3.5 billion acquisition of the software company Learning Co., she resigned abruptly and was replaced by Eckert (again, not to worry: Barad's severance package exceeded forty million dollars).

Had Eckert made the transition from the food to the toy industry a decade earlier, his corporate club confidence probably would have worked out for him. But Eckert came to the toy giant the year after Mattel saw its first annual loss in more than a decade, and just a couple of years before Barbie's biggest competitor ever was introduced by a newcomer to the toy industry. Isaac Larian believes he got very lucky launching MGA after Barad left and Eckert took over. "Barad was a product and marketing genius. She would have slaughtered us. I had lunch with her recently and she told me, 'You know that if I were there, I would have destroyed Bratz immediately when you came out with her.'" Mattel normally responded quickly to new competition, using aggressive marketing, at-cost pricing, and immediate litigation. But Mattel had become complacent.

Project Platypus

Sometimes ignorance really is bliss. As long as Mattel executives were unaware that their former Barbie designer Carter Bryant was the wind beneath Isaac Larian's entrepreneurial wings, they would attempt to decode how to regain their competitive edge. Beyond cost cutting, Eckert commissioned an expensive study from the global management consulting firm Bain to pinpoint Mattel's problems. The Bain consultants told Mattel that MGA introduced products to the market faster, and was better at advertising, promoting, and marketing. Mattel also held an internal study, producing a report titled "The Bratz Brief" on November 14, 2003. This time, the conclusion was more critical: Bratz had a unique look, and the market simply perceived them as cooler than Barbie. The report was clear. Mattel had a creativity problem.

At first, Mattel hoped to fundamentally change the culture of creativity at the company. Ivy Ross, Carter's boss at the Barbie department, was considered a luminary in the creative industries. Ambitious and confident, she was hired by the company thanks to her reputation for linking creative design and business management. Ross started out her career as a jewelry designer, but she soon crossed over into the business world and took on the direction of creative departments in some of the world's strongest brands, including Swatch Watch, Calvin Klein, Coach Handbags, and Liz Claiborne. She was brought to Mattel in that critical year, 1998, when Carter was on sabbatical and Barbie was showing signs of sagging, as Senior Vice President of Worldwide Product Design & Brand Image for the Girls Division. Her job—in other words—was to make sure Barbie comes out on top.

Eckert, who took over the reins at Mattel two years after Ross was hired, hoped to rely on her self-proclaimed talent to induce creativity within companies. Ross bragged, "I was hired to make Barbie a modern woman." In an internal Mattel memo, titled "The Vision," Ross wrote that the time had come for "envisioning creating a cultural movement via a new doll for girls ages 7 through 10. . . . The time is ripe to work differently at Mattel, to think differently and more holistically, work more collaboratively and change the culture inside and out." She used all the right buzzwords: holistic innovation, collaboration, teamwork, inside-out culture. She also first advised the company to transform its physical workspace.

Mattel was located in an open warehouse—an area reminiscent of an airplane hangar—but the cubicle-lined spaces were not conducive to interaction. Ross told Mattel's leadership that to encourage a cross-pollination of ideas, employees needed to interact more and get out of their office chairs. In Ross's view, the physical spaces should look more playful: instead of the conservative cubicle layout, there should be beanbags and giant balls to sit on. Ross also brought in creativity gurus, conducted Japanese tea ceremonies, invited a child psychoanalyst, hosted laughter sessions, hired clowns and jugglers and an expert in brainwave frequencies—all part of her project to trigger creativity through inspiration. Groups threw stuffed bunnies at each other to release their creative juices, and brainwave expert Jeffrey Thompson recorded team members humming collectively, concluding three months of group work had allowed them to reach "brainwave synchronicity in its creative mindset space."[8]

Ross even branded her own efforts at corporate revitalization, dubbing her vision Project Platypus, which is, according to Ross, an experimental process to encourage employees to think outside the box. A platypus combines elements from disparate parts of the animal world, and the plan was to remove about fifteen employees from various departments from their regular positions and offices at the Mattel headquarters and place them in a smaller, more intimate office space nearby for a period of three months. Ross promised that the framework would allow employees to "cleanse their palates."[9] She said, "I am someone who believes you can't get new ideas by being self-referential. You have to explore and be out in the world."

But Eckert soon saw the figures: leaning on Ivy Ross and her platypus magic, blissfully bringing in acrobats and jugglers and innovation gurus, did not reverse Barbie's sagging sales.

The new century arrived and brought with it Bratz, who smashed the market wide open and quickly became a worldwide hit. The new dolls' success was overwhelming. They sold billions and, during the

2005 holiday season, did the impossible—they dethroned the ice queen. It was the first time a fashion doll *ever* sold more than Barbie. Bratz captured almost half the fashion doll market, signaling the end of Barbie's fifty-year reign.

Hip Hop Designed by a Platypus Committee

It took three years after MGA released Bratz before Mattel tried to seize ownership over Bratz by claiming Carter Bryant's designs and inventions. Mattel's first intuition, it seems, was to mimic. In 2002, the year after Bratz came on the market, Mattel introduced a series of new dolls. It never wanted to put out a competing doll to Barbie, but Bratz's success demanded a response. My Scene was a new line of dolls similar to Barbie but with larger heads. Still, Mattel was unable to let go of its flagship doll; a version of Barbie was one of the three My Scene initial characters. My Scene was a flop. It failed to capture Bratz's magic. The *New York Times* described the dolls' features as "exaggerated lips and bulging, makeup-caked eyes." Isaac Larian called them "a cheap imitation" of Bratz.

Not easily defeated, a year before the trial began, a rushed Mattel introduced Flavas (pronounced *Flay-vuhs*, like "flavors") in 2003. Too little, too late, Flavas were designed as yet another response to Bratz. They were the same size as Bratz, dressed with the same urban edge, and similarly launched together as a multiethnic squad of girls. But still Mattel couldn't get it right. Flavas never felt like the real thing—rather, they looked like unwitting parodies of edginess. The dolls revealed their midriffs just like Bratz, but they lacked authenticity. By contrast, MGA, after several redesigns and tweaks of Carter's original idea, kept the creative edge Carter envisioned in Bratz, combined with Larian's sense of fluid ethnicity.

From day one, Bratz dolls had a range of skin tones. The girl squad—Yasmin, Sasha, Jade, and Cloe—were multiethnic. They roughly corresponded with Carter Bryant's original vision for the girl squad: a Latina, an African American, an Asian, and a White blonde. But Larian actually resisted Carter's rigid ethnic lines. The world as he saw it was not black and white. He wanted more fluidity, and for all the dolls to appear multiethnic; increasingly the reality of children around the world. MGA's representatives proudly refer to Bratz dolls as "ethnically ambiguous." Jasmin Larian, now working with her father on the next generation of Bratz, enthusiastically explains that Bratz fans "only know a Black president. These kids, they are so color blind. I remember being at Toys "R" Us for a launch, and seeing little girls pick out which doll they wanted, and you saw the all-American blonde girl picking out Sasha—not because of her skin tone . . . [but] just because she identified most with her style. . . . Before this brand, no one would dare to come out with a group of five girls, four of whom are ethnically diverse."[10]

Compared to Bratz, Mattel's Flavas felt stale on arrival. The six Flavas—Kiyoni Brown, Happy D, Tika, Liam, P. Bo, and Tre— were marketed by Mattel as "authentic" and with "attitude." Mattel brashly described them as "the *first* reality-based fashion doll brand." The *New York Times*, on the other hand, described Flavas as "heavily inspired" by Bratz. *Newsweek* and the *Wall Street Journal* pointed out the obvious: the success of Bratz forced Mattel to compete with itself. Mattel now had an "anti-Barbie of its own." In stark contrast to the media's positive reception of Bratz, the Flavas were mostly criticized as being overly stereotypical. The *Chicago Tribune* described them as "unimaginative stereotypes." One of the dolls was deemed to resemble a "drug-dealing pimp." Larian of course was quick to agree. He called the Flavas "gangster Barbie" and said, "The only thing that's missing is a cocaine vial."[11] The *Los Angeles Times* quoted toy industry analyst Sean McGowan as saying, "You look at Flavas and it looks like hip-hop as designed by committee. Bratz doesn't." Mattel responded to the harsh reception by pulling Flavas from shelves less than a year after their release: another utter failure. Mattel continued releasing other competing products but, like Barbie, they all paled against their bratty competition.

The Anonymous Tip from the East

In August 2002, CEO Bob Eckert received an anonymous letter. It began "Dear CEO" and contained a tip: "I have information that I think Mattel should investigate." The letter described how a former employee named Carter Bryant was the original architect behind Barbie's biggest competitor. The note further informed Eckert that Carter had "worked out a deal with MGA that let him collect a large sum of money each year from MGA in exchange for his secrecy." This clandestine missive gave Mattel insight into the origins of its nemesis, genetically linking Bratz and Barbie, plastic to plastic. Mattel was now ready to destroy Bratz as it had destroyed its enemies for decades: through litigation. For large corporations that have in-house counsel as full-time employees and outside counsel on retainer, litigation can be an extension of the boardroom. Whatever you can leverage and slow down your competition even for a few months in the consumer market is worth bringing in the lawyers for.

Once Eckert received that fateful letter revealing the inventor behind Bratz, Mattel diverted enormous amounts of resources, both monetary and emotional, to battle MGA to the bitter end. Eckert dug in and prepared for war. Faced with invincible competition, Eckert looked for answers. Was it possible that Barbie's woes were the direct consequence of failing to control one single, creative employee? Was it the illegal betrayal of a conniving insider or the overall ossification of a corporate giant? Where else could the seeds of Bratz have come from? Had Ross's Project Platypus inspired Carter? Or was it really that her decline was the cumulative result of Mattel's leadership utterly failing to pick up on shifts in consumer markets? The latter possibility was, of course, the least pleasant. Two months after the anonymous letter arrived, Mattel's in-house lawyer received a phone call from a group of Hong Kong lawyers representing a Taiwanese toy manufacturer MGA sued over infringement of Bratz. The Hong Kong lawyers told Mattel's counselors that they had some interesting information. On November 24, 2003, a meeting was set and, face-to-face in Hong Kong, Mattel's lawyers were given the contract between MGA and Carter Bryant from September 18, 2000—the contract that was signed immediately after Carter put together his FrankenBratz mock-up while at Mattel.

In war, the enemy of your enemy is your friend. Though MGA supported Carter, and allowed him to enjoy the fruits of his creative labor, it was nonetheless a corporation driven first and foremost by profit, just like Mattel. And like Mattel, Isaac Larian was militant about protecting MGA's intellectual property and preserving his products' international exclusivity. As the Bratz brand grew, MGA filed lawsuits around the world to prevent toy manufacturers from copying Bratz products and retailers from selling knockoffs. In 2002, a Hong Kong manufacturer, Toys & Trends, began marketing a doll line called Funky Tweenz, which had the feel of Bratz and appealed to the same age group. MGA filed a lawsuit asking the court to prohibit the sale of Funky Tweenz, and the court at first granted MGA's request for an injunction against the copycat dolls, but MGA eventually lost its infringement claims. The Hong Kong court characterized MGA's aggressive litigious actions against the Hong Kong company as the "use of 'a sledgehammer to crack a nut.'" Undeterred, MGA successfully went after three more companies incorporated in Hong Kong, claiming the companies infringed on MGA's copyrights and trademarks by attempting to sell dolls like Bratz. It was these same browbeaten Hong Kong lawyers who figured out Bratz might not even belong to MGA after all. The lawyers reached out to MGA's bigger and stronger competitor Mattel, urging Mattel to dig deeper and claim its rightful place as the originator of Bratz.

For the next year, at least officially, Mattel maintained its outwardly serene façade. Eckert appeared as subdued and cold as his ice queen, and the company feigned its commitment to outcompeting MGA, releasing the Flavas in 2003. Internally, however, the company was a hive of activity as executives coordinated attack plans and legal counsels exchanged strategies. Then, on July 18, 2003, the *Wall Street Journal* published an article that, for the first time, mentioned the Carter-Bratz nexus.

In the article, Carter Bryant was identified as the designer of Bratz. Someone at MGA, perhaps Larian himself, had slipped. Larian might have relaxed a little too much as his Bratz empire solidified. Perhaps he became even cockier, or had already received the news that the secret was out and Mattel was about to come after him and Carter. Whatever the reason, Larian described a doll design contest commissioned by MGA, and identified Carter Bryant as the contest's winner in the article—his design led to the launch of Bratz. The article further suggested that, inside Mattel, some were convinced that Bratz borrowed liberally from a Mattel project scrapped at the testing stage in 1998. Mattel, however, declined to comment. And yet, four days after the article was published, Mattel's chief counsel sought out Carter Bryant's current address, supposedly to get him to testify in litigation involving another claim for theft of trade secrets. The case in question involved an inventor who sued Mattel, claiming he pitched a fairy doll idea to the company and was rejected. Shortly afterward, Mattel released various fairy doll products. They told Carter Bryant that they needed him to testify about his involvement in the fairy doll's design. Little did Carter know that Mattel was already planning to sue him.

Mattel, a regular in the courtroom and already in a state of panic over its top brand's unforeseen decline, committed its vast resources to attacking Carter and MGA. In an e-mail to Tim Kilpin, his new senior vice president of girls' marketing and designs, Eckert wrote: "I'm starting to develop a line of thinking about what happened to Barbie." In a reply e-mail titled "Confidential: The Barbie Call to Action," Kilpin wrote that Mattel had "been out-thought and out-executed." Kilpin started at Mattel in 1984 but left for a few years during the 1990s to lead parts of Disney Co.'s toy division. He returned to Mattel in 2003 to fix the Barbie crisis after Carter Bryant and Ivy Ross both left. He wrote Eckert that it would require "grenades to be launched," as "complacency will kill us."

When Mattel did eventually sue, Larian explained the suit was "little more than sour grapes, it's an absolute pure act of desperation. Mattel lives in a fantasyland. They don't own Bratz and they know it. It's all fabricated paranoia from a company that's lost its leadership. Barbie, I think, has been around for too long. Kids have been looking for something new and different. They saw that in Bratz and that's why it's selling."[12]

According to Larian, Mattel wished it had the imaginative talent to develop a product like Bratz, but, at the end of the day, it couldn't imagine anything more creative than a lawsuit. Meanwhile, Larian declared that, unlike Mattel's perverse tactics, his company "will continue to beat them in the marketplace in the old-fashioned American way, through better product innovation, better sales, and better marketing."

Mattel's leadership was consumed by panic. Recognizing Mattel's downward spiral, Ross left Mattel in 2004, the year it filed its lawsuit against MGA. Unlike her employer, Ross was nimble, pro-active, and on her way up. She continues to enjoy great success in her career. After leaving Mattel, she accepted executive positions at Old Navy, Disney, and then Gap—each gave her the power to revolutionize their creative process. In 2014, she landed a dream job as the head of Google Glass. Google's cofounders have said that when they were looking to hire someone for the job, the list of attributes was so long—experience in design, engineering, marketing, new product development, consumer innovation—that they bought a stuffed unicorn for the office. When Ross was hired, she got the unicorn.[13]

Eckert, on the other hand, shifted energies to litigation. As the smoke thickened and Bratz's popularity grew, the agenda narrowed on the final battleground: the courtroom. Internal documents reflected increasing militance against MGA. These memos stated, "This is War." One PowerPoint presentation included images of fire and a flame-thrower. A memo dated April 15, 2004, included the most panicked language yet:

> *The house is on fire, sales at retail are terrible, retailer support is weak and has lost confidence, market share has dropped at a chilling rate, Barbie is losing key attribute ratings with girls. . . . Bratz is gaining share with core five to eight year olds. We must do something different around here.*

The brief's call to war reveals nothing short of hysteria:

> *Fight fire with fire, no other brand in history is as emotionally meaningful to girls and women as Barbie. In spite of this, a rival-led Barbie genocide rapidly grows. All the talent, power and history behind the Barbie brand should be focused to fight back. Product, packaging, marketing and sales must be launched that is brilliant, tactical, aggressive, revolutionary and ruthless. This is war and sides must be taken. Barbie stands for good. All others stand for evil.*

As it prepared to battle MGA in court, Mattel also took aim at Isaac Larian personally. Internal Mattel files show that the corporation gathered information about Larian's family life, his interests and hobbies, his psychological makeup, and his daily patterns. The files list Larian's children's names and ages and his elderly mother's home address. Mattel even recorded the name and address of the family's synagogue in Los Angeles. In one file, the investigator noted

Larian's love of writing poetry and described Larian as a toddler-like character who "believes he is all knowing and all powerful." The file also notes that Larian "becomes enraged if told NO."

When the Mattel documents later became public at trial, Robert Eckert admitted he was embarrassed by the explosive language used by his people at Mattel. He called some of these memos inflammatory, insisting, "I would certainly want to distance myself from this language." Distancing himself from embarrassing revelations about Mattel's corporate ethics would later become Eckert's routine defense.

PART THREE

WARRING
TITANS

7 | FANTASY, MEET PARODY

Life in plastic, it's fantastic

—AQUA

MATTEL HAS POURED POUNDS of liquid plastic in different colors into the same mold for decades. Barbie's secret to becoming a billion-dollar brand has been her versatility and ever expanding, consumerist lifestyle. Her silicon body is malleable to every aspiration, agitation, admiration, and frustration of the human mind. She embodies all professions, from nurse to astronaut, from gymnast to scientist, from babysitter to warrior, even if, most of the time, she just wants to dress up and party. For some of us, Barbie can mean blandness, but in a moment's notice she twists and turns until she mirrors our deepest anxieties and fears, pleasures and desires. Barbie is the ultimate American icon, pregnant with contrasting meaning (though never actually pregnant) and always ready to embody whatever paradigm or fantasy her user imagines. Barbie is both perfect and perfectly paradoxical: she is every woman, yet she is no woman. She is unchangeable yet endlessly mutable. She is sexual yet sexless. She is white but of all races and ethnicities.

So it should come as no surprise that Barbie has inspired artists, photographers, writers, and musicians to express their own take on Barbie's many meanings, playfully straddling the dichotomies of goddess-bitch, clean-kinky, normal-twisted, and real-fantastic. But Mattel had developed a militant sense of protectionism over its top brand. Internally, the corporation constantly shot down edgier ideas by its employees for developing Barbie's persona, and sure enough, it hasn't welcomed artistic license from outside the corporation, by fans, artists, or competitors, with open arms. Rather than embracing the play on Barbie's multiple meanings, and the accompanying publicity, the corporation attempts to control its cultural queen's image and often chases these artists all the way to court. Again and again, Mattel has asked the courts to block any creative expression involving Barbie that is not descendant from Mattel itself.

A Bad Case of Culture Control

In 1997, a decade before the Barbie-Bratz feud erupted, the Danish pop band Aqua released their worldwide hit *Barbie Girl*. The song described Barbie's life in plastic as "fantastic," and was a top ten hit on the US *Billboard* Hot 100 of the year. The pop song has an addictive sweetness that definitely channels Barbie's shallow public persona. The female singer warbles in a high-pitched voice, while the male singer's pitch is low and manly. In the music video, a real-life Ken look-alike pulls off the real-life Barbie's arm. The lyrics speak for themselves:

> *I'm a blond bimbo girl, in a fantasy world /*
> *Dress me up, make it tight, I'm your dolly*

The song poked fun at the squeaky clean values Barbie represents as well as the kinky fantasies she ignites. At the same time, the chart-topper also reaffirmed Barbie's status as a worldwide cultural icon.

Mattel focused only on the song's negative connotations, and it sued Aqua and the music company that produced, marketed, and sold *Barbie Girl*. The toy giant asked the court for an injunction to block the song, arguing that the song confused consumers and tarnished Barbie's brand.[1]

There is a corporate strategy that attorneys call "litigate to death." It involves huge businesses mobilizing small armies of lawyers to vigorously pursue baseless lawsuits. These legal teams hope to, and often do, drive their opponents—individual or small enterprises with very limited resources—to their brink until, finally, they settle and either stop competing, or just disappear. Litigate-to-death companies hope a global chilling effect accompanies isolated victories: if these industry giants successfully develop reputations as predators, willing to litigate to death, then no one will dare anger them in the first place.

Because no actual Barbie dolls or images were used in the song, Mattel could not sue for copyright infringement, which protects images and creative expression. Instead, Mattel alleged misuse of trademark for Aqua's unauthorized use of the word "Barbie," which Mattel owned. Trademark protects any word, name, symbol, or design used to identify and distinguish a seller's product. Mattel claimed that Aqua's misappropriation of the word might confuse the public into believing Mattel produced the song.

The central problem with Mattel's claim was that the song never misled people into believing that Mattel produced it. Normally, trademark litigation happens between two competitors: for example, when Mattel sued Jada Toys for its line called Hot Rigz, which sounded a bit too much like Mattel's Hot Wheels.[2] Mattel's legal team submitted two surveys that showed people believed Hot Rigz was either made or licensed by the same company producing Hot Wheels. The song *Barbie Girl*, on the other hand, was clearly a parody—poking fun at Barbie rather than trying to pass off the song as a Mattel product.

Legally, you can use a copyrighted work without the owner's permission if the use is for a "transformative" purpose, such as to comment upon, criticize, or parody the work. The idea behind the fair use defense is that ownership over expression must be balanced against our First Amendment right to free speech, which grants us the right to educate, criticize, and poke fun at other people's words and ideas. But the law in general, and intellectual property law in particular, is never that simple. For example, over the years, the courts have decided that *parody* is fair use but *satire* is not. What's the difference?

Here's how parody works: it takes an object, idea, or expression and uses it as the vehicle of a joke. Satire by contrast uses a humorous style or a character to make fun or expose the ironies of something else. For example, the Aqua song is a parody because it used the Barbie doll to comment directly about Barbie. Therefore, the court deemed it fair use. If, by contrast, Aqua used Barbie's image or name to comment on an unrelated matter, that would be satire. For example, if a video used Barbie to make fun of Ivanka Trump, the courts may find that use is satirical.

In the abstract, this line seems clear, but in reality, the line between parody and satire is blurry. For example, you may recall that during the 2008 presidential election, Sarah Palin was repeatedly referred to as *Caribou Barbie* in reference to her Alaskan roots and to poke fun at her conservative ultrafeminine manner. So would a skit of Palin as Caribou Barbie be fair use or an infringement of Mattel's trademark? In one seminal case, an author calling himself "Dr. Juice" wrote a book called *The Cat NOT in the Hat!*, subtitled *A Parody*.[3] Despite the attempt at self-categorization, the court held the book was satire, not parody. The book heavily mimicked *The Cat in the Hat* by Dr. Seuss but used the original, signature Seussian style for a poetic rendition of the O. J. Simpson murder case:

One knife?/Two knife?/Red knife/Dead wife

Could Dr. Juice write these verses without infringing upon Dr. Seuss's intellectual property? The Ninth Circuit Court of Appeals found he could not. Unlike Aqua, whose Barbie song made fun of Barbie herself, Dr. Juice criticized the O. J. Simpson case, and not Dr. Seuss. The author's use of Seuss's iconic brand was, to use the reasoning of the court, "pure shtick." So copyright law and trademark law as they stand allow new expressions that make fun of original works, but it denies borrowing that original work to ridicule other unrelated issues.

Star Wars Fan Porn—Titillating Geeks Since 1977

Mattel has a kindred spirit in its zealous fight against parody: Disney. So it should have learned from Disney's losing battles, but it didn't. Imagine a pornographic, animated film called *Star Ballz*, completely based on the characters and storyline of *Star Wars*—would that stand up to fair use analysis? LucasFilm, now owned by Disney, is, like Mattel, notoriously protective of its intellectual property. In 1985, LucasFilm even sued the United States government, when President Reagan launched the military Strategic Defense Initiative (SDI), developing space-based laser missiles and battle stations, which he nicknamed Star Wars.[4] The court was unmoved by LucasFilm's trademark infringement claim. The court explained that "when politicians, newspapers and the public generally use the phrase *Star Wars* for convenience, in parody or descriptively to further a communication of their views on SDI," LucasFilm cannot stop them.

Like Mattel, LucasFilm registers every possible trademark related to its intellectual property, slowly removing pieces of expression from the public domain. This is the primary concern with overly protecting intellectual property: that too much language, knowledge, and creative juices will be carved out and be deemed private property, making it impossible for the next artists, inventors, and competitors to continue to create and innovate. In 2009, LucasFilm registered the term "droid." Notwithstanding that *droid* is just short for *android*, which is part of the English language, and the fact that the word *droid* first appeared back in 1952 in a short science fiction story titled "Robots of the World! Arise!" that had nothing to do with the *Star Wars* conglomerate, LucasFilm jealously guarded the phrase, threatening to sue Verizon Wireless after it dubbed its new Android phones "Droid." Verizon, perhaps because it too is a corporate giant which enjoys strong intellectual property protections, decided not to risk a lawsuit on grounds of principle. The two titans quickly settled the dispute, and Verizon agreed to pay for using the name. Of course, this sort of arrangement can be mutually beneficial for the two corporate giants, as both benefit from the exclusivity that intellectual property law grants over language. But the bigger picture is this: as more intangibles—words, images, algorithms, art, and science—are carved out of the public domain, it becomes much harder for newcomers, and anyone else not already strong and wealthy, to enter, create, innovate, and compete.

Now, if you've never seen *Star Ballz*, here's how one reviewer on Amazon described it: "crude, shoddily made, and full of groan-inducing sexual humor. I've seen worse, though." The porn-lite animated film naturally makes ample use of the obviously phallic nature of light sabers, and digs into the testosterone-driven environment of Star Wars by also turning stormtroopers into phalluses. Darth Vader, for no evident reason, has Mickey Mouse ears. Perhaps *Star Ballz's* makers were poking fun at the Disney conglomerate at large, contrasting cuteness with evil. Perhaps, more fundamentally, they anticipated legal action taken by the Disney/LucasFilm empire, which alongside Mattel is one of the most infamous hoarders of intellectual property. After all, Mickey Mouse himself triggered Congress to pass the Copyright Extension Act.

LucasFilm indeed sued *Star Ballz* and, like Mattel, zealously overreached and lost. Like many Barbie parodies, the movie directly conversed with the artistic work it mimicked, making it a parody and squarely within the fair use defense. The court ruled in favor of *Star Ballz*, with San Francisco based judge Claudia Wilken writing, "The Star Wars films are so famous that it is extremely unlikely that consumers would believe that Star Ballz is associated with Star Wars or LucasFilm."[5] An amusing remix of iconic cultural themes that avoid consumer confusion is what fair use is all about.

After LucasFilm lost it issued a statement: "We feel strongly that the law does not allow for parody to be a defense to a pornographic use of someone else's intellectual property, especially when that use is directed to children." The *Star Ballz* creators then sued LucasFilm for libel, claiming that the spokespeople for *Star Wars* defamed them in suggesting that the animated erotica was "pornography directed at children."[6] More than anything, it was pornography directed at adult, tech nerds. As one devoted fan wrote excitedly about the court's decision to shield *Star Ballz* from the wrath of George Lucas: "To this day, Star Wars porn remains a safe, legally-protected way to titillate nerds and separate them from the money they earn at their systems engineer jobs."[7] Without having any direct knowledge on the matter, I am told the art of spoofing famous sci-fi in porn is alive and well. Since *Star Ballz*, there have been at least half a dozen more adult movies made, including *Private Gold 81: Porn Wars—Episode 1* and the popular series *This Ain't Star Trek XXX.*

Fan porn notwithstanding, the distinction between parody and cashing in on a recognized brand remains deeply contested. Fair use is an amorphous defense. Like many other distinctions delineating the boundaries of intellectual property protection, the fair use defense draws notoriously unpredictable and vague lines. Therefore, when the courts decide on fair use, it is often understood as a heroic act which significantly shapes the future of cultural production. In protecting Aqua's *Barbie Girl* song from Mattel, Chief Judge Alex Kozinski of the Ninth Circuit Court of Appeals, who we will soon learn is America's champion of free culture, began his decision with this memorable line: "If this were a sci-fi melodrama, it might be called Speechzilla meets Trademark Kong."[8] Mattel is the King Kong of intellectual property, intent on devouring the small artists and inventors who challenge his dominance. Speechzilla is the story's savior—Judge Alex Kozinski.

As we shall soon see, Judge Kozinski has a raunchy sense of humor, and over lunch he gave me an example of a parody he liked. He and his wife, an attorney who, among many other things, has represented the *Peanuts* conglomerate as her client, were in Las Vegas. When they were out shopping, they saw a T-shirt of Lucy van Pelt pregnant, saying, "Damn you, Charlie Brown!" Kozinski doesn't believe that kind of poking fun hurts the brand. He also happens to think it's funny.

Adjudicating the Aqua case in his courtroom in Pasadena, California, Kozinski needed to elucidate Barbie's meaning and figure out what parodying her would mean. He described Barbie's cultural role this way:

> *Barbie has been labeled both the ideal American woman and a bimbo. She has survived attacks both psychic (from feminists critical of her fictitious figure) and physical (more than 500 professional makeovers). She remains a symbol of American girlhood, a public figure who graces the aisles of toy stores throughout the country and beyond. With Barbie, Mattel created not just a toy but a cultural icon. With fame often comes unwanted attention.*

Before Judge Kozinski's Aqua decision, other judges had employed a stricter test of fair use. A parody was permitted only to use the minimum amount of protected material necessary to relay its message or idea. Kozinski diverged from precedent when he applied a more balanced approach. He explained that the song's repetition of the words *Barbie* and *Ken* were necessary for the purpose of parody. Even with the repetition, he said, no consumer is likely to think Mattel sponsored the song. (Funnily, Mattel's sponsoring of the song became something of an urban legend when I was a kid.) He wrote, "Aqua is a Danish band that has, as yet, only dreamed of attaining Barbie-like status." Aqua had the right to sing its song.

Judge Kozinski was also unmoved by Mattel's claim that the song sullied its prom queen's clean image. Mattel's argument that the song was inappropriate for young girls and therefore tarnished Barbie's reputation is built upon the controversial theory of "dilution," which has gained some power in the past few decades. It expands trademark protection beyond the original scope of preventing consumer confusion, into the realm of protecting the strength and integrity of the brand. Dilution is another way to say that a company wants to control the way a brand is presented to the public. Since trademark law's original purpose was to protect consumers from fraud or deception, with producers trying to pass off their product as associated with a leading brand, it is hard to justify any legal protection when there is no likelihood of confusion. In protecting Barbie's image and soul, Mattel aggressively pushed for the more expansive protection against any risk of diluting or tarnishing the brand. Mattel had won such claims in the past. For example, it managed to shutter an independent magazine for Barbie collectors based on a dilution claim. In a victorious statement then, Mattel explained it would not allow third parties to present unflattering public images of Barbie: "What I do, first and foremost," vowed the CEO at the time, "is protect Barbie."[9]

Judge Kozinski agreed that Aqua's use of Barbie's name was potentially dilutive because the word *Barbie* now kindled thoughts of the popular song as well as the doll herself. However, he explained that when the use of a brand involves a social meaning, such as criticism and parody, the right to free speech outweighs a risk of dilution. The fact that the song lampoons Barbie's perfectly clean image was precisely what made it fair use. As Judge Kozinski closed his opinion, he had a final piece of advice: "The parties are advised to chill."[10] Mattel did not take his advice.

When culture is freed, parodies upon parodies arise. To mark

Australia Day, a group of Aussies, swelling with national pride, uploaded on YouTube a parody of *Barbie Girl*, singing "*Aussie Barbie, let's go party. . . . Be my mate as the chops marinate. . . . Marination leads to my salvation.*"[11] In 2015, another parody of the parody, parody squared if you will, featured a viral vlogger called #SelfieGirl. In the video, #SelfieGirl, obsessed with all things social media, sings, "*I'm a selfie girl, in a selfie world, making my face known, alone with my cellphone.*"[12] And in law school parodies, where the largest bar preparation company is called Barbri, we law professors repeatedly sit through spoofs of "*I'm a Barbri girl in a Barbri world.*" Fair use has that quality of cultural remixing: Aqua's victory was not only for the band's own creativity, but also a win for the continuous expansion of cultural production.

The original *Barbie Girl* song helped sell over eight million copies of Aqua's album. In 2003, it even received the questionable distinction of being ranked by *Blender* magazine and VH1 as among the "most awesomely bad" songs ever created. That same year, Mattel bought the rights to the song from Aqua to use in its marketing campaign, changing the lyrics slightly but keeping most of it, including the line "*Life in plastic, it's fantastic,*" intact. Mattel's spokesperson explained, "The beauty of Barbie is that she can kiss and make up."[13] In the case of a single song, that may be true, but apparently not in the case of Thomas Forsythe's art.

Barbie in a Blender and Other Fetishes

In 1997, the same year that Aqua launched *Barbie Girl*, Forsythe, a self-taught Utah artist, developed a series of seventy-eight photographs called *Food Chain Barbie*. His work depicted nude images of Barbie dolls juxtaposed against kitchen appliances and food.[14] For example, *Malted Barbie* was a nude Barbie in a malt machine and *Barbie Enchiladas* showed four Barbies wrapped in tortillas and covered with salsa.

Five Moon Salutes showed five Barbies bent over to expose their perfect, and perfectly naked, behinds. Other titles included *Baked Barbie, Barbie a Trois, Barbie in a Blender,* and *Bargaritaville.* Initially, Forsythe's series received little attention and limited commercial success. The *Food Chain Barbie* series earned him less than four thousand dollars. But that didn't stop Mattel from filing a lawsuit. Mattel even subpoenaed a museum that displayed the collection, which resulted in sanctions against Mattel for overreaching and using intimidation tactics. The lawsuit over Forsythe's photography lasted five years. Forsythe was lucky: The American Civil Liberties Union (ACLU) decided to take up his case as an exemplary defense of free speech.

The Southern California chapter searched for an experienced copyright defense attorney to represent Forsythe pro bono. The problem was that going against Mattel, and its long-term law firm Quinn Emanuel, was not something that most attorneys are eager to do. "They are bullies represented by bullies," one prominent attorney told me. Another described Quinn this way: "For years it has engaged in scorched-earth representation of Mattel. A message that anytime anyone dares to challenge the corporation, the wrath of God will come down on them. It's as though they have a sign on the door: 'We're Mattel's permanent attack dogs.' " The ACLU of Southern California could not find a single law firm that would take on the case, and the branch had to turn to the ACLU Northern California chapter for help. In San Francisco, the ACLU secured one of the nation's most prominent intellectual property trial attorneys, Annette Hurst. She took on Forsythe's case pro bono and a decade later would become one of the key litigators on MGA's defense team when Mattel sued it for Bratz.

Forsythe described his artistic expression as "a pictorial antidote to the powerful cultural forces persuading us to buy the impossible beauty myth."[15] Mattel saw only copyright and trademark infringement. As in the Aqua case, the trademark claim refers to the use of the word *Barbie* itself. Mattel further claimed that the image of

Barbie, her face, her body, her expression, and her look are all protected under copyright law. Mattel argued that even if an artist buys
a Barbie doll and uses it in his art, he can be liable for copyright
infringement. At trial, Forsythe explained he chose Barbie as the subject of his art because "Barbie is the most enduring of those products
that feed on the insecurities of our beauty and perfection-obsessed
consumer culture."[16] Forsythe viewed his art as a social statement
against this plasticization and crass consumerism. He wished to flip
Barbie's message by displaying carefully positioned, nude, and sometimes frazzled looking Barbies in ridiculous, as well as dangerous,
situations. As with most artists, he wanted to offer the public something new that builds upon, as well as rejects, the old. He wanted to
create a different set of associations and context for the world's most
famous doll.

Once again, Mattel's efforts to quash creative expression with a
lawsuit were foiled when the court held that Forsythe's use of Mattel's
copyrighted doll in the Food Chain Barbie photographs was fair use.
Like the Aqua song, Forsythe was parodying the image of Barbie.
The court understood the photographs as a critical commentary of
Barbie's influence on gender roles and the position of women in society. As such, the public's interest in free expression must outweigh
potential confusion about Mattel's sponsorship of the work: "It is not
in the public's interest to allow Mattel complete control over the kinds
of artistic works that use Barbie as a reference for criticism and comment." Calling the lawsuit "groundless," "objectively unreasonable,"
and "frivolous," the Los Angeles-based judge Ronald Lew ordered
Mattel to pay Forsythe over two million dollars for the fees and costs
he incurred during the long dispute. Ironically, the lawsuit gave Forsythe street credit and increased his commercial value: if a company
as large as Mattel was interested in his work, then the show must be
worth seeing. In five short years, Forsythe was transformed from anonymous artist into a creative photographer who survived Mattel's attack.

In 2005, Mattel started a lawsuit against a Canadian leather-, rubber-, and fetishwear store called Barbie's Shop in Calgary, Canada. Barbie's Shop advertised itself as selling custom clothes "for bad boys and girls." The irony, of course, is that Mattel was suing an adult store similar to those that sold the very first Bild Lilli. But beyond that, Mattel was asserting that no one other than it could use the doll queen's name, even if the owner of the shop, Barbara Anderson-Walley, went by the nickname Barbie. The middle-aged Canadian said wryly, "I was around before Barbie was—maybe I should sue them over the name." Nickname or not, Mattel's spokeswoman coldly stated: "We own the Barbie name, clothing and dolls. Even if your name happens to be Tommy, Ralph, or Barbie, in some areas that's already a trademark." Therefore, the small Canadian entrepreneurial venture was, according to Mattel, "a simple case of Internet piracy." When a New York court dismissed the case for lack of jurisdiction over a Canadian business, Anderson-Walley was elated. "As a little guy with no money, I thought I didn't have a hope," she confessed. The Calgary community at large was also delighted by the victory. Their cornerstone fetish market shop, which catered particularly to the LGBT community, survived an American conglomerate's intimidation tactics. "It's a welcome turn of events that a small local business is able to hold their own against a corporate giant," wrote the local LGBT magazine *GayCalgary*.

Next on Mattel's docket was Dungeon Barbie. In 2001, Mattel was shocked to see a side of Barbie that was even darker than Forsythe's *Barbie in a Blender*. British artist Susanne Pitt placed the head of Barbie onto big-breasted bodies clothed in rubber bondage costumes, and positioned her as mistress of an S&M dungeon.[17] Pitt also introduced some anatomical corrections. She added nipples and a vagina to Barbie and a plastic penis to Ken. She then placed the dolls in sexual positions.[18] She called her hero Lily the Diva Dominatrix, a protagonist in a tale of sexual slavery and torture. The submissive participant in the sexual exploit was another reconfigured Barbie. Mattel was not amused. It filed a suit for copyright infringement. Pitt defended herself by drawing attention to Barbie being the reincarnation of Lilli, a European postwar sex doll. Pitt said she wanted to transport Barbie's hidden history into a "modern erotic context"—from Lilli to Barbie and back to Lily. What was the court to do with such a compelling artistic vision? Again, it turned to the concept of fair use.

Both in trademark and copyright law, fair use operates as an affirmative defense, meaning that defendants have to prove their position. The assumption is that any use is infringement and illegal, but the defendant—the artist, musician, or competitor being sued—can raise fair use as an exception. Then the alleged infringer has to convince the court that it was "fair" to borrow words or expressions owned by someone else. The analysis of fair use is one of those multi-factored legal standards that weighs and balances the particular facts of the dispute at hand. This means that parties have an incredibly difficult time predicting what will be considered fair.

One factor is whether the new artistic work is "transformative," creating something new and original rather than merely supplanting the copyrighted piece and imitating it in mundane ways. In the case of the Dungeon Doll, the court reasoned that the anatomical changes and Pitt's costumes—"Lederhosen-style" Bavarian bondage dress with rubber helmets and PVC masks—were indeed transformative. Dominatrix Barbie was a substantial departure from Barbie's official persona as a child's plaything. The court conceded that Pitt's case would have been a losing one if, for example, she had simply dressed up Barbie dolls in cheerleader outfits. Like with Forsythe's and Aqua's artistic expressions, Pitt's work was understood by the court as a parody because Pitt was commenting on, and in turn subverting, what Mattel tried to maintain as Barbie's true nature.[19]

A related aspect in analyzing a fair use defense is whether the new work will compete with the older one. In Pitt's case, the judge cunningly noted that, to the best of her knowledge, there is no Mattel line of S&M Barbies (an underserved market, if you will). She saw no danger of Dungeon Dolls supplanting the demand for Barbie dolls in the children's toy market.

Barbie bondage seems a natural step forward in the path of artistic commentary on Barbie. A woman chained was a pervasive metaphor in the late nineteenth-century suffrage movement and early twentieth-century feminism. Wonder Woman, another American icon, the greatest of female superheroes (dark haired but, like Barbie, busty with an impossibly tiny waist), is often depicted roped and chained and freeing herself from those bonds. Not coincidentally, Wonder Woman's creator William Marston was in his private life a bondage fetishist, a polyamorist, and a women's rights champion. The fair use of Barbie in bondage is a good reminder of why we protect parody against the bonds of copyright. Freeing culture is inextricably linked to freeing the mind and society from lingering inequities.

Although Mattel lost in a sequence of lawsuits against artists, even unsuccessful intellectual property litigation can chill free expression. All litigation is costly, and litigation against the world's largest toy maker magnifies these costs. Fortunately, Forsythe, Aqua, Anderson-Walley, and Pitt were able to sustain the costs and time in defending their art against Mattel. Some of them were lucky to have wealthy organizations, which supported their fight to keep culture free, sponsor their representation. Still, in the legal battlefield, even winners pay a great deal. American law doesn't ordinarily provide fee shifting—that is, it doesn't require the losing party to pay the winning party's litigation costs. There are some exceptions. The copyright and trademark statutes allow rewarding fees when the claims are abusive. This explains why Forsythe was granted two million dollars for defending himself against Mattel's lawsuit.

Mattel relies on the fact that court scare tactics can be effective even when a litigant's claims are rather weak. For example, a few years before the Pitt case, Mattel sued another artist, Paul Hansen, who lived in San Francisco. Hansen bought Barbie dolls and then transformed them using accessories, such as pint-sized plastic babies, miniature rhinestone jewelry, and Lilliputian liquor bottles. Hansen's "Trailer Trash Barbie," with black roots peeking under her platinum blonde hair, was smoking a cigarette while carrying a baby on her hip. A speech bubble accompanied the doll's packaging, "My Daddy Swears I'm the Best Kisser in the County." Hansen named other dolls "Drag Queen Barbie," "Hooker Barbie," and "Big Dyke Barbie." The dolls gained some popularity as a counterculture cult item when Madonna bought a couple for her private collection. Mattel attacked. It sued Hansen, slapping him with $1.2 billion in damages for copyright infringement, even though Hansen had made a rather meager profit selling his modified Barbie dolls.[20] A young attorney took on the case's defense pro bono. She stood at the defendant's table alone against five Mattel attorneys—"white men with no facial hair" as her colleague described the scene to me. When Mattel's attorneys began the hearing by detailing what the case was about, that second year associate cut them off and said, "Your Honor, we all know what this case is about." She looked straight at the team of Mattel's lawyers and said, "Your client has no sense of humor, that's what this case is about." The case was settled that day, with Mattel agreeing to forgo their claims of monetary damages in return for a promise that Hansen would not make any more of his cult Barbie dolls.

There are also special laws called anti-SLAPP (Strategic Lawsuits Against Public Participation), which provide rewards to defendants who are sued solely for the purpose of intimidation and silencing. The New York Supreme Court condemns SLAPPs, saying: "Short of a gun to the head, a greater threat to First Amendment expression can scarcely be imagined." In practice, fee-shifting and anti-SLAPP laws are still limited in their reach. They are certainly insufficient for offsetting the great personal and financial risks taken by individuals when a corporate giant attacks. For every artist or production company willing to take the fight to court, Mattel hopes to intimidate the multitude of ordinary artists and fans without the financial and emotional means or support to endure a legal battle against them. In reality, many artists would rather settle than fight for justice.

Indeed, not all artists Mattel has sued have been able to stand their ground until the bitter end. This is especially true in infringement cases because proving fair use is wholly unpredictable. The cases that go all the way to trial are merely the tip of the iceberg. Mattel sends out dozens of cease-and-desist letters to those all over the world who dare play with Barbie's image. Some jurisdictions are more willing than others to support Mattel's crusade. For example, Mattel sued Argentinian filmmaker Albertina Carri, who created a short film called *Barbie También Puede Estar Triste* (*Barbie Gets Sad Too*) showing Ken as a sex-obsessed businessman and Barbie as a sad housewife who finds comfort in the arms of the maid Teresa. In 2002, Mexico City's Urban-Fest festival planned a screening, but Mattel convinced a Mexican court to issue an order banning the film from being shown because the sexual content would threaten Barbie's image. The parody shielding Barbie dolls in bondage failed to protect *Barbie Gets Sad Too* in the face of zealous Mattel lawyering in Mexico.

In their book *Reclaiming Fair Use*, intellectual property scholars Patricia Aufderheide and Peter Jaszi caution that if we, as a society, don't clarify the legal doctrine of fair use and make it less risky for artists to engage in routine acts of cultural expression, we stand to lose a great deal of creativity and innovation. They warn that fair use should not require heroic courage or be the privileged rare defense of established artists, First Amendment advocates, and resourceful competitors, all of whom can risk a lengthy trial to affirm their right to free speech. Rather, fair use must be something on which anyone can rely. Free speech should be a right that all of us, from elementary schoolchildren to amateur artists, can fearlessly exercise.[21]

The most valuable examples of fair use are those that remix cultural icons and turn their mainstream meanings on their head. Feminist writers often write of a desire to connect women and girls, pointing to a disturbing gulf separating the women leading the fight for equality and the supposed beneficiaries: girls themselves. A disconnect between those who want to "liberate"—for lack of a less loaded term—and those who are captivated and confined by the chains of gender roles. Barbie, more than any other symbol, stands as the lead icon in this battle. The modern feminists speak of a Barbiphobia.[22] But rather than fear Barbie as an evil symbol of feminine stereotypes, why not recognize her strength in shaping girls' imaginations? Why not use the fact that she means so many different things, and yet at the same time means nothing— that she is a blank slate on which to shape, play, tear apart, and put back together? Barbie can lend herself to social commentary about sex, race, consumerism, corporations, and markets. In their 2000 *Manifesta*, feminist writers Jennifer Baumgardner and Amy Richards wrote that Barbie helped generations of girls-turned-women embrace their sexuality: "Barbie, who spends most of her time naked and shorn, will always be a way for young girls to imagine fucking in numerous positions." Amen.

A recent example playing with Barbie's sexual, or asexual, nature and her iconic wholesomeness is the art of photographer Sarah Haney, who shot a series of black-and-white photos of Barbie in sexual positions. Haney acknowledged the paradox of parodying a fantasy. Her photography recognizes that Barbie already embodied a range of contradictions: Barbie is the all-American Madonna whore.[23] Haney was drawn to the contrast illuminated when Barbie was placed in compromising positions, playing on her core clean, perfect image. Haney explains her take on Barbie this way: "she's marketed as this wholesome, all-American Madonna to little girls, but if you look at her as an adult, particularly at her body and clothes, she's a pretty clear embodiment of the whore." Haney says that as a child, she was always bothered by Barbie's perpetual smile. Haney recalls that growing up, she put Barbie through any number of tragedies but "no matter what befell her, she kept that fixed little smirk." As an adult, Haney decided to explore what Barbie might be hiding behind that smirk—behind the façade of perfection. Haney reasons, "After all, how great could life really be for a woman who clearly has an eating disorder, an addiction to plastic surgery, and nothing between her ears?"[24] By creating these photos of Barbie and Ken exploring their domestic selves, Haney portrays, in her own words, "the dark side of life in the Dream House: Barbie's obsession with her body, Ken's quest for sexual gratifications, all the dirty little secrets."

There is no art without exchange; no meaning without interpretation. Why are artists so intent on deforming Barbie, tearing her apart, positioning her in sexually compromising positions, casting her in sadomasochistic roles, and subjecting her to acts of cruelty and torture? Ruth Handler claimed, "I designed Barbie with a blank face, so that the child could project her own dreams of the future onto Barbie."[25] The blank slate that Barbie presents allows not only children, but fans, critics, and artists of all ages to put meaning on Barbie. Barbie parodies are not transformative in the sense they transform Barbie's singular meaning into something entirely new; say from a naïve and asexual all-American girl to a Bavarian dominatrix. Barbie herself is already a parody. A group of adult men, sequestered behind closed boardroom doors, keep the fantasy of Barbie alive: our society's dreams of plastic perfection. Those same men market her as a children's toy. Thus, Barbie, in her very essence, embodies a double nature—puritanism molded into hypersexualization. As feminist writer Jeannie Thomas observed, "The bitch-goddess identity has been with Barbie since her inception."

Barbie thus falls on both sides of the coin: she is sexual and asexual, wholesome and sullied, the misogynistic ideal of a feminist, the plastic pink of girls. If we, as a society, lock up iconic images and only give the artists the key when their work embodies an entirely fresh new break from the icon's existing essence, we might side with Mattel that no one other than that company can play with Barbie's meanings. That kind of mindset and accompanying laws would severely limit cultural expression and hamper opportunities for social change and progress.

When we look closely at intellectual property, we discover that most often corporations—rather than creators—are the primary benefactors. The idyllic image of an artist collecting royalties to support his later work is now, largely, a myth. This modern phenomenon has led many scholars to question whether the original intent of the Constitution, which gave Congress the power to grant a monopoly ownership over ideas in order to motivate artists and inventors, is being subverted. Is intellectual property law as it stands today promoting progress in arts and sciences? Or is it hindering it by blocking too many new ventures and innovations? The legacy of building on culture, adapting, developing, and remixing it, is too often crushed by the contemporary expansion of intellectual property.

Mattel does not allow others to commit the same infractions on it as Mattel inflicted on Lilli's creators. As it established its dominance over the industry, Mattel sought to freeze the remake. Mattel certainly would not allow Carter Bryant to follow his own toy dreams if they endangered Barbie. The poet Tagore wrote "All humanity's greatest is mine." Having litigated against many artists and lost, Mattel might have learned the lesson that it cannot control culture and box up creativity. Back in the corporate boardroom, Mattel's leadership should have also realized that attempts to revive the aging queen of dolls by launching lawsuits, spying on competitors, and intimidating former employees were not the path to quelling Barbie's competition.

8 | ROUND 1: TITANS, IDEAS, AND OWNERSHIP

*For 40 years Barbie was the only doll in town.
And then Bratz came in and knocked her off her
pedestal.*

—MGA AT TRIAL

*Folks, that's not the American dream, to compete
by cheating and stealing.*

—MATTEL AT TRIAL

"MOTHERS DON'T LIE. BRATZ was born on an August evening in Kimberling City," Thomas Nolan, MGA's attorney, told the jury. After weeks of testimony by Mattel and MGA employees and industry experts, beginning in May 2008, Carter Bryant's mother, Jane, took the stand to testify that Carter was inspired to create Bratz while living with her in Missouri. This timeline was intended to show that Carter was not a Mattel employee when he invented the dolls. Mattel's ownership claim over the Bratz empire hinged entirely on its argument that Carter had secretly created Bratz while he was being paid to design Barbie's wardrobe. If the jury was persuaded by the Bryants instead, then Mattel couldn't touch the Bratz product line. Carter's employment contract—assigning all his creativity to the company—was inapplicable to his time away from the company.

This Is Your Brain on Trial

The trial's drama centered on whether anyone could provide proof of Carter's "eureka" moment. Was it really in Missouri, after he saw that group of girls at the mall, or was it while he was in his office designing another dress for Barbie? How do you prove the exact moment of inspiration?

Carter claimed it was when he saw that group of Kickapoo high schoolers in Missouri. Now he had to convince the jury to believe his story. Both Carter's mother and Richard, his partner, testified that Carter showed them the designs in 1998—the year of his hiatus from Mattel. Mattel's lawyer John Quinn, on the other hand, urged the jury not to believe their testimony, saying, "Mr. Bryant's mom sees him through the filter of the greatest love you can have for someone." As for Carter's partner, Richard, "He and Mr. Bryant share a life together. They also share $30 million," Quinn told the jury, referring to royalties Carter earned from Bratz. Carter also struggled to account for why he couldn't present drawings dated from that year. "I don't usually put a date on master drawings," he explained.

Mattel took advantage of Carter's apparent disorganization and brought out the big guns to destroy his credibility. It hired a forensic expert to convince the jury that the fiber of the paper Carter used to sketch the Bratz designs matched pages from a notebook Carter used working on Barbie projects after returning to

Mattel in 1999. Next, Mattel's ink expert testified that he found ink traces matching Bratz's general shape that had bled into these 1999 notebooks.

Mattel even flew in the principal of Kickapoo High School in an attempt to show that her students were far more demure than Bratz, and an unlikely inspiration for Carter's edgy designs. The attorneys had the principal flip through the school's yearbook, grilling her for hours about teenage fashion. "They wore that? They wore that? And what about that?" one of the jurors mimicked the lawyers back to me. MGA's attorney responded by asking the principal the simple question: "Would you agree with me that the kids who make it into the high school yearbook in various photos are not always the hippest, edgiest, trendiest, kids with attitude?" "Agreed," was her reply. A fair statement, it would seem.

But the person who was grilled the most on the stand was Carter himself. Mattel's attorneys held Carter on the stand for nine days while repeatedly asking him the same questions and trying to poke holes in his story. As one lawyer told me, "It was ugly."

Bratz Funded a Luxury Home in Arkansas

By the time the legal battles were waged, Carter Bryant had severed his relations with both companies. He lost nearly all of his $30 million fortune—the royalty received for his brainchild—in bad real estate investments his then-partner Richard Irmen had pushed him to make. Carter says he invested in the real estate market at exactly the wrong time and that he and Richard had business partners who cheated them. Michael Page told me a different story. He described Richard himself as a "parasite" who chewed up the small fortune Carter made: "Richard spent on an over-the-top house with a massive orchard. All he wanted to do was show off their success. He radioactively spent all the millions of Bratz royalties." Another insider said that among Richard's acquisitions was a luxury mobile home in Arkansas ("You heard it right," she told me, "an Arkansas luxury mobile home! Talk about an oxymoron!"). By the time the trial was over, Carter and Richard had broken up. With just $1.4 million left, overwhelmed, exhausted, and disillusioned, Carter wanted nothing more than to escape the crossfire of the upcoming battle. He felt neglected by both sides, and worried MGA wouldn't support his personal legal defense. He settled the lawsuit with Mattel before the trial began, handing over all that remained of his fortune to his boss-turned-accuser.

As one of Carter's attorneys put it, the case was about "two big kahunas." Carter was simply "a pimple on the problem." Carter was not just frightened of Mattel; he also felt that MGA was unsupportive, and its legal team was distancing itself from his claims. MGA focused more on its own defense: even if Carter stole from Mattel, he lied about it to MGA, and in any event, MGA ended up developing Bratz, a line different enough from Carter's drawings that Mattel couldn't claim ownership over it. In the words of Carter's attorney, "Carter didn't have a pot to piss in." Each company made him sign contracts which "tied Carter to a mast and committed him to making sure that their ship would not go down."

Broke, and with no real stake in the fight, Carter nonetheless became the central witness in the billion-dollar corporate fight. Attorneys hammered away at him, but throughout the first round of trials he tried to stay positive and upbeat. He told his story of inspiration with such detail and conviction that, at some moments, it sounded almost too rehearsed. In turn, Mattel's attorneys went to great length to paint Carter as a conniving double agent who manufactured a fake story about inventing Bratz in Missouri. In his closing statement before the jury, MGA attorney Thomas Nolan parodied Mattel's disparaging image of Carter by saying, "Oh, he has an evil heart"; Carter is evil "as long as he's testifying against Mattel, or as long as he came up with an idea that Mattel so desperately wants but doesn't deserve."

A Living Bratz in Our Ranks

To win a case before a jury, you need to accomplish two goals: tell a compelling story and destroy your opponent's version. Unfortunately for MGA, the judge presiding over the first trial made that task exceedingly difficult. Judge Stephen Larson, who was rather inexperienced at the time MGA and Mattel arrived at his court, was assigned to sit in the first trial. This was one of Larson's first, and last, cases, having been appointed to the federal bench by President George W. Bush in 2006, and leaving the judiciary by 2009. Larson set the tone of the trial early with a series of evidentiary rulings that made it exceedingly difficult for MGA to defend its case. Larson refused to allow MGA to show Mattel was struggling creatively and morally, or that it opted to litigate its competitors to death rather than compete. In the second trial, Isaac Larian was allowed to mention Mattel's history of suing any competing doll maker who threatens Barbie's popularity. He testified: "I didn't want to get into a lawsuit with Mattel. They sue everybody." But in the first trial, the jury was not allowed to hear any of that. Judge Larson also rejected the vast majority of MGA's motions, and he refused to allow MGA to disclose any of Mattel's financial struggles. In fact, he even forbade anyone from mentioning Barbie by name, ruling the case was about stealing Bratz, not about Bratz's competition with Mattel's queen.

Mattel, meanwhile, was free to construct its own counter story to demolish Carter's narrative of Midwest inspiration: Lily Martinez, a Barbie designer, created a line called Toon Teenz. Mattel painted Carter not only as a disloyal corporate employee, but also as a thief guilty of stealing his coworkers' ideas. It asserted that Carter saw Martinez's sketches when they were both at Mattel and copied her idea to develop Bratz. Mattel never developed the Toon Teenz sketches beyond the idea stage into actual toys, nor did it immediately file to register copyright for the drawings. Four years after the Toon Teenz were sketched and shelved, and mere months after discovering

Carter Bryant designed Bratz, Mattel finally registered a copyright for Martinez's sketches. All of a sudden, Lily Martinez was plucked out of her cubicle and groomed to be Mattel's manna-from-heaven doll designer.

In the courtroom, Mattel transformed Martinez into its secret weapon. She always entered court gorgeously put together, wearing a different designer outfit each day; her shiny, flowing hair professionally primped and her makeup impeccably done. MGA's defense team believes Mattel footed the bill for the grooming and wardrobe of its supposed star inventor during the entirety of the trial. It further believes that Mattel's legal team hoped Martinez, young and beautiful, would wow the men on the jury. One juror I talked with had a particularly interesting theory about Martinez's role: she was there to show the court that Mattel had a living Bratz doll within its ranks. Martinez herself testified that Toon Teenz looked "like me; it's how I look." In other words, the juror's theory was that Mattel hoped the jury would decide that, rather than a quiet gay male artist creating his dream girl, it was more plausible that an attractive young woman created Bratz in her own image. This would, in turn, convince the jury that Carter's inspiration came from his Mattel coworkers rather than a group of teenaged girls in Missouri.

Mattel created the following story through its questioning of Martinez on the stand: Like Carter, Martinez was an aspiring fashion designer, and she was always sketching small figures with oversized heads, eyes, lips, and an edgy style. Mattel hired Lily Martinez as an intern while she was still a student at the Fashion Institute in Los Angeles. Martinez describes how, as a girl, growing up poor jumpstarted her interest in fashion: "I would design one-of-a-kind outfits for my Barbie dolls using my ruffled socks that I lost the mates for because my parents couldn't afford to buy me fashions." Like a talking doll, she speaks in inspirational one-liners: "Always listen to your heart and to your gut instinct" and "Do what you really love because that's what's going to make you happy." At Mattel, she rose to assistant designer and eventually senior doll designer.

Like Carter, Martinez never received much appreciation from Mattel before MGA introduced Bratz. Mattel had not developed any of her lines, and she was rather low in the corporate ranks. So the war against Bratz was an unexpected stepping stone in her career. After years of relative invisibility, Martinez suddenly received a lot of her bosses' attention. Mattel quickly promoted her and arranged TV appearances. Right around the trial's start, Mattel arranged a spot for Martinez as a guest judge on Heidi Klum's reality show *Project Runway*, appearing in a special episode where contestants designed clothes for dolls. At trial, Martinez was designated Mattel's corporate representative. Each side in corporate litigation must choose someone from the company to appear in court every day of the trial on the business's behalf. The idea is to allow the jury to associate a "face" with the corporation and for that person to provide in-house assistance to the legal team throughout trial. Instead of CEO Bob Eckert or another executive from the top of the corporate hierarchy, Mattel named Martinez its representative.

Mattel's executives testified Martinez was given the green light to work on Toon Teenz, though Mattel never developed the product line. Martinez herself testified that she posted her sketches on her cubicle where anyone passing by could see. Carter swore he never saw Martinez's drawings, yet Mattel brought evidence that Elise Cloonan, his close friend and roommate, sat in a neighboring cubicle to Martinez. The big boss, Ivy Ross, testified that Carter actually saw the designs, and even complimented Martinez on their "cuteness," saying, "Mattel will be sorry someday that they didn't make those dolls."

Ross explained to the jury how Toon Teenz and Bratz were linked by their general air of "defiance." More than that, she implied in her testimony that Carter snuck around planning his coup. "There were rumors," Ross later said about Carter being the man behind

Bratz. When he left, she conducted the exit interview, and, she said, he outright fooled her, telling her he was planning to altogether leave toy design. Ross, however, focused much of her testimony on her own role as the company revolutionary; an energizer and font of creativity. Mattel's attorney hoped to show the jury that Mattel was a place sizzling with innovation, from Project Platypus to workshops with clowns and creativity gurus. It was this environment that must have inspired Carter.

The biggest problem with Mattel's accounts about Martinez's sketches and Ross's mentorship was that, even had Carter seen Toon Teenz, those sketches bore little resemblance to Bratz. Further, Mattel had thrown Toon Teenz into the intellectual *basura*. The doll lines it launched post-Bratz felt like poor imitations of MGA's blockbuster line, and they demonstrated Mattel could never even conceptualize something as edgy and fresh as Bratz. In fact, Carter was never even invited to participate in Ross's Project Platypus or creativity sessions. But MGA was forbidden from revealing Mattel's long history of intellectual stagnation; all the company's attorneys could do to refute Ross's story was simply ask Carter, "So you were being inspired by actual teenagers, as opposed to a union analyst or a clown, true?" It was like channeling the great Anais Nin, who said, "My ideas usually come not at my desk writing but in the midst of living." But, during the first trial, the jury seemed to be buying what Ross was selling.

Creativity Without Ownership

And what if Carter had been partly inspired by his time at Mattel? What if he developed at least some of his designs while back at Mattel? Wasn't he free to think up and own Bratz while working as a fashion designer for Barbie? Couldn't he work on his own ideas at home during the weekends? Who owns the creative mind (and thereby the doll's body)? To answer this question, we must combine two fields of law: intellectual property and contract law. On the one hand, intellectual property has a pretty straightforward answer to who owns creativity: under both copyright and patent law, the creator is the lawful owner. On the other hand, these days, employment contracts used in every industry, and covering nearly all types of professions and jobs, routinely include clauses that assign all of an employee's creativity and innovation to the corporation. So how can these seemingly oppositional legal theories be reconciled and coexist?

First let's unpack the concept of initial allocation of ownership under copyright law. The author—whether an artist, poet, or musician—is a copyright's default owner. If Carter Bryant drew pictures of a new character, then he is the author of those expressions under copyright law. And yet there is one big exception, already embedded in the law, even in absence of a contract. The Copyright Act's work-for-hire doctrine says that if a company hires an employee specifically to produce creative work, say, as a designer like Carter or a software programmer, the company owns the copyright to the creative work for which the person was hired. So, for example, when Carter was designing new dresses and accessories for Barbie, any copyrightable expressions belonged to Mattel, his employer. This is true for all work created while under another's employ, even if the employer gave very little direction on the final product. For example, when famed choreographer Martha Graham fought with her employer over the ownership of dance moves she created, the court decided the rightful owner was her employer: "The fact that Graham was extremely talented understandably explains the Center's disinclination to exercise control over the details of her work, but does not preclude the sort of employee relationship that results in a work-for-hire."[1]

Still, if the employee was not hired to create something, but to do different work, or if he creates something different from the creative work for which he was hired—say, a marketer who writes jingles also writes a hit song—the song isn't considered a work made for hire.

If an employee creates something outside the scope of what he was tasked with, copyright law aims to leave the employee the ownership of his or her creation because, as we've explored, the original idea behind copyright law was to reward innovation by placing ownership in the hands of the creative person. Copyright law, according to the Supreme Court, is "based on the belief that by granting authors the exclusive rights to reproduce their works, they are given an incentive to create."[2] Individual authors—artists, musicians, designers, architects, and photographers—create, not corporations, and by keeping some of an employee's productive activity outside the scope of work made for hire, copyright law hoped to strike the right balance between corporate and individual ownership.

These days, however, contracts have kicked through traditional copyright assumptions and expanded the reach of corporate ownership. Like many workers, Carter signed a broad employment contract, effectively assigning his innovation beyond what intellectual property law envisioned.

When he began working for Mattel, Carter signed the standard employment contract, which included a clause assigning all of his future inventions to Mattel. Carter's contract was not unique—it is a standard form that companies all over the country, across a multitude of industries, require their employees to sign. Mattel's contract required Carter not "to engage in any employment or business other than for Mattel or invest or assist (in any manner) any business competitive with the business or future business plans of Mattel." It also required him to assign:

> *All inventions (as defined below) conceived or reduced to practice by me (alone or jointly by others) at any time during my employment by the Company.*[3]

The contract defined the term *inventions* to include:

> *All discoveries, improvements, processes, developments, designs, know-how, data computer programs and formulae, whether patentable or unpatentable.*

Notably, the word *ideas* did not appear in this long list.

Companies use these blanket employment contracts to demand that everyone, from low-level manufacturers up to the office's top creative minds, assign the company exclusive rights to their knowledge and talent. I was recently invited to present my research about the expansive use of such contracts across all industries at the White House and before representatives from the Treasury Department. My research shows that the vast majority of managerial and technical employees sign such agreements. While eight states—California, Delaware, Illinois, Kansas, Minnesota, North Carolina, Utah, and Washington—have labor codes limiting the reach of these assignment clauses, most employers can demand ownership over almost all our ideas, from inventions to creative concepts. Even a state like California, which poses some limitations on post-employment restrictions—it voids noncompete clauses, as well as any assignment agreements that extend to completely unrelated inventions—allows very broad assignments like the one Carter signed. And as we saw earlier, unlike other high-patenting countries such as Germany, Finland, Japan and China, which all require that businesses pay employees for their inventions for the company, American intellectual property law has no parallel requirements.

Long-time Mattel attorney Michael Zeller explained it to me this way, "Being in the creative industries, there ain't a lot of job security. The studios, the toy companies, Internet start-ups, tech industry in general, people are always looking for the next thing to do. So that's their motivation of planning to compete with their employer, to move to competitors, to develop their ideas on the side, to take trade secrets. But you can't socialize your losses and privatize your gains." This is why Mattel, like so many other conglomerates, goes to extreme measures to deter employees from leaving and competing with them. I've shown in my research that this can quickly backfire: motivation is suppressed when employees stay with their employers out of fear. But Mattel holds a hard line regarding the contractual obligations of its employees. In its lawsuit against Carter and MGA, Mattel asked the court to read the contract as all inclusive—everything an employee conceived of belongs to the company.

When Mattel's CEO Bob Eckert took the stand, MGA's attorneys asked him a key question on assignability: "When an employee agrees to go to work at Mattel and signs a confidentiality agreement with Mattel, is it your view that they transfer all of the ideas and dreams that they had before they began to work at Mattel?" Eckert paused, and meekly responded with a "no." But what if a Mattel employee developed the idea during weekends and nights? Eckert answered an uncompromising "Yes, Mattel owns it." Carter's attorney tried unsuccessfully to attack the contract itself as unconscionable and thereby void. He told the courts that "somehow, someone within Mattel came up with a nifty idea for an agreement with terms that only an advanced patent attorney would be able to know and understand." He continued, explaining that Mattel used to print these clauses in a very readable type, but over the years shrank the print to nearly an illegible size. The contract was then routinely presented to employees during orientation with no opportunity to negotiate or object. But the court ruled early in the trial that the contract was valid. So the question became how to interpret it.

Ivy Ross testified for Mattel that naturally creative people like herself are hired for their ideas. Carter too, she insisted, owed his former employer all of his ideas. Ross pointed to the literal interpretation of the contract, especially the word *conceived*, which appeared in the assignment clause. " 'Conceived' is anything you think of," Ross explained to the court, "So there are times when, as a creative person, you think— you're on 24/7—you think of things that relate to your industry, not necessarily when you're even just at work." She herself, she told the jury, had often been inspired outside of work and brought her ideas to the company: "When I was at Coach handbags, I was in an airplane and I was looking at the way a propeller spins, and I thought to myself that would make an incredible lock on a handbag. So that was something I conceived of while in an airplane on my own time but employed by Coach. So I walked in on Monday and played with that idea."

She testified that, as a creative, you just can't shut your mind off. When your ideas relate to your employer's business, regardless of whether you do think of them on your own time—in the shower, on an airplane—they are owned by the company. Ross therefore was Mattel's key witness to refute MGA's "weekend and nights" argument, which held that Carter was allowed to own ideas he created during his free time off the job:

> *If your creativity is about looking in the world, taking things in, putting it into your filter and kind of coming back out with something new or something that takes parts of things that you've seen in the world and reinterprets it—yes, you can clock out, but you're thinking about what you do creatively. You may not be making it, but you are taking in information. That's how creativity works.*

It was also beyond Ross to see why any designer, or specifically why Carter, would be unhappy working at her division, notwithstanding the fact she earned nearly ten times more than he did. Ross testified that she was particularly surprised by Carter's unhappiness after his name was featured on a Barbie collectible box, explaining, "It was a big honor to be asked to do one of the collector dolls where we celebrate the creator."

Romantic Fiction and Comic Relief

Carter may have thought up Bratz, yet he lived in a world where corporations had a strong hold over intellectual property. From

Thomas Edison to Steve Jobs, Leonardo da Vinci to Picasso, individual inventors and artists are heroes in popular imagination. We celebrate the power of individual creativity and, from a very early age, we have strong notions of a person's right to own the fruits of his or her mind. And yet today, as the *Harvard Business Review* recently announced, this image of a lone genius inventing from scratch may be "no more than romantic fiction."[4] Unsurprisingly, with more corporations demanding employees preassign all forms of intellectual property to them, as well as their rights to move freely in the job market, inventor-owned patents and copyrights are at an all-time low. A couple of decades ago, people owned about 25 percent of all patents granted in the United States. Now, individuals barely own 10 percent; 90 percent are corporate owned. And this disparity is about to become even more pronounced. In March 2013, the America Invents Act—the most significant patent law reform since 1952—went into effect, shifting our patent system from a first-to-invent to a first-to-file rule. This act, while extremely beneficial to corporations, harms individual inventors who lack the funding to file a patent for their invention before a corporate competitor. The contemporary expansion of the law has meant that small inventors and artists are left frustrated with few rewards from, or control over, their creations.

Take for example another group of cultural icons born around the time of Barbie: the Fantastic Four, the Incredible Hulk, Thor, and X-Men. Jack Kirby, the King of Comics, created these properties for Marvel Comics. Kirby began working for Marvel in 1958 as a freelance artist. During his first five years at the company, Kirby and Marvel never defined their relationship with any kind of formal contract. Instead, Kirby sketched stories and characters he thought Marvel might be interested in and showed them to Stan Lee, Marvel's president, who, if interested, purchased the drawings at a per-page rate. Kirby was not promised royalties for the artwork, nor was he promised that Marvel would even use or publish the pages. Like

Mattel, as Marvel grew, so grew its bargaining power vis-à-vis its artists, and it began requiring that artists release all prior work as works made for hire. In 1972, Marvel asked Kirby to sign a contract that assigned all of his intellectual property to Marvel.

Many years later, in 2009, shortly after Disney announced its four-billion-dollar acquisition of Marvel, Kirby's four children attempted to reassert Kirby's copyright over his drawings, claiming Kirby—and his heirs—own the rights to the characters, and as a result hundreds of millions (if not billions) of dollars in royalties. Kirby died in 1994, and his children explained that their father "didn't have the stomach lining to fight Marvel over copyright" during his lifetime. The court found in favor of Marvel, reasoning that Kirby's creations were works made for hire as a matter of law, even absent a contract. He was hired specifically to create super heroes and fantastic storylines, which meant, under the court's reading of the law, that even as a freelancer Kirby implicitly conceded his copyright to Marvel. Late in his life, when asked about Marvel, Jack Kirby said bitterly: "They can act like businessmen. But to me, they're acting like thugs."[5]

For Carter Bryant, there was no bigger thug than Mattel. At trial, Carter claimed he saw nothing wrong with pitching his personal idea for a racy, urban doll while still employed by Mattel. He honestly believed that because his serendipitous encounter at a Missouri mall occurred while on leave and seemingly beyond Mattel's corporate grasp, he owed the company nothing. Upon returning to Southern California, he felt free to send his artistic rendering to a talent agency. At Mattel, he was never asked to invent a new doll line, only to design Barbie's clothes. He felt that his creative talent during his time away and during weekends and nights should not be owned by his employer. In their closing statement, MGA's attorneys urged the jury: "The only theft that will occur in this case is if you allow Mattel to take ideas and drawings they did not conceive of, that they did not draw and dolls that they did not make. That's what this case is about."

Your Teddy Bear Looks a Lot Like Mine!

Even if Mattel convinced the court in its claim that it owned Carter's initial concept and designs, it still had to prove another claim: that it owned the copyright of MGA's Bratz. MGA could viably fight back by arguing the doll MGA eventually released was different from what Carter envisioned. Even if Carter conceived a bratty doll line a year later than he claimed, why should the law prevent MGA from developing the idea of a bratty, edgy new doll line? Copyright law, as broad as it currently is, has limits: you can own expressions but you can't own ideas. MGA argued that even if Carter had assigned his ideas to Mattel by contract, as a competitor, copyright law only prevents MGA from copying the expressions of those ideas, and not the ideas themselves.

Copyright protection is one of the most controversial areas of contemporary law because copyright, compared to patents, has a very low standard for originality while, at the same time, lasts far longer. Patents are granted for 20 years, but nowadays a standard copyright exists for the life of the author, plus an additional 70 years—virtually an infinite amount of time from a human perspective (a copyright for an anonymous work, or a work made for hire, lasts either 95 years from the work's first publication, or 120 years from its creation, depending on which of the two dates occurs first). These two features taken together have muddled the actual purpose of copyright law, and perhaps no longer encourage progress in the arts. Companies can own relatively unoriginal works of art, and prevent others from building on those expressions, for longer than an entire human lifetime. There are two ways out of this bind, and each is limited. We saw earlier the fair use defense as one way to limit the reach of copyright. But equally important is that copyright is granted over concrete expressions only, not ideas.

The idea/expression distinction is notoriously elusive. The Copyright Act states that "*in no case* does copyright protection for an original work of authorship extend to any *idea, procedure, process, system, method of operation, concept, principle, or discovery*, regardless of the form in which it is described, explained, illustrated, or embodied in such work." But that elusive distinction, though subtle, is essential. It simultaneously ropes off copyrightable material and lays a welcome mat at the entrance to the public domain. This balance is meant to reflect the goal behind copyright: to incentivize authors, artists, and creators by protecting their expression from being copied, but keep ideas free and the intellectual public domain rich, enabling others an opportunity to freely build upon what came before. Assume I have a script idea. The idea-expression distinction occurs along a continuum from the most specific to the most general. My script expresses the following:

> *Steve, 25 years old, 6' 1" with brown hair and brown eyes, a slight stutter that embarrasses him enough to keep him quiet in groups of people he doesn't know, is passionate about nachos, New Balance running shoes, and always wears red sweatshirts because the last time his father saw him, Steve was wearing a red sweatshirt. He falls in love with Alice, 26 years old, 5' 9" blonde with blue eyes, a dimple on her left cheek. Alice is the daughter of Steve's father's longtime nemesis and her family prohibits her from dating him.*

Behind this expression is my idea: a boy meets a girl from a different background, the families are opposed to the union, and conflict ensues. Think *Romeo and Juliet, West Side Story,* or *Abie's Irish Rose.* The law would likely deem the short synopsis, along with my script, protected expression, but the idea of a boy meeting a girl from a different background is not unique. If the idea were protected, would we get stuck with just one variation of star-crossed lovers? Would we have creative expansions and remixes of classics? Would we have, for example, the movie *Avatar*? A ship lands in a new world searching for valuables; our hero is supposed to search for valuables but meets and falls for one of the natives. The native teaches our hero important life lessons, and they fall in love. The young couple must then fight against the invading forces, which the visitor was once a part of. This is the same exact plot as *Pocahontas*, but the *Pocahontas/Avatar* connection is far enough down the continuum toward an "idea" that it is not protected. The general plots and themes span the history of storytelling. The movie business provides us with many such examples: *Deep Impact/Armageddon, Dante's Peak/Volcano, Mission to Mars/ Red Planet, Emma/Clueless,* and *Harry Potter/Star Wars.*

Similarly, a creator cannot claim the elements of an image— *scènes à faire,* as they are referred to in the copyright law, that flow naturally from the concept. For example, when a Kate Spade fashion campaign included an image of a woman's feet in stylish, colorful shoes as she sat on a toilet with a handbag on the floor, Spade successfully defended a lawsuit from a photographer who also had the idea of using a woman sitting on a toilet to showcase stylish shoes and other fashion accessories. If fashionably sitting on the toilet is an idea, then elements that necessarily flow from the toilet *idea,* like a bathroom floor framing a woman's legs and handbag, also cannot be protected.

Over the years, copyright protection expanded and became the heart of heated conflict among artists, authors, businesses, and policymakers. Increasingly, it seems that corporations demand their copyright extend to concepts and ideas, rather than just concrete expressions. Take James Bond, for example. Metro-Goldwyn-Mayer, the owners of the James Bond copyright, sued Honda over a commercial featuring a man in a tuxedo, a beautiful woman by his side, racing around in a new Honda. The California court compared the commercial and the James Bond films. Both had suave, tuxedo-clad male heroes with beautiful females by their side, facing off against villains, and escaping from said villains during a high-speed chase. The court found the two pieces were so substantially similar—there was a sameness in the style of dialogue, music, and resulting escape from the villains—that Honda had infringed MGM's copyright. My research shows that this is an overly broad interpretation of copyright law, paradoxically limiting human creativity rather than encouraging it, which was the original intent behind copyright protection. And yet, despite empirical evidence pointing to the contrary, increasingly over the past few decades, courts have accepted this expansive construction of copyright, and Mattel has pushed hard to extend this new definition into the toy industry. So when it came to the Bratz doll line, Mattel was set on defining its copyright ownership broadly to include the concepts behind the particular sketches that Carter originally drew. MGA by contrast argued that even if Mattel owned Carter's original sketches, it was still free to develop the *idea* of Bratz. How do you separate the ideas and expressions of toys: cars, airplanes, teddy bears, and dolls?

In the toy industry, companies vigorously wield their right to intellectual property so they can fight copycats and wannabe competitors. Innovations involving technological advancement, such as a new mechanical feature like a sensor that can detect movement and make a doll talk, are patentable, granting toy manufacturers twenty-years of exclusivity over the invention. For the other components of a toy—names and logos—toy companies rely on trademark protections. But it is the copyright wars that are the most heated in the industry: copyright protects the toys aesthetic features, images, shapes, expressions, and storylines.

If you think about it, most of Mattel's toys are replicas of larger originals—whether human or human-made—guns, dolls, miniature pianos, airplanes, and cars. And indeed, until the 1980s, toys received little copyright protection. The courts held that, most of the time, toymakers were trying to protect the idea behind a toy, rather than an artistic expression, and ideas can't be owned. For example, when, in 1983, a toy company wanted to protect its toy airplane, the court found the plane "permits a child to dream and to let his or her imagination soar." That's a conceptual idea and, therefore, a toy plane cannot be copyrighted. Even more basically, the court explained that toy airplane models are not copyrightable because a toy airplane is modeled off a real airplane.[6] Now take teddy bears. Because those cuddly stuffed animals represent the basic features of a cute bear, competitors can produce similar products.[7] When, for example, Toys "R" Us dropped a manufacturer's toy and started making a very similar one, the manufacturer sued. Toys "R" Us hired an army of teddy bear experts who testified the similarities between the teddy bears were simply the general *ideas* we have of cute teddy bears: the requisite ears, eyes, nose, mouth, belly, arms, and legs. Since copyright does not protect ideas, but only a particular expression or authorship, the court dismissed the lawsuit against retail partner-turned-competitor Toys "R" Us (as in so many disputes, here, the major corporation won against the smaller competitor, but at least the law came out on the right side to protect a greater public domain of ideas free for all to copy). In one case in the 1980s, even stuffed cuddly dinosaurs were dismissed from the courtroom when one producer sued a competitor producing stuffed dinosaurs: the court held that gentle, cuddly characteristics of toy dinos are not protectable under copyright law. Rather, these elements are too generic and conceptual—they represent an idea, not expression.[8] Snowmen too have lost in court—two plush snowmen of the same height, with the same black button eyes and V-shaped mouths, red buttons, and a black hat were not similar enough in copyrightable elements for a legal claim. Since most of these elements represented generic ideas we have of snowmen, small differences in their stitching, contours, and features were enough for a competitor to exist.

So planes, teddy bears, cute dinosaurs, and snowmen are tough litigants, but what about dolls? Since dolls have inherently similar features—all resemble humans in some way—courts historically rejected copyright infringement claims. Until the mid-1980s, toy companies generally lost when they sued a competitor for producing a similar-looking doll.[9] The courts have held that dolls will usually have common human features, including faces, along with locomotive ability and plastic construction.[10]

Times have changed. Over the years, Mattel has fought to protect the copyright of all its toys, but most of all Barbie. By the 1990s, Mattel took the lead in convincing the courts to expand copyright protections for toys and thereby prevent competitors from selling similar products. The courts now reasoned that, just as a painting of a plane had copyrightable elements, so too did the artistic side of toys. This expansion of monopoly over images and storylines has been especially problematic when it comes to the toy industry, which for years has consisted of a virtual duopoly between Mattel and Hasbro (in 1996, Mattel tried and failed to take over Hasbro, offering $5.2 billion). Once Mattel owned the expansive rights that prevented copying toys, it became almost impossible for newcomers, such as MGA, to enter the market. Intellectual property began perversely stifling competition and innovation.

In the turn of the century, the judgments were stacking the deck toward expansive copyright protection. When Radio City Music Hall created its own doll in celebration of the millennium, the Rockettes 2000, Mattel immediately filed a copyright suit claiming the doll looked too much like Barbie.[11] At first, the district court dismissed Mattel's lawsuit after relying on early cases, which reasoned that basic human-like features—the eyes, nose, mouth—are all unprotectable. Mattel, however, appealed and won. The Court of Appeals determined that any artistic feature that possesses some level of creativity, if only a "*slight amount*," deserves copyright protections, even when on a toy doll. Copyright law protects standard or common features, opined the higher court, and features "*need not be particularly novel or unusual.*" Features need only to have been "independently created" by the author and possess "some minimal degree of creativity."[12] The court explained that because there are innumerable ways to upturn noses, bow lips, and space eyes, the features of Barbie, which were independently created (the court apparently was unaware of Barbie's German doppelganger Lilli) had the minimal degree of creativity necessary to afford copyright protection. After lowering the bar for originality dramatically, the court found that Mattel's copyright for a doll's face with fairly standard features was protectable. However, the court trod carefully, clarifying that the *idea* of a doll with similar features—an upturned nose, bow lips, and widely spaced eyes—was not protected, but rather it was the execution and concrete expression of these ideas that infringed upon Barbie's domain. An elusive distinction indeed!

Armed with new expansive interpretation of copyright, Mattel continued to use litigation to try to drive out competition, not only on its home turf, but also around the world. Perhaps the most ironic of the international lawsuits, given Barbie's appropriation of Lilli's image, was Mattel's suit against German toy maker Simba Smoby, which developed a doll named Steffi Love. Mattel tried to convince the German court that Steffi was riding Barbie's success, copying her ideas and marketing similar accessories. The German court didn't buy it. It held steadfast to the distinction between unprotectable concepts and copyrightable expressions. But back home in Los Angeles, where Mattel sued MGA under federal copyright law, armed with its victory against Radio City, the company felt it was on solid ground.

At trial, Mattel claimed that Carter's original drawings and MGA's Bratz line were similar enough that, if Mattel owned the drawings, it also owned the doll line. If Carter owed his creations to Mattel, then MGA too, having developed Carter's two-dimensional drawings into a full-fledged doll line, owed its empire to Mattel. With precision and conviction, Mattel's lawyers detailed all the ways in which Bratz's final formation was the essence of Carter's vision:

> *The proportional placement of the eyes, hair, and lips, which define Bratz's sultry look, match nearly identically between the drawings and*

the dolls. The eyes are a similar distance apart as are the eyebrows. The cheek color application is in the same place. The faces have a similar shape, from the brow, to the eye socket, to the outward curve of the cheek. Even the moles are in the same location.

To counter Mattel's claim of copyright infringement, MGA tried to show that even if Mattel owned the copyright to Carter's original drawings, and even if Carter himself had contractually assigned not only copyrightable material but also his ideas to Mattel, MGA as a competitor was under no obligation to avoid using Mattel's ideas. It was only prevented from using whatever Mattel could lawfully claim to own as a copyright. MGA claimed that the similarities between Carter's sketches and Bratz dolls were all similarities of features that represented ideas. To support this logic, MGA brought evidence of other earlier characters—Betty Boop, Japanese Anime characters, and Sailor Moon—showing the jury that the very concept of bratty, cartoonish characters, with big heads and a defiant attitude, was not new and that all of these girls shared the same abstract ideas.

To further sever the connection between Carter's creations and MGA's eventual product, MGA's attorneys also told the jury about the crucial role that Isaac Larian played in developing Bratz. They leveraged Larian's underdog immigrant status as a way to bolster their claims that, without Isaac Larian at the helm, Carter's undeveloped idea would never have succeeded—it would have remained an abstract, worthless idea. MGA's opening statement began:

Now, times have changed since 1959. Today's teens are hip, they are urban, they are likely to have friends of all different ethnicities. They are more attuned to iPhones and MP3s than Barbie's dream house. And teens in 2000 were just as likely to be hip, urban and multiethnic, they were more attuned to Napster and their play stations back then than prom dates with Ken.

The jury was reminded: "Kids these days are no longer 90 percent White-European. They might be Asian or Latina or Middle Eastern or Caribbean or African or Indian, all kinds of different ethnicities. We don't have such a modalistic society anymore." And given these realities, the jury was asked to recognize that Larian—an immigrant, a bold and different kind of entrepreneur—was the one who could grasp and capitalize on these market shifts in ways Bob Eckert, a professional CEO who thinks selling culture is akin to selling American cheese, never could: "This is something Mr. Larian was keenly attuned to just from looking at his own kids and their giant variety of friends. He would look around and look at his own kids and look at the dolls that were out there on the market, and he saw opportunity, the thing he came to this country for."

In the Heat of Biases

As the companies became increasingly embroiled in war, grown men personified their billion-dollar rival dolls. Isaac Larian and his family were present in the courtroom every day, and he bubbled with emotion, eagerly spouting verbal jabs at his enemies to anyone who might listen. Bob Eckert, the all-American professional CEO, rarely appeared at trial and refused to give interviews.

Before the trial had begun, but after Mattel filed the lawsuit, a married couple from San Diego sued Carter Bryant and MGA, claiming that Bratz was copied from the airbrushed T-shirts they sold at county fairs. During this "warm-up" trial, the majority of attorneys who actually showed up to court didn't represent either party to the suit. Instead, the back of the courtroom was filled with Mattel attorneys, huddled together to compare notes taken while observing the seemingly small trial.

The case was a loser. Carter had never been to a county fair (as one person close to Carter told me, Carter, who shied away from crowds and enjoyed edgy and sophisticated offerings, "would be the last person to be wandering around the county fair eating pumpkin-glazed deep fried turkey legs."). Not only had Carter never seen the T-shirt, but the images on the T-shirts bore very little resemblance to Bratz. Yet, despite the seemingly frivolous nature of these claims, the trial in San Diego was a spectacle. Isaac Larian and his family showed up every single day at this "trial run" trial. Larian never passed up any opportunity to show off his many perfectly tailored suits, and his wife and daughter seemed to have stepped straight off the runway. The women wore dresses from Dior and Chanel, and heavy, flashy jewelry. One insider confided with me that to him, "it felt as though the Kardashians had arrived to court." The Larians, seated as defendants in the front row of the courtroom, contrasted sharply with the working-class jurors of San Diego County. Regardless, the case was quickly dismissed when it became clear that there was no shred of evidence to suggest Carter had copied the hand-painted images sold on their T-shirts.

But while Larian and his family appeared to be the hotshot lit-igants when they were fighting a San Diegan couple who sold T-shirts at the local fair, up against Mattel, the Larians seemed like the small family business attacked by a ruthless corporate giant. Even the body language of the two CEOs was diametrically opposed. Larian appeared eager to please, eager to connect. Eckert made no eye contact. He rarely showed emotion and carefully limited his public appearances. "He acted like he was too good to be there though he was behind these lawsuits that were making his competitors' lives miserable," one juror told me. He sent a clear message to his under-lings: my time is too valuable and I am above all of this. One of the jurors described to me an underlying vibration in the courtroom of Mattel, simply the biggest player in the industry with a team of over a hundred attorneys working for it. Day in and day out, there were dozens of Mattel attorneys in the courtroom. MGA was a smaller fish, a family-run company, and it had less consistent legal representation.

Isaac Larian took much of the lead in overseeing his case and working closely with his lawyer du jour to win his argument. On the first day Eckert took the stand, MGA's attorney highlighted the disparity between Larian's presence and his absence: "You know that when Mr. Larian is sitting here every single day and you are not, it looks bad to the jury, right?"

A few weeks into the trial, Larian received an anonymous letter warning him that Mattel executives "have collaborated to spy on you and your family at your home and your children's school." The letter ended with the word *Shalom*, the Hebrew word for goodbye as well as peace. To this day, the sender of the letter remains unknown. But evidence unearthed later proved Mattel's surveillance of the Larian family, including the children. "The Mattel folks hated Larian so much that they investigated his children," one juror told me. "We were shown how they filmed the kids coming and going from their home. I mean, that's where you have to draw the line. You don't go after someone's home and wife and children."

Judge Larson's prior rulings meant the jury heard a fairly lopsided story about a small, possibly jealous upstart allegedly stealing ideas from an industry giant. However, Judge Larson's evidentiary rulings did not stop at keeping out Mattel's financial and moral imperfections. He also allowed the jury to hear evidence that, in retrospect, seems particularly problematic. One of the lead MGA attorneys told me, "The case was pervaded with every racial, sexual, ethnic stereotype imaginable." During the discovery stage, the pretrial procedure through which the parties can demand that the other side produce evidence, Mattel's attorneys got a warrant to scan Carter's computer. On his computer, they found eliminator software as well as some porn. Judge Larson allowed Mattel to present that porn to the jury and to question Carter about it. One of MGA's lead attorneys told me that "the subtext was that Carter, a gay man, had an unhealthy interest in children; that the porn was male pornography, perhaps child pornography. It was nonsense and there was also no evidence that there had been elimination of any evidence. Carter testified that he used the program in order to delete certain explicit material he had on his computer." Another experienced litigator explained that the atmosphere set in Judge Larson's courtroom was central to understanding the arch of the trial: "You can't underestimate the tremendous influence that the judge has on a jury. Evidentiary rulings as well as nuances during the testimonies, comments he makes, facial expressions."

In the courtroom, the exchanges between the attorneys and the litigants became increasingly rocky as the trial dragged on. Isaac Larian believes that he was incrementally subjected to various racist comments. One example that Larian likes to retell is when one of Mattel's attorneys read one of Larian's work e-mails back to him, which Larian sent in response to Paula Garcia's request for twelve thousand dollars to pay for a doll sample. Larian originally wrote, "All the women in my life—my wife, my secretary, you—want so much from me." But on the stand, Mattel's attorney asked Larian why he wrote that his wives, secretary, and so forth make demands. Larian, face bright red with anger, exploded, "Wives?!? What did you say? Wives!?! You racist! I am not answering any more of your questions until you apologize to my wife who is sitting here in court. You are a racist!" Mattel's attorney said it was only a slip of the tongue; Larian's Iranian heritage had nothing to do with his accidentally saying "your wives," rather than "your wife." He turned to Larian's wife and apologized, but asked for an apology himself. "I am not a racist," he insisted. Larian refused to take back his accusation. Rather, he repeated, "You are a racist."

Larian has multiple examples of Mattel's personal attacks, though when listening to him talk about the courtroom experience, it becomes clear that both sides indulged in attempts to tarnish by innuendo and insult:

They tried to dig all sorts of false dirt on me. They found an e-mail that I received on my fiftieth birthday from my best friend's wife. She wrote me, "You're a big boy now." They asked me who this woman is. I said she was a close family friend, the wife of my best friend. Zeller asked, "And what other kinds of relationship do you have with her?" I blew up and yelled at him, "You nicotine chewing druggy with your mail-ordered wife—cause Zeller, you see, he has a Filipina wife. How dare you offend my wife of thirty years who is sitting in the courtroom?!"

(So much for rejecting offensive biases. Zeller's wife is a highly educated Asian American attorney.)

All the identity-based subtexts that pervaded the trial culminated in a statement of racial bias by one juror. Near the end of the trial, a juror came forward and reported to Judge Larson that a fellow juror had made disparaging comments about Iranians. The juror had told the other members of the jury during deliberations that Iranians were "thieves" who were "stingy, stubborn, rude," and steal other people's ideas. She told the other jurors that her husband was a lawyer who dealt with a lot of Iranians and knew their character. It wasn't the first time Larian dealt with potential prejudice in the courtroom. One of his attorneys, Patricia Glaser, told me that when she represented Larian in litigation against LucasFilm (which he eventually won), the trial was set to take place right after 9/11. She asked the judge for a continuation, to try the case a bit later so the prejudice against Iranians would be less likely to affect the trial, and the judge in that case granted her motion.

In Judge Larson's courtroom, when the juror's comments were reported, MGA demanded a mistrial. According to an MGA attorney, "When Judge Larson was told about a juror who had expressed his biases against Persians, he basically just shrugged his shoulders." That was a bit of an overstatement—in reality, Judge Larson dismissed the juror and brought in an alternate. He ruled that the remarks, while "grossly inappropriate," were made after the jury decided on all of the major issues (though not yet on the damages) and that the juror in question was rebuked by all of the others. Larson called the juror prejudiced and her comments "a cancer" but decided that the comments had no legal implications on the continuation of the jury trial. Still, MGA's attorneys were not satisfied. One of them told me that "Judge Larson seemed oblivious to the racial undertones in the trial." To this day, Larian continues to claim that the verdict in Judge Larson's courtroom was based only on racism.

After hearing all the testimonies, at the end of the trial, Judge Larson instructed the jury that any Bratz-related idea, concept, drawing, design, or work Carter created while employed by Mattel is owned by Mattel, regardless if he thought up the ideas outside of working hours. In other words, he knocked down MGA's two central defenses—that Mattel's contract didn't extend to work Carter did on his own time on nights and weekends and that the contract didn't include "ideas" so a *concept* for a new product line was not covered.

Next, Judge Larson told the jury that neither general resemblance to human physiology (the mere presence of hair, head, two eyes, eyebrows, lips, nose, and mouth simply track human anatomy), nor the idea of age, race, ethnicity (as well as "urban" and "rural" looks) were protectable under copyright law. And yet, he told the jury, the particularized compilation of these elements imbued Bratz with a distinct look—"aggressive, contemporary, youthful style"—and the particularized expression of the doll's features, including the exaggeration of certain anatomical features relative to others—lips, eyes—and de-emphasis of others features—nose and body—are all copyrightable.

In late 2008, having heard all the evidence and Judge Larson's instructions, the jury unanimously accepted all of Mattel's claims. The jury interpreted Carter's contract as assigning all of his ideas to Mattel and believed that Carter had developed his Bratz idea during the period when he came back from Missouri to Mattel. The jury concluded that Carter invented every aspect of the Bratz line—from its very name down to the doll's specific design—while employed at Mattel and that many elements of his creations that eventually made it to the final doll were protected by copyright. Therefore, they found that by developing Bratz, MGA infringed on Mattel's intellectual property. The jury awarded Mattel one hundred million dollars in damages, but much more damaging was that Judge Larson issued a worldwide injunction keeping MGA from selling any Bratz product. The judge ordered MGA to immediately cease production, stop selling Bratz dolls, and refrain from ever using the Bratz name, or licensing the line to another company. The sketches and everything they inspired, even subsequent generations of dolls and the hundreds of related products, were now Mattel's.

The all-inclusive injunction would be one of Judge Larson's last orders—he retired in 2009 at the age of forty-four, blaming the low pay of federal justices. He explained that he had to support his seven children, and Congress' failure to increase judicial salaries made it difficult for him to stay on the bench. If you believe Isaac Larian, Judge Larson was better off not judging the Barbie versus Bratz case: "I am tolerant to all religions. I have mezuzahs everywhere in my company and house, I respect all faiths. But in any religion, extremists become fanatics. Larson, with an altar in his house, had it out for us. I believe he thought God put him on the bench to get rid of the newest slutty influence on America, Bratz." As reflected in his over-the-top remarks, Larian obviously came to detest anyone who ruled against MGA.

Most companies, after suffering such a devastating loss, would have quit, but Larian went to the media and vocally opposed settling with the enemy. "I need to sleep good at night; I can't get in bed with them," he said. And indeed, he wouldn't.

9 | TAMING BARBIE: STARRING JUDGE ALEX KOZINSKI AS SPEECHZILLA

Nowadays people know the price of everything and the value of nothing.

—OSCAR WILDE

OF ALL THE JUDGES in the world, none was better suited to tame Barbie than Judge Alex Kozinski, who is the most colorful judge sitting on the US Court of Appeals for the Ninth Circuit. Kozinski's reputation as a staunch supporter of free culture and competition meant MGA was delighted to have him overseeing the case.

Until recently, Judge Kozinski was the court's chief judge, a position he held for seven years, from 2007 to 2014. Judge Kozinski was only thirty-five years old when President Reagan appointed him to the bench in 1985, making him one of the youngest federal appellate court judges in the country. His Senate confirmation was also one of the closest votes over a judicial appointment. At the time, he seemed too conservative—a wild card from the Democrats' perspective. On many fronts, he is still quite conservative. He tolerates the death penalty and believes in deregulation. He believes government intervention is suspect. He also fervently resists judicially created powers and rights, and, like the late Justice Antonin Scalia and the newly appointed Justice Neil Gorsuch, Kozinski is an originalist, meaning he considers the "original" intent of the founding fathers who drafted the Constitution. Therefore, he prefers interpreting the Constitution narrowly. He rejects the liberal idea of "a living Constitution" and once referred to the prospect of judges deciding cases according to their personal and political views, rather than formal legal rules, as "horse manure." Like all horse manure, he warned, it contains little seeds of truth from which tiny birds can take intellectual nourishment to distort legal judgments. Judges have quite a bit of discretion but must be bound by the narrow letter of the law. Still, Kozinski's worldview isn't easily pinned down to black-and-white rubrics. Since becoming a judge, he has gained supporters and fans from all colors of the political rainbow thanks to his sharp judgments, raw intellect, wicked humor, and quirky charm.

Judge Kozinski describes his path to the bench as rather serendipitous. An only child, Kozinski was born in 1950 in Bucharest, Romania, to parents who survived the Holocaust. His mother, Sabine, was confined to a ghetto. His father, Moses, survived four years in a concentration camp. In 1962, when Kozinski was twelve years old, the family immigrated to America, first to Baltimore, then to Los Angeles, where his father ran a small grocery.

To this day, Judge Kozinski's heavy Romanian accent remains unshakable. In his mouth, *the* becomes *zha; copyright law* becomes *copyride lah.* When he and I converse, I need to pay particularly close attention to his words and sometimes ask him to repeat himself. But beyond these small pronunciation quirks, his English is, of course, perfect.

As a child of an immigrant family in Los Angeles, the young Alex worked hard, studied hard, and was a zealous self-advocate. Still, Kozinski admits, he was often distracted by his weakness for chasing girls. As a student at UCLA Law School, Kozinski never quite played the part of an aspiring "Big Law" attorney, eschewing the typical clean-cut style of a law student, opting instead to sport long hair and a beard. Today, he continues to defy convention and behaves far from the stereotyped stuffy judge. He seems more multidimensional than most. Partly, it's because he's refused to allow the bench to define him.

He is passionate about his interests, many of which do not involve the law. When he is not draped in judicial robes, he is snowboarding, writing movie and video game reviews, and hosting parties (the first thing he did when we met was to invite me to his KFF parties: *Kozinski's Favorite Flicks*, a monthly event at the Pasadena courthouse where Kozinski is a perfect host, walking around with a tray of Philly cheesesteaks and local beer). He makes friends, smiles, and laughs easily.

Though a hard worker, he requires some escape. Recently, over lunch, he told me that he still doesn't have a smartphone because he enjoys time away from e-mail and electronics. He admitted, though, that if he needs to call an Uber or wants to show someone a funny YouTube video, perhaps one featuring himself, "There are always people around me with a phone—a law clerk, my assistant, my kids." He has raised three sons with his wife in Los Angeles in their house by the sea and now has five grandchildren.

Kozinski's love of pop culture eclipses that of any judge I've met. I've clerked for the most wonderful judge in the world, Justice Itzhak Zamir of the Israeli Supreme Court, but I admit that no one, including my beloved Justice, comes close to matching Judge Kozinski's cool factor. Perhaps that has made Kozinski too cool for one particular school—Kozinski admits he has given up on his dream of sitting on the Supreme Court of the United States. He has not exactly played by the book. But life is too short for such calculations or regrets. Kozinski doesn't sit waiting for the president's call from D.C. Instead, he embraces life in sunny Los Angeles and has become a prominent fixture in the Hollywood community.

Judge Kozinski has seen every film ever produced and remembers each in vivid detail. He has his own IMDB profile, from which he has rated 1,101 films. He poses with celebrities and gossip columnists. He writes columns online and once described attending a lingerie party at a Malibu villa, calling it a "scandalous haven of sleepless nights." In one famous case about the movie industry, *United States v. Syufy Enterprises*, he weaved over 200 film titles into his written opinion.

Kozinski sits on the Ninth Circuit, which spans all of California, south and north, as well as Oregon, Washington, Montana, Hawaii, Alaska, Arizona, Idaho, Nevada, and the territories of Guam and the Northern Mariana Islands. It is by far the largest of the thirteen courts of appeal, covering a territory of 60 million people. The Ninth Circuit is thus hugely influential in shaping American law. That Kozinski is the Ninth Circuit's most recognizable and iconic judge tells us much about how this circuit shapes intellectual property and contract law as well as many other fields of law.

Kozinski's personal philosophy, which influences both his private life and his judicial approach, is that you need to build your brand through aggressive self-marketing, rather than by preventing others from competing. For example, Kozinski heard the Winklevoss brothers argue that Mark Zuckerberg stole the idea for Facebook when he worked on their idea for a social network at Harvard where they all were college students. In dismissing the Winklevoss complaint Kozinski wrote: "The Winklevosses are not the first party to be bested by a competitor who then seek to gain through litigation what they were unable to achieve in the marketplace."

Kozinski himself likes to compete and to win. Before he was married, Kozinski appeared, not once but twice, as an eligible bachelor on the *Dating Game*. He won as a contestant but then his date stood him up. Still, despite the subsequent off-screen rejection, he loves to show the clip of his win on YouTube. More recently, when leading legal gossip site *Underneath Their Robes* (a blog like *People* magazine but about "legal celebrities") nominated members of the bench based on their *hotness*, Kozinski was utterly disappointed by his apparent snub. His solution wasn't to mope around—he took action. He e-mailed the contest organizers with a long letter explaining that "discerning females and gay men find graying, pudgy, middle-aged men with an accent close to Gov. Schwarzenegger's almost totally irresistible." His persistence paid off big time. Kozinski was added to the roster at the last minute, the votes came in, and *Underneath Their Robes* officially named him the #1 male Superhottie among the federal judiciary.

Complementing his love of free-market competition, Kozinski is passionate about a thriving culture and adamant about free speech and the right to individual expression unconstrained by government control. In one memorable incident, Judge Kozinski recused himself from an obscenity trial because he had stored among his online files a folder with what the media outlets described as "bestiality porn." This was in 2008, when the judge was presiding over a case involving a filmmaker accused of criminally distributing obscene depictions of bestiality and defecation. In response to a *Los Angeles Times* article about his personal online graphic materials, he declared a mistrial and recused himself from the case. He also requested the Judicial Council of the Ninth Circuit initiate proceedings with regards to the allegations, maintaining that he had done nothing wrong.

His wife, Marcy Tiffany, a successful Los Angeles attorney, leaped to his defense against the media's alarmed coverage of "the judge who posts porn." She explained, "The fact is, Alex is not into porn— he is into funny—and sometimes funny has a sexual character." In a long letter, she pointed out how the media distorted the actual issue. She was especially angry at the egregious misrepresentation of one video as "bestiality porn." In fact, she wrote, it was "a widely available video of a man trying to relieve himself in a field when he is attacked by a donkey he fights off with one hand while trying to hold up his pants with the other. . . . Crude and juvenile, for sure, but not by any stretch of the imagination is it bestiality." Even the tiny percentage of Kozinski's posts that were sexual, she said, were all humorous.

The newspapers, she counterattacked, used "graphic descriptions that make the material sound like hard-core porn when, in fact, it is more accurately described as raunchy humor."

Unlike his wife, Kozinski was less willing to dissect each image and refute allegations that they were porn. On the images and their value, Kozinski was unapologetic: "I think it's odd and interesting. It's part of life."[1] He is, after all, a great defender of free speech, and to simply deny that the posted materials were obscene compromised his First Amendment freedoms, as an adult, to view and enjoy anything legal that comes his way. The judicial conduct investigation found that Judge Kozinski originally intended his website to be a private server on which he would store "a large agglomeration of files" that he had "collected over very many years." At the same time, the committee found that when the judge's link became public, and he became aware of it, he failed to take corrective action.

Kozinski apologized before the judicial committee that convened to investigate the incident:

> *I have caused embarrassment to the federal judiciary. I put myself in a position where my private conduct became the subject of public controversy. While this was painful for me personally, my greatest regret is that I was identified as a federal judge, indeed, as a Chief Judge of the nation's largest federal circuit. And thus whatever shame was cast on me personally, it reflected on my colleagues and our system of justice as well.*

The site was found to be in contravention of the Code of Conduct for United States Judges but the judicial committee found Kozinski's apology enough to warrant closing the investigation without further admonishment. Today, anyone visiting alex.kozinski.com is greeted by a lone message: "Ain't nothing here. Y'all best be movin' on, compadre."

Kozinski's zealous belief in free speech is tightly linked to his wariness of intellectual property. He firmly believes that all creators draw from the work of those who came before. In one of Kozinski's favorite opinions, he gave Vanna White and the *Wheel of Fortune* a piece of his mind over their complaint against a Samsung ad featuring a shapely blonde look-alike Vanna White Robot—her successor on a futuristic *Wheel of Fortune*. While the Ninth Circuit Court of Appeals affirmed the right of Vanna White to block the Samsung ad, Kozinski, in the minority, wrote a powerful dissent. Eyes sparkling, he told me that the Vanna White case anticipated his eventual call to tame Barbie and, in both cases, he maintained a deep commitment to remixing culture. He wrote in his Vanna White dissent, "We call this creativity, not piracy." Vanna White should have lost, he reasoned, because icons exist to be evoked by all:

> *If you want to refer to someone as a nebbish, you call him a Woody Allen type; or if it's someone who throws his weight around, you might call him the Arnold Schwarzenegger of his profession. Or if you want to evoke the image of a blonde with a waxen smile, wearing a glitzy evening gown on a game show, who could easily be displaced by a robot, you'd refer to— never mind, don't even think of it.*[2]

"Parody, humor, irreverence," says Kozinski, "are all vital components of the marketplace of ideas. . . . The right to draw ideas from a rich and varied public domain, and the right to mock, for profit as well as fun, the cultural icons of our time."[3] On famous marks and famous cultural icons, he says, "The originator must understand that the mark or symbol or image is no longer entirely its own, and that in some sense it also belongs to all those other minds who have received and integrated it."

Most importantly, Kozinski has warned that "overprotecting intellectual property is as harmful as underprotecting it. Creativity is impossible without a rich public domain. Nothing today, likely nothing since we tamed fire, is genuinely new: Culture, like science and technology, grows by accretion, each new creator building on the works of those who came before. Overprotection stifles the very creative forces it's supposed to nurture."[4] And so, when Mattel appeared again in his courtroom after Aqua's Barbie song, this time attempting to prevent a competitor from selling a fresher doll, Kozinski was ready to give the company another piece of his mind.

Unsurprisingly, given Kozinski's views about creativity, culture, and intellectual property, Barbie's victories ended, and Bratz's good fortune began, once Mattel's case against MGA came before him on appeal. Kozinski confessed to me, "Mind you, I had never heard of Bratz, which proves I had been living under a rock for some years." It fell to his fellow appeal panel judge, Judge Kim McLane Wardlaw, to explain the dolls to the two older men on the panel, Kozinski and Judge Stephen Trott. Judge Wardlaw had two young daughters and attested to the recent popularity of Bratz. Kozinski, a father to three boys, also did not know much about Barbie as a doll but was well acquainted with her legal entourage. What he remembered was his advice to Mattel to chill: "Well, they didn't listen to me."

When I told the judge that I grew up with a feminist mother who taught me that Barbie sends girls the wrong message about body image, Kozinski looked puzzled. "What's wrong with her body image?" he asked. I explained that her proportions represent unattainable female perfection and weight. Kozinski answered jokingly, "The only thing wrong that I saw when I held Barbie is when I lift her skirt there is nothing underneath." After his decision came out on appeal, a legal magazine drew a caricature of Kozinski holding the dolls and whispering to the other judges, "Let's keep them."

On appeal, MGA's attorneys urged the Ninth Circuit to reverse Judge Larson's jury instructions, the flawed findings made by the jury based on those instructions, and Larson's award of damages and worldwide injunction. Specifically, MGA argued that Judge Larson interpreted Carter Bryant's contractual obligations to Mattel too broadly. Moreover, even if Mattel owned the copyright and trademark to Carter's original sketches, the lower court erred in finding this meant everything MGA created thereafter also belongs to Mattel. As the Court of Appeals described the erroneous result by the lower court, "Barbie captured the Bratz."

It takes a judge with confidence in his professional rigor to pepper humor into his decisions. Reversing the lower court's victory for Mattel, Judge Kozinski set the tone of his judgment with this major statement: "America thrives on competition; Barbie, the all-American girl, will too." In his opinion he wrote about Mattel's unwillingness to compete: "Bratz became an overnight success. Mattel, which produces Barbie, didn't relish the competition. And it was particularly unhappy when it learned that the man behind Bratz was its own former employee, Carter Bryant." To Kozinski, the case was about a corporate giant trying to prevent competition in its market. Mattel had two central claims in the case—Carter's contract breach and MGA's copyright infringement. For Judge Kozinski, a culture-loving libertarian, contract and copyright claims are distinct issues. He had always been more comfortable with limiting copyright. But when it comes to contract, libertarians are keen on enforcing whatever two parties have freely agreed upon.

Kozinski thus followed his natural inclinations: look at the contract closely, interpret what it says, and figure out what each side thought it meant. Kozinski realized the contract never mentioned the word "ideas," instead using narrow and concrete terms, such as designs, processes, computer programs, and formulas. Ideas, Kozinski explained, are ephemeral and often reflect bursts of inspiration existing only in the mind. Kozinski admitted that other words appearing in the contract, such as "discoveries" and "know-how," seemed closer to the amorphous nature of ideas. He also thought the word "conceived" in the contract could hurt Carter, since conception precedes the concrete expression of an idea. Still, Kozinski overturned the first jury trial. He believed that a better-drafted contract could corral all ideas, abstract and ephemeral, but he was not convinced that Carter had signed such an expansive blanket agreement. He therefore sent his inquiries back for a second jury trial to have the contract's terms more carefully interpreted. Similarly, he rejected the holding that all inventions, even those made outside of working hours, were owned by Mattel. He considered the contractual phrase "at any time during my employment" as too ambiguous. "'At any time' could mean when I am at work. . . . Does this mean when I go to the bathroom? When I am asleep?" Kozinski asked. Thus, he also overturned the prior judgment that the contract automatically included all of Carter's innovations, during and outside of working hours, and held that a new jury would decide about the correct scope of the contract, especially what "conception" meant.

The divide between the scope of intellectual property law and the contractual pre-innovation assignment is illuminating. An unintended side effect of Kozinski's and other courts' analysis of contracts is that assignment agreements are getting broader and broader. Contracts now regularly subvert the lines drawn in patent and copyright law. Google, for example, requires employees to sign an assignment agreement that defines *inventions* to include "designs, developments, ideas, concepts, techniques, devices, discoveries, formulae, processes, improvements, writings, records, original works of authorship, trademarks, trade secrets, all related know-how, and any other intellectual property, *whether or not patentable or registrable under patent, copyright, or similar laws.*"[5] These types of explicit assignment clauses expand company ownership, and some, like Google, even expressly defy the bounds of patent and copyright law. Intellectual property law's Goldilocks bargain—getting the incentives just right so that employees will want to be inventive—is nullified by this contract. The standard employment agreements are now making ideas akin to a physical object and assigning automatic ownership over abstract ideas that would otherwise be part of the public domain, which would allow the person who thought it up to develop it.

I asked Judge Kozinski about the inherent tension between his willingness to interpret contracts broadly and his refusal to expand the boundaries of copyright law. Always open to discussing inconsistencies in his own jurisprudence, he considered how to reconcile his positions. Kozinski concluded that there actually wasn't much conflict in his interpretations. He explained that contracts are between two private parties and so, in Kozinski's view, the court must respect their right to strike a deal: "In theory, one could approve slavery within the bounds of law and contract. Of course if the state puts limits on such contracts, for example on sex services or physical abuse, that is all fine, but otherwise a contract is a contract. It is the private free will of the parties and should be respected." Still, a contract cannot give away more than is legally cognizable. So while it is well within the rights of two parties to contractually preassign ideas, that right does not suddenly afford those ideas copyright protection. The judge admitted that governments are empowered to void some contracts pursuant to public policy. California, for example, voids noncompetes and restraints on trade contracts. Kozinski said he would enforce those restrictions, but beyond that, it was not within his judicial purview to invent policies that are not set forth in statute.

As for intellectual property, despite his unwillingness to encroach on the legislature, Kozinski personally believes that copyright lasts too long. In a 2006 interview with *Reason* magazine, four years before he decided on MGA's appeal against Mattel, Kozinski said,

> *Nobody writes anything from scratch. We all build on the past from a shared public domain of ideas. We use copyrighted ideas to communicate with each other. For instance, when you say someone has a Barbie personality, it provides a description, and leaves no need to go into a thousand details. But Mattel, the inventor of Barbie, hates when you say that. People who own those trademarks and copyrights want to control the way people communicate, and they have the ear of Congress right now. Congress just extended copyright terms again [in 1998].*

So while Judge Kozinski was rather comfortable with contractual expansion over employee creativity, provided it was drafted diligently, he was far more suspicious of wholesale copyright protection. Kozinski, always conscious of the threat copyright law posed to human creativity, believed interpreting copyrights too broadly would allow the monopolization of an idea by the first person who expressed it. As he states, "There are gazillions of ways to make an aliens-attack movie." Looking at the final Bratz doll and its connection to Carter's original drawings, Kozinski warned that overly broad copyright protection could chill innovation. In his decision, Kozinski writes that "the kicker" of the case was whether Mattel even held a copyright over Carter's initial sketches and sculptures and whether the Bratz dolls actually infringed on that copyright.

Copyright only covers the particular expression of the bratty-doll idea, not the idea itself. As we have come to expect from the judge's storied lineage of intellectual property findings, Kozinski believes excessively strong controls over information threaten innovation and creativity. Examining the sizable leap from Carter's sketches to MGA's development of a doll line, Kozinski reminds us of the distinction between idea and expression at the core of copyright law:

> Degas can't prohibit other artists from painting ballerinas, and Charlaine Harris can't stop Stephenie Meyer from publishing Twilight just because Sookie came first. Similarly, MGA was free to look at Bryant's sketches and say, "Good idea! We want to create bratty dolls too."[6]

Even if the court's interpretation of the contract granted Mattel copyright over Carter's original sketches, Kozinski stated that Mattel was "entitled to only thin copyright expression against virtually identical copying" because "the concept of depicting a young, fashion-forward female with exaggerated features, including an oversized head and feet, is . . . unoriginal as well as an unprotectable idea."

Kozinski thus held that the lower court erred in so quickly finding copyright infringement. Larson failed to instruct the jury to remove the unprotectable elements of the dolls and sketches when assessing their similarities. Human characteristics, personalities, and features cannot be monopolized: "Mattel can't claim a monopoly over fashion dolls with a bratty look or attitude, or dolls sporting trendy clothes—these are all unprotectable ideas." Producing small plastic dolls resembling young women is a staple of the fashion doll market. The fact that Bratz added exaggerated features, such as her oversized head and feet, does not erect a wall precluding everyone from using those elements. Exaggerating a girl's features is therefore unoriginal and unprotectable. Kozinski rejected Mattel's argument that, since there were so many ways to exaggerate the human figure, the particular iteration of Bratz belonged to it. Granted, a company could make a fashion doll with a large nose and a potbelly, but there isn't much of a market for those iterations. Given these constraints, there are only so many ways a company can design an attractive, young, female doll with exaggerated proportions and therefore there should be no copyright protection for such a cluster of iterations.

However, some dolls seem so unique that their distinctiveness seems worthy of copyright protection. Take Pull My Finger Fred and copycat Fartman. Judge Diane Wood, of the Seventh Circuit Court of Appeal, described Fred as "a white, middle-aged, overweight man with black hair and a receding hairline, sitting in an armchair wearing a white tank top and blue pants. Fred is a plush doll and when one squeezes Fred's extended finger on his right hand, he farts." He also voices ten humorous and crass comments. Judge Wood then compared Fartman, who also wears a white shirt, blue pants, and farts when his finger is pulled. Moreover, "two of Fartman's seven jokes are the same as two of the 10 spoken by Fred."

In this case, Judge Wood accepted the claim of copyright infringement, hypothesizing that a competitor could create another doll of a middle-aged farting man that looked nothing like Fred: "He could, for example, have a blond mullet and worn flannel, have a nose that is drawn on rather than protruding substantially from the rest of the head, be standing rather than ensconced in an armchair, and be wearing shorts rather than blue pants." Judge Wood emphasized the distinction between exact copying and more general similarities when she noted that there was another farting doll out there—Frankie—who was blonde, stood up, and donned a tattoo and red-and-white striped tank. In Wood's case, the competitors admitted that they had visited the toy fair and based their idea for Fartman on Fred. But even with such easily shown knockoffs, it is unclear that either the toy industry or the public gains anything long-term by preventing copycats.

Unlike the doll industry, which is so concentrated and ridden with copyright litigation, the fashion industry is notoriously prone to knockoffs, and yet it thrives and is hyperinnovative. The fashion industry has tried unsuccessfully to copyright clothing, but courts generally refuse to protect functional items. However, courts have protected copyright when it comes to doll clothing because they don't see them as being functional as human clothes are, and when something is merely aesthetic without functionality, it is more prone to be protected by copyright law. Dolls do not actually need clothes to keep warm or keep their private parts private. As the court explained in the Bratz case, "Dolls don't feel cold or worry about modesty." But again, the effects of these distinctions seem to be perverse—often, the more an industry benefits from copyright protection, the less likely it is to be innovative and dynamic.

Kozinski sensed this perverse effect in the expansive nature of copyright law. He therefore emphasized the boundaries between ideas and expressions and explained that MGA could copy many of the elements of Carter's designs without being liable for infringement.

Beyond remanding the questions of contract interpretation and copyright protection to the lower court, Kozinski found a third major error in Judge Larson's analysis. (Though MGA also appealed Larson's ruling to allow the trial to proceed despite the racial remarks made by the jury members, Kozinski told me over lunch that he was glad his court didn't have to rule on that question. It was easier to vacate the decision because of the substantive legal errors than finding that a juror's biases tainted the entire lengthy trial.) The third error was that even if Carter was responsible for the initial creative energy behind Bratz, MGA's investment, development, and marketing actually created the brand's value. Kozinski found Larson's worldwide injunction over Bratz to be draconian. He found that Larson abused his discretion by effectively transferring MGA's Bratz trademark and copyright portfolio to Mattel. Kozinski adamantly rejected this result. Mattel, he explained, had, through litigation, acquired the fruit of MGA's labor. Even if a Mattel insider came up with Bratz, Kozinski thought MGA should benefit from its investment. The underlying legal issue was how to deal with an infringer's unjust enrichment. According to the rules of equity, if the legitimate owner is scammed into selling or giving away his property, the owner is entitled to every bit of profit earned once the scammer sells to someone else. So if I, hypothetically, take your land through fraudulent means in 2010, and that land appreciates in value by a million dollars, and then I sell it, you get every penny. Legally, you still held a right to that property, and therefore should get any profit from its sale.

But when the defendant, in this case MGA, puts in its own labor and legitimate effort, the law should "avoid taking the defendant's blood along with the pound of flesh."[7] We call the legitimate efforts and talent input by a defendant "sweat equity." For example, if Leonardo da Vinci stole some paintbrushes and pigments, and used them to paint the *Mona Lisa*, the owner of the paints should not be entitled to the painting's staggering value, or to da Vinci's genius; however, the law should compensate the owner for the brushes and paint. The same concept translates to ideas: "Even assuming that MGA took some ideas wrongfully, it added tremendous value by turning the ideas into products and, eventually, a popular and highly profitable brand. The value added by MGA's hard work and creativity dwarfs the value of the original ideas Bryant brought with him, even recognizing the significance of those ideas." Kozinski concluded that transferring a billion-dollar brand—the value of which is overwhelmingly the result of MGA's legitimate efforts—because the brand may have started with a few misappropriated ideas was inequitable. Handing Mattel the keys to MGA's entire Bratz kingdom—a constructive trust of all of the Bratz brand—was "drastic" and "unprecedented." Even if the court decides that MGA owes some damages to Mattel, those must be assessed far more narrowly, considering only what the idea at its undeveloped state was worth when Carter brought it to MGA.

Before the new trial between MGA and Mattel began, Judge Kozinski's ruling was already influencing courts around the country. For example, early in the original Mattel/MGA trial, recall that Carter admitted he was particularly inspired by the full-page Steve Madden ad *Angel/Devil Girl*. This spurred new litigation against him. Bernard Belair, the photographer who worked on the campaign, claimed the exaggerated features of the models and their abnormally long limbs, large heads, and unusually tiny torsos—which he created by incorporating numerous photographs of the same model with manipulated features—were stolen by Carter and MGA and used to create the first Bratz doll. Carter had even admitted to using the ad as a reference when creating the first prototype.

In 2011, a New York judge, Shira Scheindlin, considered Kozinski's holding in the MGA/Mattel litigation when she quickly dismissed the claims made by this new litigant.[8] The judge found that the Bratz dolls were not substantially similar to the models in Belair's *Angel/Devil* photo, at least in their protectable elements. The photo featured two models: one dressed as an angel with wings, a halo, and a bare midriff; the other is the devil, dressed in black leather, sporting horns, a black choke collar, and an orange tail held like a whip. Both models' features are extremely exaggerated. There were, admittedly, several important similarities between Belair's models and

Carter's Bratz: large heads, eyes, and lips; smaller noses and waists; long limbs; heavy makeup; and fashionable women's clothing. But as Judge Kozinski explained, these aspects could not be copyrighted. Citing Kozinski's decision, the judge noted that these "exaggerated and idealized proportions are (distressingly) commonplace in both children's toys and the fashion industry, and Belair cannot assert a protectable claim to them." Moreover, the judge ruled that courts should consider copyright infringement only when looking at the final product, not the prototype. She concluded that Belair "cannot monopolize the abstract concept of an absurdly large-headed, long limbed, attractive, fashionable woman." Mimicking stereotypes, the court explained, was not problematic under copyright law (though surely problematic in other ways).

Although the New York judge easily applied Kozinski's understanding of copyright law in the rather straightforward case of the Madden ad, it took a bit longer to resolve the Barbie-Bratz conflict. The Barbie versus Bratz case was remanded back to federal district court in Southern California to be decided by a new judge and jury, and guided by Kozinski's ruling.

10 | ROUND 2: THE PLAYGROUND BULLIES

I can't understand why people are frightened of new ideas. I'm frightened of the old ones.

—JOHN CAGE

THE CHINESE PHILOSOPHER CONFUCIUS counseled: before you embark upon a journey of revenge, dig two graves—one for your enemy and one for yourself. The case once again went to trial, and just when it seemed that the fight couldn't get any uglier, it did. Larian's legal team planned their counterattack while Mattel prepared for another go-round in the ring. Once Mattel's claims were up for rehearing, MGA filed new counterclaims accusing Mattel of vast anticompetitive behavior. After nearly a decade-long litigation, with Judge Kozinski reversing the first jury award in favor of Mattel, MGA now countered Mattel's claims of ownership over Bratz with its own allegations of trade secret theft, economic espionage, and unfair competition schemes designed to prevent retailers from shelving Bratz dolls.

A Fresh Start

The new trial had a very different judge, a different jury, and, most importantly, a new attorney representing MGA. Jennifer Keller made a last-minute entrance as lead counsel, coming into the four-month jury trial just twelve days before jury selection. Her firm, Keller Anderle, is a small 100 percent women-owned law firm in Irvine, California. In part, Keller was hired because Larian had been unable to get along with the highly paid lawyers from some of America's biggest law firms—Skadden; Orrick; O'Melveny. Also, after years of litigation with Mattel, Larian couldn't afford them. His insurer AIG refused to pay the soaring legal fees and Larian became entangled in side suits, brought by the same law firms that initially represented him, now demanding payment. An insider told me, "The satellite litigation on attorney fees has been immense. It's possible that Larian paid none of the law firms he hired their full fees. He had hired some of largest law firms in California, ran through them, and ended up owing all of them money."

Despite their dispute with Larian over their unpaid fees, Orrick, one of the law firms that represented him in the first trial, continued preparing for the second trial. But just weeks before the trial began, Larian notified the firm that he was bringing in a new firm to take the lead. From Orrick's perspective, the co-counseling situation was far from ideal, but the firm made it work. At least in the eyes of the jury, MGA's varied counsels operated like a well-oiled team; after all, that's what good representation is all about. Just as he always sought new talent and fresh ideas for MGA, Larian wanted fresh blood in his legal team. Partly, Larian did not want to solely rely on attorneys with whom his relationship was already strained, but beyond that,

Larian has good instincts and he felt it was time to trust a different kind of trial lawyer. He had been through enough legal disputes to appreciate Robert Frost's famous words that "a jury consists of twelve persons chosen to decide who has the better lawyer."

For this trial, representing Larian in his fight against the industry's greatest bully, Keller was the better lawyer. She made more sense as a voice for Larian. A bit of a renegade herself, Keller is an outsider to the "Big Law" attorneys who specialize in intellectual property disputes. She started her career as a criminal defense attorney, but what she lacked in intellectual property experience she made up for with passion and work ethic. In her eyes, civil copyright or trade secret litigation is not that different from run-of-the-mill criminal defense. Many colleagues warned her that taking over where so many legal giants had failed—and knowingly representing a serially disgruntled client—could be career suicide. Behind closed doors, Keller was further cautioned that, as she wasn't an intellectual property expert, she should let more seasoned attorneys call the shots. But for Keller, technical knowledge is not as important as presenting the story to the jury in a compelling and simple way. It's about putting together the pieces of the puzzle to show who is in the right and who is in the wrong. In other words, it's all about justice.

Keller is sharp and competitive, but she is also relatable and open. She is a self-described "brat," a trailblazer, liberal attorney living and working in conservative Orange County. Like me, she grew up in a home that discouraged playing with Barbie. Instead, she and her brother played with blocks handcrafted by their father, and they constructed forts and mazes around the house for their pet hamsters and rats. Now, in court, Larian was not the only brat on the toy-industry block—his attorney was, too.

According to one insider, Mattel's Quinn Emanuel attorneys treated Keller condescendingly: "At one point John Quinn said about Jennifer dismissively, 'She's behaving like a state court attorney.' " Except, unbeknownst to opposing counsel, she wasn't exactly new to the game. She and the new judge, Judge David Carter, went way back. Keller had appeared before Judge Carter many times as a public defender. Carter was most proud of his time on the state court bench and, suffice it to say, did not appreciate demeaning comments about state courts, which fancy Big Law attorneys who are used to only appearing in federal court like to gratuitously dispense. The clash of personalities was so stark that the jurors took note. In contrast to Keller's calm, relatable demeanor, one juror told me, "None of Mattel's attorneys were particularly likeable. In the closing argument, the attorney for Mattel was practically yelling at us: 'You better make the right decision!' He seemed as though he was actually mad at us."

As in the first trial, the dolls' sharply contrasting personalities were reflected in the demeanor of their respective attorneys and, most of all, in their clients. The litigant CEOs, Eckert and Larian, once again displayed very different attitudes toward their investment and interest in the trial. As in the first trial, Larian and his family attended court daily. Eckert, on the other hand, was still noticeably absent. Instead, Mattel again designated Lily Martinez as its corporate representative. But unlike the first trial's judge, Judge Carter was not willing to let this imbalance stand. Early in the trial, when the ground rules were being set, Keller pointed out the disparity: Why was Mattel's designated corporate representative a low-level employee when the case was about a mammoth corporation litigating a multibillion-dollar dispute? When Judge Carter asked Eckert about his noticeable absence, Eckert mumbled an excuse that he believed witnesses were barred from sitting at trial. Judge Carter disliked Eckert's answer: Eckert should have known that the corporate representative is exempt from witness sequestration, thus enabling him or her to listen to all testimony. Judge Carter then sided with Keller, announcing that he too was worried about the bad optics for the jury: the CEO of MGA, Isaac Larian, sits in front of the jury every day, while Mattel's executive leadership is notably absent. The jury might believe Eckert's absence signals Mattel's disinterest in the dispute. The judge ordered Eckert's presence in court every day for the next three months of trial. After this decree, the parties convened outside of the courtroom in separate rooms and Eckert could be heard screaming at his handlers behind closed doors, "You better get in there and fix this!" He was so angry that he returned to court fuming. Despite—or because of—Eckert's rage, Judge Carter's decision stood.

Eckert felt the order was a huge imposition. One day he asked the court to excuse him because of a board meeting, and Judge Carter ordered he directly obtain Larian's consent. Eckert looked even more enraged at the court throwing him on Larian's mercy. One of the attorneys involved in the trial told me, "Eckert behaved like he is above it all. He blew through the court marshals without acknowledging them. He had a 'do you know who I am' air to him. Sharp contrast with Larian who chatted with the marshals, they showed him pictures of their kids, took pictures with him. They called him their 'friendly neighborhood billionaire.'"

Throughout the trial, Eckert remained aloof and disdainful. He hated having to sit on the busy freeway while his limo driver took him from Los Angeles to Orange County, where the trial was held. Again, the CEO—master of delegation—commanded his underlings to fix things. Although Mattel suffered from all sorts of innovative problems on the toy front, Eckert's employees were surprisingly creative when trying to please him. They suggested he use the company helicopter every morning to avoid L.A. traffic. The only problem was that, other than the helipad used by law enforcement, there was nowhere to land near the courthouse. Not easily deterred, Eckert's people made some calls. The Orange County Sheriff Department explained that the helicopter landing was not for sale because it was reserved for public helicopters in case of emergencies. Unable to comprehend such a restriction, Mattel's response was "Name your price." Eckert's handlers even issued an implied threat to the public administrators, asking them to consider how the media would react when Mattel leaked that the sheriff's department turned down a huge pot of money for no good reason. Eckert and his entourage had a hard time accepting that some things are not for sale. The sheriff didn't budge, and Eckert was stuck in traffic like every other commuter in the Greater Los Angeles area.

The new trial lasted nearly four months and, as Keller puts it, the case was "nothing short of gargantuan." With over ten thousand filings, a record in the district, the case crashed the district court's server. To keep up the pace, the trial often included hearings on Saturdays and Sundays. The proceedings demanded so much in overtime pay for the court marshals that, during those weekends, Judge Carter would send the marshals home and take over their tasks. He would arrive alone at the courthouse's main entrance in jeans, sometimes as early as 6 a.m., to open up the gates for all.

The jury appreciated the way Judge Carter ran his courtroom. He is a particularly engaged judge, has a sense of humor, and humanized the dispute in a way that Judge Larson had not. As one seasoned litigator put it, "David Carter is a judge who desperately wants to get it right and no one works harder than him." The trial was run like a marathon. The attorneys were on a tight clock as the judge set time limits for each party. Judge Carter started his mornings early at the courtroom gym, and he would take his seat on the bench with his hair still wet from the shower. He set a no-nonsense tone and demanded that all show the same rigor, efficiency, and focus he practiced, though he made a point of accommodating the jurors as much as he could. At the outset, he warned the attorneys that if any phone ever went off during trial, he would confiscate it. Then he turned to the jury and said, "Not you, you are here performing a public service and you have lives, you have kids, you have jobs. You are free to use your phone." One afternoon a juror's phone went off. Judge Carter stopped the trial and gave everyone a ten-minute break so the juror could take the call. But, when one of the attorney's phones rang, Judge Carter took it away. He turned to the jury and reassured them,

"Don't you worry, he can afford a new one." Once when Eckert's attorneys complained about the toll the trial was taking on their boss's time, Judge Carter reprimanded, "Is his time more valuable than any of these jurors?!" At various points during the trial, Judge Carter even ordered all present in the courtroom to stand up and stretch and often joked, "Now give me ten jumping jacks."

We Don't Own People

In the new trial, Jennifer Keller made a key strategic decision to not throw Carter Bryant under the bus. She believed the lawyers before her had focused too much on the argument that, no matter when, how, or why Carter invented Bratz, MGA had no reason or duty to question the representations he made to the company. Keller decided on a different strategy. She wanted to convey the injustice that Mattel inflicted on the actual inventor. The problem was that Carter had avoided any attorney hoping to speak with him before he took the stand again. It was not even clear whether he would actually appear in court to testify. Judge Carter had to issue a special order warning Carter that he was legally obligated to show up or else he would face contempt charges. MGA's legal team had no idea how to even prepare for questioning him.

At the eleventh hour, only as Carter took the stand, did Keller realize how much the first trial had affected him. When she met him just minutes before he was about to testify, she was struck by the stark contrast between his appearance then and how he looked in the photographs from the first trial. The pictures showed a happy, slightly chubby man who appeared comfortable in his own skin. But before her stood someone thin, frail, and clearly depressed. The artist with the soulful eyes had physically transformed. Those eyes were now sunken, and he was pale and prematurely aged. Carter looked as though he had been sued to death: "He was just done; head to shoulders beaten down," Keller says. He came to court in a T-shirt, was unshaven, had not brushed his hair, and seemed not to have showered in a week. He slumped in the witness stand. He answered many of his questions with whispers of "I don't know; I don't recall." Still, Carter came across as honest although his answers were fragmented and pained. He only came to life when Keller showed him the sketches he hadn't seen for years—his face lit up when he saw his original Bratz sketches.

Keller believed Carter's inspiration story, and she wanted the jury to believe him too. She particularly wanted the jury to understand the inherent injustice in a world where a creative person's former employer could so deeply intimidate him or her. Rather than both corporations kicking Carter's already beaten body, Keller wanted the jury to see what had befallen the inventor who dared to leave Mattel. She wanted the jury to see how Mattel destroys a person who gets in the company's way. She also wanted Carter to understand she was different than the previous lawyers he had met. She designated him as the tragic hero of Mattel's legal wars.

Keller purposely began questioning Carter softly: "These last years have been hard on you?" she asked empathetically. Mattel's attorneys tried to portray Carter as a liar by focusing on the fact that he could not remember everything that had happened, detail by detail, ten years prior. In contrast, Keller gave Carter the opportunity to describe how rough the decade-long litigation was for him: "It was very exhausting. A lot of little things that were hard to remember. It was scary. It was pretty tough. Very stressful," he said.

Keller asked, "How did it affect your sleep?"

Carter responded, "Greatly. I basically had to start relying on sleeping medications, Ambien, Lunesta. I definitely have been suffering from a lack of sleep."

Keller continued, "Right now as you sit here, you really pretty much have lost everything because of this case, right?"

Carter replied, "Most everything, yes."

"Still have your talent?" she asked him.

"Who knows," he answered meekly.

Keller asked, "And one reason you don't know is because at this point, no other toy maker wants to hire you, you're kind of radioactive, right?"

Carter answered, "It seems that way. I mean, it feels that way."

Judge Carter stepped in to protect Carter as well, nipping any inquiry into the porn on Carter's computer in the bud. He said that bringing it up "will result in obvious prejudice, personal embarrassment, and undue invasion of Bryant's privacy." Directly criticizing Judge Larson's previous rulings, Judge Carter continued, "In fact, I'm rather shocked in reading the transcript that Bryant was asked what his sexual persuasion was, where he was forced into the position, either willingly or not, of having to respond truthfully under oath that he was gay."

Keller was thus freer to create a compelling narrative about that summer when Carter Bryant was free and inspired. Keller vividly described to the jury the time gap between Carter's moment of inspiration and the never-ending legal battles propelled by Mattel: "So this was the summer of 1998. That was the year Google was founded, the year Apple unveiled the iMac, Exxon Mobil merged. The popular music was the Dixie Chicks and the Spice Girls and Shakira, and the biggest movie of the year was *Titanic*. *Ally McBeal* was still on TV, so it's a while ago." Once again, Mattel argued that Carter created Bratz while working for the company, and that he stole his ideas from designs floating around the workplace. Mattel's strategy was to badger Carter about his creativity, or lack thereof, for seven days straight, but this time around, attempting to present the worn-down artist as a thief and a liar did nothing but hurt its case. Some jurors even teared up during his questioning.

Keller explained to the jury that Carter's disappearance at Bratz's launch was due to fright, rather than guilt, as he knew Mattel was aware of his impending exit, and the company was a known legal predator. He didn't think he had done anything wrong, but he knew well that his former employer would be ready to attack.

Bob Eckert took the stand days after Carter. During his testimony, Keller asked him a hypothetical: "Say I am eighteen, doodling away, I place my doodles in my parents' house in one of the drawers of my teenage closet. Twenty years later, I am hired by Mattel. I visit my parents' home and find the doodles. Does Mattel own them?" Eckert's robotic response was "Yes, very probably yes." Keller thinks that if Eckert had responded "like a normal person," saying instead, "Ms. Keller, your hypothetical is too farfetched, it doesn't apply to our case; if you drew something twenty years before coming to Mattel, you would own it," he might have more effectively convinced the jury that Carter owed Mattel his drawings. He could have focused on narrower claims to employer ownership. But Eckert's hard-line answer that everything ever made by an employee is owned by the corporation was unreasonable and off-putting. His responses were the responses of the company man and the perfect embodiment of the cold creative void Mattel had become. Although Eckert reluctantly showed his face at trial, Mattel came across as faceless. Keller wanted to show a pattern of the company's treatment of its rank-and-file employees as disposable. She asked Eckert about the firing of the Mexican sample makers because they had moonlighted for MGA a decade earlier. These seamstresses spent their off hours stitching and sewing in their garages to make ends meet. Keller asked Eckert on the stand whether he cared at all about these workers. In his characteristically cold tone he gave an answer that made jurors cringe: "To the extent I care about people, then, yes."

Larian, wanting to show the jury just how detached Eckert was from the creative process of toy design, floated an idea by Keller. He suggested that she present two boxed dolls—one a Bratz doll and the other a doll from Mattel's Monster High line, one of Mattel's later responses to Bratz—and ask Eckert which was which. Keller was skeptical, worrying it was too simple. But she also knew that

Larian, despite having no legal training, had killer legal instincts. Larian grinned at Keller and told her in his heavy accent, "Trust me, that cheesehead won't know the difference." And indeed, the moment was powerful. After Keller handed over the dolls, Eckert looked perplexed. He stared at the boxes, turned them over, trying to find the mark that would indicate whether the doll was Mattel's or a competitor's. Mattel's own CEO looked as though he couldn't tell the difference between his and his competitor's products. He eventually picked one, and got it right, but the effect Larian had hoped for was achieved by the long while in which Eckert seemed lost. As one juror later described that awkward moment: "He was the CEO, and he came across as if he could have been selling canned peaches for all he cared. The corporate culture at Mattel is so formulaic. It's all about metrics, numbers, sales, and their sales were plummeting."

The jury could tell that Eckert wanted to be as far away from the courtroom as possible, but in this new trial, Eckert's leadership was about to be scrutinized from all perspectives: Did he do anything to save Barbie; did he support the "genocide" rhetoric that was bubbling within his company; did he consider the sufferings of the seamstresses he abruptly fired after decades of service; did he order surveillance and illegal spying on the competition?

But first, continuing the testimonies as to whether Carter owed his ideas to Mattel, Isaac Larian took the stand. With his flair for the dramatic, Larian built on Keller's theme, articulating his own notions of justice regarding what employees may or may not do upon leaving an employer: "I don't think, whether it's MGA or Mattel," he said, "that we own the people, especially the creative people, forever." He went on to say that there was no problem with somebody spending weekends and evenings working on an idea he or she had before being hired. "Maybe Mattel is different, but I don't think I own people's evenings and nights when they are not on my payroll." Beyond presenting a more reasonable sense of fairness in allocating the fruit of creativity between employers and employees, Larian's deep involvement in bringing Carter's designs to reality came out as he testified: he selected the names of the dolls, was involved in their look, their technical functions, and even held patents in his name. Larian was passionate, and he cared. One juror told me, "He almost seemed possessive and paternal over those dolls. It was devastating for him to lose them."

As for Lily Martinez, this time around, she came off as another Mattel pawn. "She was left in shreds," says Keller. The jury simply didn't buy the story that Martinez's undeveloped designs inspired Carter. According to Keller, "Once the jury saw how ugly her designs were and how genuinely creative Carter was and how many other points of inspiration he had, while Martinez didn't appear that inspiring and she herself never had a hit—Mattel had never developed any of her creations—the whole Martinez narrative collapsed." One juror confided in me:

> My gut told me all along that the only reason she was there on the Mattel side at court was that they dressed her up to look like a Bratz doll. Mattel wanted to show that it had a live Bratz doll in the Mattel headquarters. I felt sorry for her. Martinez seemed like she was trying to look confident and composed but in fact was quite scared and intimidated. And of course she would say anything Mattel prepped her to say: What's she going to do otherwise if she wants to be a designer? You obviously can't leave Mattel.

Martinez, in fact, did leave Mattel after the second trial ended and, like Carter, left the toy industry altogether. Instead of designing toys, she did what any unemployed stylist would do: she began an independent lifestyle blog. I reached out to her, but she didn't want to be interviewed. Martinez's timing in leaving Mattel upon the conclusion of the second trial, after seventeen years in the toy industry, speaks volumes.

Keller leveraged Mattel's reputation as stodgy and antiquated the minute Mattel's attorneys brought Ivy Ross to testify that the term *Bratz* had floated around the Mattel compound common areas. Keller pushed Ross to admit Mattel would never use the name "Bratz." She asked Ross to pinpoint the time she first heard it. Ross responded that she heard the term refer to a Mattel line eventually released with the name "Diva Starz." Keller snapped back, "I remember hearing it in second grade too. Applied to me." She may as well have said, "Bratz *c'est moi!*" Judge Carter quickly reprimanded Keller, "That's not a question!" and struck the comment from the record. Keller argued that the connotation of a *brat* went against Mattel's jealously guarded image of a clean, wholesome Barbie. Ross continued to testify about the creativity buzz she had brought to Mattel but after the second trial, a juror told me, "Ivy Ross and her platypus project was a distracting side trip—sand in our eyes. Bells and whistles. Beyond all the minutia, the window dressing, the clouds of confusion, when all was carved away, we saw the core issue—Mattel didn't like competition."

In the new trial, Judge Kozinski's warning about overcontrolling culture imbued the proceedings with a sense of caution. The second trial was, in fact, framed entirely differently, largely due to Kozinski's instruction on remand that the jury read Carter Bryant's obligations narrowly. Judge Carter instructed the jury to find for Mattel only if Carter had worked on Bratz during working hours and while performing tasks for Mattel, or if the jury interpreted the contract to also cover nights and weekends. He also closely guided the jury about all the *nonprotectable* elements in Carter's drawings under copyright law: resemblance to human form, exaggerated features, including oversized head and oversized almond-shaped eyes, and idealized features such as luscious lips, a slim waist, a barely-there nose, and long limbs. But it didn't end there. He listed before the jury further nonprotectable elements:

> *The idea of a young fashion-forward female with an attitude, and the expression traditionally associated with that idea, including but not limited to heavy makeup, an urban look, defiant poses, defiant gazes, angular eyebrows, trendy clothing, shoes and accessories. Features shared by a particular race or ethnicity, for example, skin tone. Postures that mimic*

the human form and postures that are standard for the effective display
of fashionable clothing.

In effect, building on Judge Kozinski's jurisprudence, Judge Carter
instructed the jury that protectable elements included far less than
Judge Larson allowed, and were narrowly constrained to the precise
shape, size, and placement of the doll's anatomical features, hairdos,
face paint, and specific fashion outfits and accessories.

MGA's arguments from the first trial seemed to be gaining ground
this time around. Keller presented a full picture of inspiration: there
were already dolls with big heads, styled after Japanese anime art,
on the market; Carter pulled ideas from many different sources, and
most elements of a doll are not copyright protected because you can't
own the human form or abstract ideas.

MGA nearly made the same mistake as Mattel in drafting its counterclaims to mirror Mattel's controlling mentality. MGA had entered
the trial claiming copyright infringement, arguing that Mattel's later
doll line My Scene looked too much like Bratz. One of MGA's attorneys, who wished to remain anonymous, told me that dropping this
claim mid-trial was a strategic decision that MGA made. It was important because it was completely inconsistent with MGA's defense—that
only the expression, and not the idea of a bratty doll, was protectable.
In the second trial, MGA's legal team wisely focused on the princi-
ples emphasized by Judge Kozinski: free competition and a narrow
interpretation of copyright protection.

And in fact, MGA didn't need to counterclaim that Mattel had
been infringing on MGA's copyright of Bratz by releasing a cheap
imitation immediately thereafter. It now could present a better
argument: Mattel was illegally stealing trade secrets from MGA and
using those secrets when it released competing products. In other
words, Judge Kozinski's rulings were not the only reasons MGA could
orchestrate what one of the most seasoned trial attorneys in the country, and an insider on the case, told me was the greatest reversals of

any case he can recall. Mattel's arguments about justice and rightful ownership were completely undercut by a plethora of illegal practices discovered by MGA just prior to the second trial: evidence that Mattel spies snuck into private showrooms with fake IDs, stole competitors' secrets, and pressured retailers to shun MGA. Mattel went from innocent victim of corporate espionage to one of the practice's worst culprits. As MGA's legal team told me, once the illegal practices at Mattel were revealed, "Everything was cast in a different light. The halo was gone."

Brain Rape at the Toy Fair

> **Brain Rape:** *Intellectual property robbery thinly disguised as acquisition talk. Usually committed by a big company on a startup.*
>
> —SILICON VALLEY DICTIONARY

Jennifer Keller fought vigorously to try to convince the jury that Carter Bryant owed Mattel nothing, but she did not stop there. After MGA's attorneys presented its defense against Mattel's claims of intellectual property theft, they went on the offensive and zoomed in on the evidence of trade secret theft by Mattel. Just before the start of the second trial, Judge Carter allowed MGA to file counterclaims accusing Mattel of illegal economic espionage at toy fairs and of conspiring with retailers to keep Bratz off the shelves. MGA argued that the reason Mattel was coming out with similar product lines wasn't because it had been legally *inspired* by competitors' products after they hit the market, but rather because Mattel had been illegally *spying* on its enemies. Larian told me that he had long before the trial believed there was a mole—or possibly wiretapping or some other improper means by which Mattel was competing against his company—because Mattel kept releasing the exact products and marketing campaigns MGA was about to launch, only a few days earlier and for two dollars less. MGA couldn't figure out how Mattel was anticipating its every move until a Mattel insider jumped ship and revealed shocking information about Mattel's practices. Keller told the jury that Mattel was the worst type of offender in the corporate espionage world—the kind that maintains its own corporate espionage department. She described to the jury Mattel's conduct as "unlawful, outrageous, despicable" and argued that it cost MGA tens of millions in losses.[1]

MGA presented evidence that while Mattel was preparing for its final attack on MGA in the courtroom, it was also engaged in illegal economic espionage. MGA termed it Mattel's "scorched earth strategy." Together, these two frontiers—litigation and spying—became Mattel's greatest weapons in the innovation wars: litigation brought to drive competition out of the market and spying to gain an unfair advantage over the hearts and dollars of consumers. As MGA told the jury, "Barbie was flailing and Barbie was failing," and Mattel executives were in a state of panic. Mattel's desperation grew as Bratz' popularity exploded. Ivy Ross brought in the clowns, the neuroscientists, and the creativity gurus, but the real focus was crushing the competition in questionable ways. Mattel operated like a well-oiled undercover rival. In internal memos, Mattel employees were instructed to use the code name NHB instead of MGA. Can you crack the code? NHB is one letter off MGA, bringing to mind another shift in letters: in *Space Odyssey*, the sentient computer HAL is often thought to be based on a one-letter shift from the name IBM, though this has been denied by director Stanley Kubrick. Mattel too denied that NHB was a code. When questioned on the stand, Eckert explained that NHB simply meant "North Hill Bratz," referencing the location of MGA's offices.

But a code name doesn't grant access to an enemy's information, which is exactly what Mattel sought. In its despair, the company turned to Salvador Villasenor. Sal Villasenor had worked at Mattel for fourteen years, making his way up to head of the Market Intelligence Department. His job was to know everything about rival toys and ensure Mattel stayed ahead of the competition. But over the years his job shifted from collecting publicly available data to actively training his team to infiltrate MGA's as well as other competitors' private showrooms. He learned how to spy on the job at Mattel because of the mounting pressures he faced from his bosses. As Mattel executives became increasingly obsessed with exterminating Barbie's nemesis, they demanded more access to MGA's plans. They sought MGA catalogues and price lists before the information hit the market. They asked Villasenor and his colleagues to bring back confidential loot from the restricted meeting rooms at toy fairs.

The oldest and most important toy fair, launched in 1903, happens in New York City. Each February, after everyone has recovered from the holiday season, the toy fair marks the start of next season's preparations. The New York Toy Fair, like other fairs, includes highly confidential spaces within which the industry shares Vegas's mantra—*what happens at the fair stays at the fair*. When it comes to the next hot plastic toy, loose lips can sink a plastic toy ship. Mattel, in fact, is so secretive of its own product launches that it has long forgone toy fairs, opting instead to send scouts to the fair to contract with lone inventors, identify industry trends, and, well, to improperly spy on competitors. Mattel prefers introducing its own products at private Southern California events with its invited guests basking in the sunshine. Every year, Mattel flies out toy buyers to the posh Renaissance Hollywood Hotel, where they are treated to several luxurious days spent viewing Barbie, and Mattel's other toys, while sipping pink cocktails poolside—a scene reminiscent of the Barbie fantasy it sells. (Choosing Hollywood over a cold Manhattan winter may help Mattel for other reasons as well. Psychologists have long studied the best environments for negotiating a deal. Psychologist Thalma Lobel (aka my mother) has recently highlighted in her bestseller *Sensation: The New Science of Physical Intelligence* how better weather and better optics, such as the Pacific Ocean and a poolside blue, induce more favored feelings, which warm people up for a purchase.)

When you're as big as Mattel, you can afford a secluded solo venue to present your new products and bypass the risks of competitors infiltrating private showrooms. But for a smaller company like MGA, the toy fair is the primary place to make a mark. Bratz was the belle of the ball from the minute she arrived at the fair. Buyers go to the fair to watch what are called "sizzles"—videos showing a product and its use. Bratz was sizzling, and retailers lined up for MGA's showroom. Access to the Bratz private lounges, offering sneak peeks of upcoming collections, was a highlight for retailers. Larian and his team made painstaking preparations ensuring competitors could not access their newest plans. Indeed, at trial, Mattel's own employees testified that they thought MGA's security was "a little bit excessive." For example, guards were stationed in front of each showroom, entry was by appointment only, and visitors signed a nondisclosure agreement upon entry. All documents— price lists and yet-to-be-released toy catalogues—are marked *confidential*. Gaining access to these documents is like getting access to the playbook of the opposing football team just before the start of the NFL season.

So how does one access competitor information with such extreme measures in place? A quick read of Mattel's internal documents offers some ideas. Mattel's Market Intelligence Department put together a manual, which Jennifer Keller cleverly dubbed in trial the *How to Steal Manual*. It is a step-by-step guidebook on infiltrating a private showroom at the toy fair. Mattel employees are instructed to create fake retailer IDs, fake resale tax certificates, fake business licenses, fake invoices as toy buyers, and fake business cards. The manual is detailed and user-friendly: accounts payable will proctor invoices upon request, and the Kinko's "around the corner" can design and print fake business cards, as long as they are given "at least one week." The manual also states that employees need at least three recent industry manufacturer invoices for at least five hundred dollars in order to demonstrate that their fake business exists.

The manual offers other practicalities: think in advance about your imagined store and then build a story in your mind to avoid mistakes. Prepare fake advertisements for the fake businesses. Disguise your physical appearance by, for example, using a fake moustache. Those sent to the European toy fair in Nuremberg were advised "It's best to go as a US retailer since you will not be asked as many questions (for example, 'Where is your store?')." In preparing for the New York Toy Fair, the manual directed employees to "think about the size of your store. Try to keep it reasonably small; what types of toys you sell; how many employees; where exactly your store is located; how many stores you have." The manual also advised scheduling appointments with competitors at the last minute so that there is no risk they might run a background check that would unravel the cover story. As for names, the spy team members learned it was best to use real names while forging an identity because they would often need to present a picture ID. In short, the practice required creating fake personas but using real names and home addresses and, of course, never including any information that may link them to Mattel.

Villasenor's persona worked for a company called Toy Shop. Other Mattel employees created similarly unimaginative names: Toy Tree, Toy Harbor. Creativity, clearly, was not the central focus of the intelligence department. Rather, they were tasked to infiltrate toy fairs and bring information back to the mothership. Villasenor's team members documented their covert siege with small video recorders and cameras. Undercover Mattel agents hit toy fairs around the globe, trekking everywhere from New York to Hong Kong to Nuremberg. For example, in one internal e-mail correspondence, two members of the intelligence department, Carey Plunkett and Tyler Snyder, proudly report gaining access to MGA's restricted showroom by masquerading as buyers for a large retailer. One by one, armed with their freshly printed business cards, manufactured storylines, and small recording devices, Mattel's intelligence agents infiltrated their competitor's private showrooms, accessing upcoming marketing plans, pricing, and new products. They retrieved secret release dates. They took photos, notes, price lists, and catalogues, all before the products were launched.

Once home, these undercover agents presented their findings to hundreds of Mattel executives and employees in the corporate auditorium.[2] Mattel also created an easily accessible internal "Market Research Library" to house all the looted information. Despite Mattel's initial attempts to hide the boxes containing the files of espionage before the trial, the boxes were eventually retrieved after repeated court motions—thirty-five in all. Beyond what was contained in those thirty-five disappearing and reappearing boxes, MGA also accused Mattel of attempting "to conceal, suppress, and destroy evidence of that theft" by altering or tampering with evidence and inducing witnesses to lie under oath.[3]

Knowledge is power. Mattel didn't just want to know what its competitors were doing—it also wanted to profit from its illicit access. According to MGA, Mattel used the confidential information in refining its own products, price lists, marketing, advertising plans, and strategies. MGA argued at trial that Mattel stole its dolls' stylistic details (for example, a symbol that lit up on the doll's clothing), the idea to introduce male characters as part of the line (rather than a stand-alone Ken), and even the smallest creative elements like the doll's fashion accessories (tattoos, rhinestone watches, glowing rings).[4]

Sal Villasenor's job at Mattel was his first position in the toy industry, and he credits his entire bag of market intelligence tricks to Mattel's corporate teachings.[5] He publicly admitted entering the showrooms of many of Mattel's competitors at Mattel's behest. According to Villasenor, Mattel's leadership not only condoned but also coached the espionage activities of its Market Intelligence Department. His supervisors carefully advised his team on everything from which fake company names to distribute at the toy fairs to what type of suitcase or briefcase to bring along—these illegal espionage practices were extended, according to the evidence MGA presented in court, to nearly every company in the toy business.

To Mattel, Villasenor was invaluable, and the company rewarded him handsomely—"nice fat promotions and bonuses, stellar promotion evaluations"—for his team's illicit activities. In one e-mail, Mattel praised Villasenor for obtaining a competitor's price list: "This is great. You just saved Mattel close to 1 million." And yet, despite the glowing reviews and financial rewards, Villasenor grew fearful and remorseful just around the start of the first trial. Villasenor knew he was committing illegal economic espionage by stealing secrets, which is a serious federal crime. In fact, in the last few years Congress twice amended the Economic Espionage Act, a 1996 statute that criminalizes trade secrecy misappropriation, to increase criminal penalties and expand the definition of the crime. The FBI has channeled more and more resources into investigating trade secrecy cases, and the number of criminal prosecutions under the act has dramatically risen. The FBI estimates that economic espionage costs the American economy billions of dollars annually and classifies such activities as a national security risk.[6] My research shows the side effect is that employees are increasingly found liable for taking secrets with them to new employers. New York University law professor Rochelle Dreyfuss and I argue in a recent article that lateral movement between employers is chilled by the threat of trade secret litigation by the former employer.[7] The criminalization of employee mobility is far more problematic than the comparatively straightforward crime of one competitor illegally infiltrating, either virtually or physically, another company's private space. What Mattel did was direct targeting of the secrets of a competitor. So Villasenor was right to worry. He knew that lawsuits have a tendency to reveal a company's darkest secrets and correctly predicted that MGA would dig into Mattel's corporate practices.

On December 25, 2005, Villasenor wrote to Bob Normile, general counsel at Mattel. He also copied Mark Kimball, Vice President for Human Resources, and Michael Moore, Mattel's lead intellectual property attorney. The letter began, "I have worked for Mattel, Inc., for almost 14 years. I am currently the manager of market intelligence." He continues with astonishing honesty in the face of his own delinquency:

> I'm writing to complain about Mattel's directives and instructions to gather market intelligence from competitors through unlawful means. I no longer wish to engage in misrepresentations and undercover assignments in which I am paid by Mattel to attend trade shows and events. I fear that my actions may expose me to personal criminal liability, and I am stressed about the fallout which may occur.
>
> My conscience does not allow me to continue in this role, and I do not feel I can take the pressure to engage in misrepresentations any longer.
>
> I know that Mattel has gained a superior competitive advantage through my hard work and I appreciate your consideration of my complaint. Because of my fears, I have retained a legal representative, and I would ask that you direct all future communications concerning this complaint and my continued role with the company to my attorney.

Immediately after sending the e-mail, Villasenor took sick leave, citing stress. Six months later, Villasenor officially quit. As the former director of Mattel's infamous Market Intelligence Department, Villasenor's decision to step down from his post and testify against Mattel was a coup for MGA. Before the new trial began, MGA gleaned most of its insight into Mattel's competitive practices from Sal Villasenor's deposition. It was thanks to Villasenor that MGA could accuse Mattel of espionage with such specificity. Of course, Mattel called Villasenor a Benedict Arnold and accused him of trying to extort Mattel to pay for his silence. In addition to branding him a blackmailer, Mattel tried to paint Villasenor as a rogue, isolated employee who along with a couple of others—a secret society—acted outside the chain of command.

At trial, Mattel tried to depict Villasenor as a greedy and disloyal former employee who only blew the whistle to try extorting money from the company. After sending the initial letter condemning his own behavior, Villasenor asked for a severance package comparable to those Mattel offered other management level executives. Villasenor's attorney sent Mattel a letter providing Mattel a floor and a ceiling of acceptable numbers. On the low end, he said, one executive was paid a severance package of $5.4 million. At the high end, former CEO Jill Barad received over $40 million in severance (and recall that her departure from Mattel was triggered by staggering losses she had brought on the company). His letter ends: "Mr. Villasenor is not making a demand for a specific sum; instead, he asks that Mattel acknowledge his contributions, the risks he has taken, the value of his services, and the toll it has taken on Sal's life and his career in order to resolve this matter on fair terms." Mattel paid Villasenor a small amount in return for silence. He promised not to disclose any confidential information about his work at Mattel and agreed that, if anyone inquired into his termination, he would respond obliquely, "I left to pursue other opportunities." And yet when MGA litigated its trade secret theft claims against Mattel, Villasenor couldn't lie under oath. On the stand, Villasenor physically shook as he testified, and his eyes welled up with tears. The jury could tell that Villasenor left Mattel because he couldn't in good conscience continue leading Mattel's illegal reconnaissance.

After Villasenor testified, Mattel executives, who Villasenor thought were his "personal friends," took the stand and denied not only the friendship he spoke of but even knowledge of his existence.

One such "friend" who distanced himself from Villasenor was Matthew Turetzky. Turetzky was a high-level executive at Mattel. As Vice President for Strategic Planning, Business Development, and Consumer Research, Turetzky wore many hats and performed many functions for Mattel, one of which was supervising the Market

Intelligence Department. Turetzky insists, however, that the intelligence department was not a separate and specialized division within Mattel but rather a small group of "business analysts."[8] If you believe Turetzky, the Market Intelligence Department was an informal subgroup of two inexperienced people. Turetzky testified that this informal team never received instructions from superiors to engage in illegal espionage.

While denying ever sanctioning the Market Intelligence Department, Turetzky confessed meeting Mattel's general counsel to brainstorm appropriate (in another word, *legal*) ways of gathering competitive information. In court, Turetzky was first in line to denounce Villasenor's illegal activities. He then admitted being "uncomfortable" with some of the activities of the intelligence department, "but because it had been an established practice, I didn't object to it." He distanced himself further from Villasenor's team by insisting, "When they were at the toy fair, I had no responsibility for any of them." And yet when pushed, Turetzky confessed he knew what happened at the fairs, but he still insisted he forbade the infiltration activities. Turetzky claimed that as soon as he found out about the "business analysts" conducting espionage, he gave strict instructions to cease and desist, even implementing a new policy that expressly denounced these kinds of actions. In 2003, Mattel indeed officially introduced a new internal policy prohibiting gathering competitor information through "misleading means."[9]

MGA noted a striking distinction between Mattel's official memos and its practices. Keller told the jury that corporate statements are notorious for being broad and legally appropriate, and the gaps between the written words and executive actions run deep. Keller takes particular pride in her idea to highlight for the jury the gap between Mattel's written corporate code of conduct, which requires all employees to "play fair," behave ethically, be good corporate citizens, and the actual, long-standing institutional practice of spying. "Barbie does not 'play nice' with others (particularly her competitors)," MGA told the jury. Keller urged the jury to recognize that Mattel's' actions spoke louder than its words: in writing, Mattel's top executives are the guardians of the business's ethics and should know the actions of its employees. And yet here they were, denying any knowledge or involvement.

Matt Turetzky insists that he personally met with Villasenor in 2003 to discuss the new policy, and that he expressly told him to stop using fake credentials. He admits, however, that he did nothing to follow up or discipline Villasenor for the department's criminal practices. On the contrary, in 2004, a year after Turetzky claims to have ordered the department to stop posing at the toy fairs, Turetzky approved an expense report for the Pomona Toy Fair, which itemized "Kinko's for tradeshow business cards."

As for Villasenor, he recalled events quite differently. He insisted that Turetzky never once instructed him to stop his department's sanctioned corporate espionage. Instead, he remembers a meeting with Turetzky to discuss recent difficulty in accessing MGA's showrooms, as Villasenor and his team had become too recognizable.[10] The two men then discussed using new faces to infiltrate the showrooms. Ultimately, they decided to entrust the mission to Sharon Rahimi, who had worked with Villasenor in the past and was hired as an independent contractor so she could infiltrate private showrooms using fake credentials.[11] She was asked to impersonate a journalist and "trend expert" when attending toy fairs. Although Turetzky testified that Rahimi was hired as a journalist tasked with writing a "kids' trends newsletter" based on publicly available information, he couldn't produce or recall a single article ever published by Rahimi.[12]

Not only did the managing leadership encourage unlawful activities, but it also seems that Mattel's robust legal department, that crew of attorneys which so zealously protect Mattel's intellectual property, failed to prevent any of these practices until they were exposed. Like Turetzky, each Mattel executive who took the stand played the blame game, the game of plausible deniability, or both. Each asserted no knowledge of, and no responsibility for, the fraudulent activity.[13] Jill Thomas, Mattel's chief counsel at the time of the trial, testified that the new policy was implemented as soon as Mattel executives discovered the fraudulent activities of a few renegade business analysts. She insists that using fake business cards "certainly isn't something that Mattel would have condoned even pre-2003."[14] But again, Mattel's official words contradict its unofficial actions. For example, Thomas admitted that she was aware of some of Rahimi's actions while Rahimi was working for the Market Intelligence Department, but that because Rahimi's conduct predated the new policy advocating corporate ethics, she was never penalized in any way. In fact, despite Mattel's official reprimand of the Market Intelligence Department, the entire department, including Rahimi, Villasenor, and Turetzky, received bonuses and raises for their work.[15]

When the face of Mattel, CEO Robert Eckert, finally took the stand to be examined on Mattel's espionage practices, he laid the blame for the corporate spying squarely on the lower ranks. Eckert testified that other Mattel employees were uncomfortable about sneaking into competitors' showrooms, but they were wrongly guided by Villasenor and Turetzky. Eckert condemned and distanced himself from the behavior of Turetzky, who, as a relatively senior executive at Mattel with a Harvard MBA, knew the code of conduct and should have known "right from wrong," and understood he was operating in a "gray area." The CEO chastised a senior executive for his lack of accountability for illegal business practices, yet swore he himself did not know of their existence. One juror, who wished to remain anonymous, showed me notes taken during Eckert's testimony: "Appears to be a practice of plausible deniability. Leaves things out." Following another part of his testimony, the juror jotted down "LIAR." The jurors of the second trial particularly remembered that there was no evidence of Mattel's spies being reprimanded, but plenty of evidence that those people got promotions and bonuses. The jurors also noted that, though Eckert spoke with the royal *we* rather than *I*, he took no responsibility for the company he led.

Boiling Frogs and Toxic Dirt in the Playground

Mattel's Market Intelligence Department exemplifies how companies can quickly cross the line between healthy market competition and fraud. Competitive intelligence is the legal counterpart to corporate espionage. It includes examining corporate publications, websites, patent filings, and visiting stores and the public spaces of trade shows. All of that is fair game. And yet, too often, corporations have practices, and even entire departments, that straddle the gray area between the two worlds. At the same time Carter was reaching for discarded materials in his cubicle's *basura*, Mattel's spies-for-hire were engaging in a different kind of illegal dumpster diving. Mattel has always aggressively kept competitors, as well as artistic Barbie fans like Aqua and Tom Forsythe, at bay through its litigate-to-death strategy. Hand in hand with these legal attack plans are the aggressive and questionable methods of gathering competitor information.

Of course, economic espionage is not unique to the toy industry. But unlike Mattel, most companies, when caught red-handed, are quick to acknowledge wrongdoing and distance the corporation from what they term an isolated unethical incident. For example, when Procter & Gamble (P&G) gained proprietary information by having employees rummage through trash bins on restricted competitor grounds, not only did P&G agree to pay Unilever ten million dollars, but it fired the employees responsible and quarantined the information gathered.[16] Whether P&G was truly ignorant of its employees' illegal activities, or whether it threw its employees under the bus to cover a bigger practice, the company effectively mitigated the damages from this embarrassing blunder. MGA produced evidence that Mattel, especially its Market Intelligence Department, employed clandestine practices that spanned over seventeen years and affected dozens of competitors. And yet Mattel failed to present evidence of meaningful corrective measures.

Eventually, when all the evidence was shown at trial, John Quinn, Mattel's longtime attorney and one of the country's toughest trial lawyers, admitted before the jury that the Market Intelligence Department's activities were "unsavory." Quinn said, "It was wrong for people to misrepresent themselves. It was wrong and it was stupid." But Quinn asked the jury to see this espionage as the actions of a few self-aggrandizing individuals gone rogue, without support from the top. More than that, faced with undeniable evidence of improper conduct, the last line of defense at trial was trying to convince the jury that this was simply standard to the industry. Quinn said, "It is, I acknowledge, an unfortunate regrettable fact that apparently a number of employees did use phony IDs at certain toy fairs, phony business cards to gain access to showrooms. But, folks, this isn't something that only Mattel did. Sneaking into toy fair showrooms, competitors' showrooms, was commonplace in the industry. It is something that MGA did." MGA, according to Quinn, pretended to be "shocked and appalled" by what it called "espionage at toy fairs." But, Quinn nearly yelled at the jury, waving his fist, "I'm telling you this is something that's commonplace. . . . Everybody tries to do the best they can to find out what products others are coming out with." The toy fairs, according to Quinn, reveal how "competitors compete . . . you know, the rough and tumble of American competitive enterprise that we're all familiar with."

Keller, in contrast, urged the members of the jury to remain unjaded and asked them to see things differently. This was no case of a few rogue employees acting unbeknownst to Mattel's executives, but "quite the contrary, this was a carefully constructed scheme orchestrated and supervised by Mattel's most senior executives to steal its competitors' trade secrets for its own competitive advantage."[17]

Sometimes moving to the dark side, if done incrementally, feels like a natural progression. In every industry and every market, in both private and public settings, from Wall Street to Hollywood to Silicon Valley to Washington, we find examples where even some of the most experienced leaders fail to recognize that they are in hot water until they are completely scalded. This behavior is best encapsulated by what behavioral psychologists term the "boiling frog syndrome." The metaphor is based on early biology experiments hypothesizing that if a frog is placed in boiling water, it jumps out, but if it is placed in cold water that is incrementally heated, it will not perceive the danger and will be gradually cooked to death. In reality, this scientific premise is false—a submerged frog slowly cooked will make the leap to save itself. But as a metaphor, it holds true for too many contemporary business leaders. To mix some metaphors, in today's business world, we encounter not only many top-office ostriches digging their heads into the sand, unwilling to react to threats which occur gradually, but also a garden variety of corporate frogs warming up to wrongdoing until they forget the feeling of moral behavior.

Quinn's notion, "but everyone is doing it," echoes a related behavioral ethics phenomenon. Cheating is contagious. In my research on corporate culture with my longtime collaborator, law and psychology professor Yuval Feldman, I study the behavior of employees who encounter corruption in the workplace. When employees perceive an unethical practice as widespread, they are more likely to adopt that behavior. And when corruption is institutionalized, it is incredibly difficult for insiders to go against it. As Albus Dumbledore tells Neville Longbottom in *Harry Potter and the Sorcerer's Stone*: "It takes a great deal of bravery to stand up to our enemies, but just as much to stand up to our friends." As our experimental research on whistleblowing shows, it takes great bravery for employees to muster resistance to patterns of corruption from within a large organization, leaving most employees silent.[18]

Beyond crossing the line from market intelligence to illegal market espionage, Mattel adopted other means of pushing deep into the competitive gray area. By 2004, Mattel's war against MGA had reached new heights. MGA claims that Mattel began threatening retailers, licensees, and service providers that it would scupper their contracts if they bought Bratz in large quantity. It pressured leading stores to relegate Bratz to the back shelves. In 2004, Kohl's was selling over five million dollars' worth of Bratz products, but in 2005, it abruptly ceased business with MGA. Foreshadowing the end of the Kohl's-MGA partnership, in December 2004, Tom Maskel, a buyer for Kohl's, approached Mattel with an e-mail titled "Huge Opportunity":

> As you are well aware, I have zero love for Bratz. In my humble opinion, this is just a fad that is done. As you are aware, we have approximately 4 feet of POG [or planograms, retail shelves] space designated for Bratz this Spring. What would Mattel think about me throwing out Bratz and replacing the space with our friend Barbie? Here is the kicker: If I throw them out, I will need some help with markdowns on old Bratz. We can talk money later. I think you would agree this might be a nice opportunity for Mattel to take back a little market share.

Sure enough, Mattel paid Kohl's $1.25 million to sweeten the deal. In January 2005, an e-mail titled "Kohl's Great News Barbie" circulated within Mattel. The e-mail said, "It's final. Kohl's has agreed to the following: Double Barbie's retail space to 8 feet for a minimum of two years. . . . [T]he competitor will not be represented in the toy department for two years. . . . Let's congratulate . . . for this outstanding accomplishment."

Mattel attempted backdoor deals with other retailers as well. In a meeting between Mattel and Target, Matt Bousquette, president of Mattel's Brand, and Eckert's number two, repeatedly used the word "unfair" when he said to Target: "We, as a vendor, want to be treated differently than the other guys. We want to do it bigger than the others, larger playing field, give us *unfair* benefit. Place *unfair* bets on us for *unfair* benefits." That same year, in light of Barbie's continuous losses and despite his seventeen years of boundless devotion to the company, Bousquette was asked to resign. Barbie essentially flat-lined during his term, yet the toy executive received a golden parachute of over $5 million in cash plus a $1.5 million contract to serve as a consultant for two years, along with health insurance, a company limo, membership in a country club, and tax services until he could find another job. Most importantly, Bousquette got to keep $31.5 million he had in stock options. In short, Mattel paid him nearly $40 million to leave the company and become a consultant for a limited time. This had become a regular practice at Mattel: executives fail and fall but they are guaranteed a golden parachute on their way down even as the company and its shareholders take a hit. Compensation experts have commented that Bousquette's post-employment terms were particularly generous for someone who is not the company's CEO. One expert noted that the murkiest part of the agreement was the consulting arrangement: "Why would you provide a consulting agreement for someone you just threw out?"[19]

Evidence of Mattel's unfair practices spanned beyond just Kohl's and Target. MGA discovered that Mattel's national merchandisers, ranging from Florida to California, were systematically removing Bratz dolls from the store shelves at Toys "R" Us and replacing them with Mattel products. Some instances of this practice were reported to Mattel by retail partners. When asked whether he knew about any of these incidents, or investigated the allegations about such practices when brought to his attention, Eckert flatly denied any knowledge. Keller considered Eckert's head-in-the-sand approach and asked, "And so if you insulate yourself from knowing about it, then you can't report it, right?" Eckert responded simply, "That's right." Still unsatisfied, Keller pushed further, "As captain of the ship, as the head person, as the guy responsible for reporting, not just to the federal government, but to all of your shareholders about what's going on in your company, you need to know if your largest customer is complaining to you that your people in three states are engaging in anticompetitive activity, right?" Eckert responded that the complaints the company received were not specific enough to require his personal attention.

Keller took full advantage of having Eckert on the stand. She asked him if he knew that the United States was the global origin of antitrust laws, the leader of free market competition perfected through governmental oversight to prevent monopolies and cartels. Eckert said he wasn't aware. "Back in the days of Teddy Roosevelt, the trust buster," Keller enlightened him, "And so in the United States, would you agree that robust competition is kind of—is almost an American principle? And protecting robust competition is enshrined in our laws, isn't it?" "It is," Eckert replied. After dancing around the question, Eckert admitted that he considered and discussed killing deals with licensees who were also doing business with MGA. Keller pushed, "And is this the unwavering integrity that you brought with you from Kraft?" Eckert coolly responded, "Accusations don't mean a lot to me."

According to the motions MGA filed in court, Mattel's manipulation of the market went beyond retailers.[20] For example, Isaac Larian believes that a leading market research firm in the toy industry, NPD Funworld, was strong-armed by Mattel to drop MGA as a member and manipulate sales data to make it appear MGA was selling fewer fashion dolls. MGA also claims that the Children's Advertising Review Unit, an industry association that attempts to maintain standards in advertising in the toy industry, placed onerous restrictions on MGA ads under pressure from Mattel. The Toy Industry Association, the leading trade association in the industry, was itself accused of rigging the yearly awards. When Bratz first came out, the Toy Industry Association presented Bratz with the People's Choice Toy of the Year Award two years in a row. But according to MGA, Mattel insiders pressured the association to change its process from a consumer's choice to a vote by industry members, and the next year, Mattel's Hokey Pokey Elmo overtook Bratz Formal Funk Super Stylin' Runway Disco. Larian even believes that Mattel blocked MGA from sponsoring Nickelodeon's Kids' Choice Awards. Larian basically views the entire industry as rigged and conspiring against newcomers, the underdog outsiders.

Another one of MGA's accusations was unique to the doll industry. Larian believes Mattel attempted to manipulate the market for Saran doll hair—the locks that adorn the heads of both Barbie and Bratz dolls—by buying up the supply from the two main hair-supply companies in the hopes that the competition would go bald.[21]

The accusations have been endless, but not all corroborated by evidence. For example, Isaac Larian told me that Mattel, whenever it fears that kids are developing a taste for a competing toy, sells its toys at prices below cost to kill any new line, and it did so to compete with Bratz. The Fair Trade Commission regularly examines such claims brought by competitors in all industries about predatory pricing— the practice of below-cost pricing by a dominant competitor to knock its rivals out of the market, after which prices are hiked to above-market levels—but generally today such practices are legal and not an antitrust violation. Larian also believes that Mattel falsely told the press that "Bratz sexualizes girls and that Bratz dolls say the "F" word (which they do not) as part of Mattel's 'Operation Cast Doubt on Bratz.' "[22] "How dare they accuse Bratz for being a slut when their Barbie hails from red-light district of Hamburg?" Larian posed to me.

Mattel's covert competition tactics also extended to monitoring its own troops. As Mattel realized the cost of Carter Bryant's departure, it became increasingly suspicious and wary of all its employees' loyalty. Employees were leaving as MGA became the hotter, sexier toy company for which to work. Over the five years following Bratz's launch, 115 ex-Mattel employees moved to MGA. In California, talent wants to be free. Unlike most other states, California has a unique policy which voids all noncompete clauses. In other words, California employers are prohibited from demanding absolute restrictions of post-employment noncompetition. This policy means that employers like Mattel focus on requiring strong innovation assignment agreements, such as the one Carter signed, as well as developing strong deterrent policies against employees who jump ship. Companies in the United States are generally allowed to monitor all their employee's electronic communications, and Mattel wanted to know exactly what these employees might potentially take with them—company secrets, ideas, perhaps sketches for a doll line. The company monitored its employees' incoming and outgoing e-mails, its filter flagging any emails that contained specific keywords, one of which was, of course, "MGA." Other keywords included the names of other toy competitors, like Hasbro and Spinmaster. In her deposition, Mattel's general counsel revealed her involvement in at least four investigations into departing employees.

Mattel even targeted its own executives. Suing an employee is a strategic move. In a memo to Richard de Anda, Mattel's head of internal security, investigators submitted a surveillance log from a private detective monitoring the home of Ronald Brawer, a Mattel vice president and general manager who left to work for MGA. Mattel hired private detectives to watch Brawer's Manhattan Beach house, follow his car around town, and even videotape his child. Eventually, Mattel sued Brawer, alleging he passed company secrets to MGA. It relied on its code of conduct that forbade employees from discussing confidential information in public places, including "planes, restaurants, and elevators." The lawsuit was dismissed.

Although increasingly paranoid, Mattel's fears were not groundless. MGA was battling fire with fire, and the two companies became more and more locked in battles plagued by irrationalities and high emotions. Not only had MGA been hiring Mattel employees, but in 2005, Larian also wrote to his high execs at MGA, "[W]e want to kill Mattel once and for all." The desire for vengeance went both ways.

And yet the romantic David and Goliath story resonated with the jurors of the second trial. They saw a large corporation behaving vindictively when faced with competition from a newer and smaller company. In sharp contrast to the first trial, where Judge Larson had prohibited MGA from even mentioning Barbie, MGA was allowed to paint a full picture of Mattel's crisis for the jury. The jurors later recounted to me the following story: while Mattel was facing Barbie's first serious competitor and stagnating sales from unforeseen shifting markets and tastes, it also turned a blind eye to tragedy.

Toys That Kill

In the first trial, MGA's attorneys were not permitted to tell the jury about Barbie's woes, which had started before Bratz came along. Judge Carter, however, allowed Keller to relate the information. With that, Keller was able to achieve two things: first, show the jury that Barbie had popularity problems unrelated to her competition, thus refuting the claim that her sinking sales were all due to Bratz taking her market share. Second, she could present some of Mattel's most notorious scandals to the jury. Since the early days of the Handlers' leadership at Mattel, toy production had largely moved abroad. The Handlers originally produced some toys in Japan, but over the years, like so many other American companies, Mattel moved its manufacturing primarily to China and Indonesia. In the summer of 2007, the news broke that Mattel toys manufactured in China contained lead paint, toxic and deadly for children when found in large enough quantities. Specifically, Fisher-Price, acquired by Mattel in 1993, had manufactured toxic versions of characters such as Dora the Explorer and Sesame Street's Grover using lead paint that exceeded 180 times the regulatory limits. The lead was first detected by the Europeans, who generally have stronger consumer protection standards, and the scandal quickly crossed the pond into the United States.

When the news broke in both markets, Mattel was forced to recall nearly one hundred different kinds of toys—approaching a million units of sold toys. Eckert was asked to testify before congressional committees, where consumer advocates described Eckert's leadership as "disturbing." Eckert admitted in interviews that Mattel didn't move forward with the recalls as fast as the law required, but instead took its time to conduct internal evaluations before alerting the Consumer Protection and Safety Commission (CPSC). It was months before Mattel finally announced it would cease subcontracting with the Chinese manufacturer that produced the affected toys. Zhan Shuhong, the fifty-two-year-old owner of the Chinese manufacturer, committed suicide by hanging himself in the factory.

Evidence emerged of more toxic toys produced in China, and the recalls expanded exponentially, with Mattel recalling tens of millions of toys and paying a two-million-dollar governmental fine for concealing information and delaying recalls. The Mattel lead paint scandal was especially significant because it revealed inadequacies in both corporate and governmental oversight. The tragedy not only shed light on Mattel's inadequate safety processes but also uncovered the United States' weak governmental regulation over the toy industry. The CPSC, it turned out, had just one toy inspector, Robert Hundemer, who had worked at the agency for three decades. He alone was charged with testing toys for the entire United States market. He resigned immediately after the Mattel recall fiasco. The agency's top commissioner was also accused of ignoring the risks of defective products, and members of Congress called for her resignation.

Exposing Mattel's inadequate safety measures to the sunlight revealed other risks that were lurking in the shadows. Barbie accessories, along with other Mattel toys, contained small magnets that were deadly if swallowed by children. In 2006, three children in Indiana, Colorado, and Wyoming swallowed the tiny magnets of Polly Pockets and became gravely ill. Mattel tried to erase the tragedies by paying off the families. However, no amount of money could hide the company's tarnished reputation. Angry parents around the world accused the corporation of deadly greed. A class action on behalf of millions of children was filed in California, demanding that Mattel provide lead testing for children exposed to the dangerous toys. Mattel announced another round of recalls.

The problem with recalls is that often only a small percentage of the hazardous item is returned to the company. This is especially true for toys, which have a large secondary market. Sadly, a recall heightens the differences in the consumer protection of the rich and the poor. It's one thing if a batch of bad cheese is recalled. If, while Eckert led Kraft, a batch of American Singles got contaminated and started turning into French Blue Cheese, he could confidently ask the stores to throw out the tainted cheese. Food is perishable and will go off the shelves either way, but recalled toys can stick around for a long, long time. Only a fraction of recalled toys, less than 10 percent, are ever returned, and the rest continue to haunt the playrooms of small children, garage sales, Craigslist, eBay, and Goodwill stores. Sadly, more often than not, children whose parents don't have time and resources to follow the latest in recall news are the ones exposed to the risky toys.

In 2011, as the trial proceeded in court, outside of the courtroom Mattel launched a desperate love campaign, featuring a heartbroken Ken professing his renewed love to his ex, whom he had met in 1961 on the set of their first TV commercial together, and with whom he had split in 2004. On Facebook, Ken made a very public effort to woo Barbie back. As Valentine's Day neared, Ken's unwavering devotion was displayed on billboards and on the Times Square Jumbotron: "Barbie, I want you back," "Barbie, you're the only doll for me," "Barbie, we were made for each other," and "Barbie, we may be plastic but our love is real." Naturally, Isaac Larian had plenty to say on Barbie and Ken's reunion. He was quoted in the *New York Times*, calling the reunion "stupid publicity" and stated, "Ken is not going to save Barbie."[23] And he was right.

11 | THE JURY DELIBERATION ROOM THAT LOOKED LIKE A TOYS "R" US

ON APRIL 20, 2011, after months of trial, when all the evidence was presented, Judge Carter was ready to read the jury its instructions. But first he turned to his jurors and asked them, "Do you have time for a story?"

In 1835 a French gentleman named Alexander de Tocqueville came to the United States. I met him. He's a wonderful man. And he had two things to observe about America that sets us apart from any other country in the world. And I hate that phrase "second to none." He said, in studying our political system and the judiciary, he didn't believe a judge in his home country, France, or a panel of judges—because in France, in the European system, they often sit as a tribunal of three judges—that their judges would make a significantly different decision than an individual American judge. But he was amazed at our system and by our system, because he said two things occur. For some reason, in America you have decided to empower people in your country and make them jurors, and when you do that, you give them a sense of ownership in your great

231

democracy. They're not dictated to by somebody, they share and participate in this democracy, and therefore you give everyday people with common sense and wisdom, the ability to apply your laws. The second thing he said that was so astounding about our country was that our community accepts the verdicts from you, the people, much more readily than from an individual jurist or judge.

So therefore, when I instruct you on the law and throughout your deliberations, you are now held to that same high standard that you have exhibited throughout these proceedings. You'll eventually become judges of the facts and the application of the law. That's my story for today to you. Alexander, by the way, is dead, but his thoughts live on.

As if in response to Judge Carter's story, the jury took its responsibility seriously and deliberated for almost two weeks. The deliberation room itself looked like a Toys "R" Us store. "We got access to everything—we had tons of toys and sketches, and we were diligent in comparing everything side by side," recalls one of the jurors. For the most part, the jurors were in agreement: hearing everything together, MGA looked like David fighting Goliath. But in federal courts, whether the trial is criminal or civil, the jury must reach a unanimous verdict, and there were two wild-card jurors. One was an Asian immigrant who during the deliberations informed the other jurors that the economic espionage and trade secrets theft that Mattel engaged in was nothing compared to the cutthroat corporate practices in China. To him it was all relative, and what Mattel did was not so bad. He also thought "a contract is a contract is a contract" and that Carter Bryant was bound by the contract he signed with Mattel. None of the others could predict how he would cast his vote. MGA's psychology expert, sitting in the back of the courtroom analyzing the jurors' facial expressions to predict their votes, was even more in the dark about a second juror: the youngest juror, a beautiful, petite blonde woman in her early twenties, seemed to him the wildest card. She had first served as an alternate, then joined the jury, and admitted to growing up loving Barbie during the voir dire—the preliminary examination of potential jurors for the jury selection process. On the day the jury reached its conclusion, she came to court wearing a Barbie-pink jumpsuit. The MGA psychologist was certain MGA was doomed.

But on that day, the jurors brought a stunning conclusion. On April 21, 2011, in unanimous decision, the jury found for MGA on its counterclaims for trade-secret misappropriation while finding against Mattel in its claims that it owned the Bratz brand. The jurors believed that, for the first time, Barbie faced a serious challenge to its fifty-year iron-fisted grip on the doll market, and all hell broke loose. They agreed with MGA's assertion that with new competition, "Mattel did not take kindly to the challenge. Either unable or unwilling to compete against Bratz fairly in the marketplace on a level playing field, Mattel took a more expeditious approach, resorting to unfair and anti-competitive business practices including, but not limited to, corporate espionage."[1] One juror said after the trial, "I don't think anyone should be able to bully someone and own everything."

The jury felt that an employee's creative mind is not owned by his or her employer. Jury members thought employees should have a right to their ideas unless they very specifically assigned those ideas to their employers. The jury never accepted the theory that everything in your head becomes a company's property the minute you are hired, and your ideas remain company property years after you've left. They agreed with Judge Kozinski's point on appeal that Mattel's contract was missing the word *ideas*, and they interpreted that to mean Carter's ideas were not assigned to his employer. As a juror said to me, "You don't get to claw back to the past every idea that an employee might have just because they've started working for you." Moreover, they believed Carter when he said Bratz was born in Missouri. As a juror told me: "He wasn't paid during the time away from Mattel and he had made the sketches at his mother's home. He was a costume designer at heart and he was struck by the urban gritty look of the school girls in Missouri." About Mattel's attempt to examine the principal of Kickapoo High School in an attempt to refute Carter's story, a juror told me, "They were throwing dust in our eyes." Another juror told me after the trial, "Carter had used no resources of Mattel. Mattel hadn't taught him how to be a designer. He had been creative all his life and he knew how to draw dolls from the first day he joined Mattel. If you aren't sitting down at your desk under the direction of your supervisor to create something specific, you should be able to own the idea." The juror asked me a follow-up hypothetical: "Say I dedicate all my weekends to inventing in my garage a new type of lawn sprinkler and quit my job—the company can claim to own that too?"

The conclusion was that Mattel did not own the idea behind Bratz, or even the sketches that led to their creation. Even if Mattel had a claim to an abstract idea, under the new jury instructions, these were too abstract to claim copyright ownership over the final doll line. Thus, the jury sided with MGA and unanimously found no copyright or trademark infringement stemming from the development of Bratz. The jury rejected each of Mattel's ownership claims over the early Bratz sketches, the first Bratz models, and the final Bratz line.

As for MGA's counterclaims about Mattel's unlawful practices, the jurors believed Sal Villasenor was telling the truth—Mattel's top executives knew about, and even condoned, corporate espionage. The jurors I talked with felt that the trade secrets theft "further vilified Mattel." One juror expressed utter shock at the company's behavior: "What corporation would so blatantly be unlawful, create fake IDs, write up a *How to Steal Manual*?" The juror told me she owns a manufacturing company, knows how much time it takes to get products to market, and what a fortune it costs to develop them. To think that a competitor would deceptively infiltrate private showrooms and then hurriedly develop almost identical products shocked her.

While Mattel had described the counterclaims as "a cynical attempt to deflect attention from MGA's own wrongdoing,"[2] the jurors concluded that Mattel was the cynical bad actor. The jurors I talked to believed Carter was right to want to leave Mattel's unimaginative and corrupt bureaucracy and join the nimble, adventurous MGA. So in a dramatic turn of events, after hearing testimony from Mattel's most senior leadership, the jury found the corporation liable for willful and malicious theft of MGA's trade secrets. The only claim that the jury found against MGA was Larian's intentional interference with Mattel and Carter's contract, for which he had to pay the symbolic, and laughable, sum of ten thousand dollars. As for MGA's claims on unfair competition in manipulating consumer markets with deals with retailers and other manufacturers and undue influences on industry associations, the court found against MGA.

As a result of the jury's decision, Judge Carter awarded MGA $309 million.[3] Mattel was ordered to pay MGA $172 million in damages, including punitive damages, with the addition of over $105 million in attorney's fees, and over $31 million in litigation costs; nearly the same amount the previous, overturned jury ordered MGA to pay Mattel. Judge Carter further awarded MGA its fees under the Copyright Act because of Mattel's abuse of discretion in suing MGA. The judge explained that MGA's efforts "secured the public's interest in a robust market for trendy fashion dolls populated by multiple toy companies." Judge Carter called Mattel's claims for billions of dollars in damages and ownership of Bratz "stunning in scope and unreasonable in the relief it requested." He said that the protected features of subsequent generation Bratz dolls "are nothing like" the concept sketches and sculpts to which Mattel claimed ownership. He explained the great risk Mattel's lawsuit presented to society at large:

> Mattel's claim posed a serious threat to the public's access to free and competitive expression. . . . MGA's contribution to the state of intellectual property law in a case of this magnitude and notoriety cannot be

understated. Failure to vigorously defend against Mattel's claims could have ushered in a new era of copyright litigation aimed not at promoting expression but at stifling the competition upon which America thrives.

Judge Carter emphasized that for years, other courts reminded Mattel of the black letter law concerning the boundaries of copyright ownership. The punitive damages were designed to send an important message to Mattel and the rest of the business world. Keller convinced the court that this monster of a case should set a precedent for other corporations everywhere:

Companies are watching around the world. And that's especially true because Mattel has held itself out publicly as an industry leader as one of the world's most ethical companies and, yet, it was engaging in a systematic pattern of utterly unethical conduct, utterly reprehensible conduct. It hasn't shown any remorse whatsoever. None. Zero. And instead it has tried to blame MGA.

On the damages for Mattel's unlawful economic espionage practices, Keller continued depicting an alternative path that Mattel had not chosen. She emphasized that Mattel's leaders chose not to apologize to the court, to the public, or to MGA:

You would expect that Mattel would be taking steps to make sure nothing like that ever happened again. You would expect that they would be in here showing you a new compliance program, showing HR pamphlets on this, showing you training videos to keep anything like this from happening again. You would expect that you would hear from some special committees of the board on corporate governance. You would expect to hear from an audit committee. You would expect to see an apology of some kind for the conduct in a reassurance, Don't worry, Your Honor, we don't need to be deterred. We have learned our lesson. We're going to make sure nobody in the company ever does these sorts of things again.

Instead, Keller said, Eckert took the stand and said "literally, anything that his attorneys suggested he say." She noted how he kept changing his testimony to mirror Mattel's best position. First, he completely denied the existence of a market intelligence library. Then, when confronted with evidence of multiple well-organized employees and the involvement of Mattel's accounting department, Mattel took the position that the whole thing was not a big deal. Mattel, which had initially called the case against MGA "the greatest intellectual property heist of all time," minimized its own theft—stealing a competitor's lines was all part of the game. Instead of playing the victim, Mattel presented itself as just playing the game—something everyone does.

The jury didn't buy Mattel's vacillating stories. Instead, the jury agreed with Keller. The jurors felt outraged by Mattel's practices, and compassion for the immigrant family-run company that took a stab at the doll market and on which Mattel rained hellfire. Of course, that close-knit immigrant family was together in court to hear the final verdict. The reading lasted for three long hours and in the end all the Larians—Isaac, Angela, Jason, Jasmin, and Cameron—leaped out of their seats, jumped up and down with joy, and hugged each other in their elation. Larian wept with joy. The court bailiffs too were happy for the Larians. They came over to congratulate the family members for their victory and lined up for selfies with these colorful self-made billionaires. "The American dream lives," Larian declared as he exited the courtroom. He announced that the verdict was "a victory for all entrepreneurs, immigrants who came here."

The Mattel team, including Bob Eckert, who came to the reading, sat cold and shocked. Eckert issued a corporate statement. Mattel was "disappointed by the verdict, but we remain committed to protecting the intellectual property that is at the heart of business success." In an unusual move, when he completed the reading, Judge Carter came down from the bench and hugged each one of the jurors. "You did good," he said.

As for Carter Bryant, the father of Bratz, he was not there to witness MGA's victory. He was far from the courtroom, California, and anything that had to do with toys, designs, or fashion. He was penniless, with his creative dreams crushed. Months before the verdict, as he left to the airport to return home to Missouri, Carter experienced stroke symptoms and was rushed to an L.A. hospital in an ambulance. In the end, even the sight of Bratz in his home was too painful to endure. In 2014, he auctioned off his entire collection of Bratz dolls from his home in Missouri. He enclosed a letter for the winner to hold on to: "Hello Bratz Fans! This is Carter Bryant. I am the creator of the Bratz concept." He tried later to channel his artistic energy in other directions, attempting to release a record with his sister. Like the story of so many other inventors, despite the eventual win, Carter's story is an unhappy one. Carter had lost everything, handing over what was left of his fortune to Mattel in a settlement prior to the first trial. But more than money, Carter, whose creativity drove the entire decade-long battle, lost his passion, which tragically disappeared into the virtual *basura* of discarded talent.

Isaac Larian continues to be bold, colorful, outspoken and enraged. He has publicly stated that "the people at Mattel are crooks," adding that he is happy to be quoted.[4] In his typical provocative style, he likes to brag that he has made $5 million by shorting Mattel stock. Indeed, Mattel's stock fell after the loss. Not exactly the biblical David, MGA is currently estimated to be worth $1.1 billion, with Larian controlling over 80 percent of the still privately held company. And yet, over Mattel's objections, Larian accuses Mattel of creating the stress from the long trial that caused not only Carter Bryant's stroke but also the death of Larian's father in the midst of the long litigation. Larian says that his experience with Mattel's attorneys making racist remarks was particularly hurtful. He told me that his youngest son Cameron, who turned nineteen right when the trial ended, said, "Sure we won, but I haven't seen my father for ten years." Larian admits, "That's when I started crying. My wife kept telling me to just give it to them, 'give them Bratz and they will leave us alone,' she kept telling me. I guess you need guts and stupidity to fight the bullies."

After the trial, Larian invited all the jurors to a gourmet dinner. He personally talked with each juror, asking if they needed toys for their children or their grandchildren. He made donations on their behalves to their favorite charities. At the request of one of the jurors, he donated ten thousand dollars' worth of MGA toys to Laura's House, a domestic violence shelter in Orange County. Mattel mailed invitations to the jurors, also asking them to attend a dinner. The jurors deliberated and collectively decided not to go to the Mattel shindig.

Despite the winning verdict for MGA in the Barbie/Bratz saga, everyone lost. In the end, both companies ended up paying hundreds of millions of dollars in legal fees to pursue the deadlocked trials. One prominent attorney described to me the staggering legal fees billed to Mattel, estimated at over $450 million, as "distasteful." It is possible that the litigators, as well as top executives who left Mattel with millions in golden parachute severance packages, were the ones who gained the most from the decade long battles.

And the war isn't over. It was now Mattel's turn to appeal the decision to the Ninth Circuit Court of Appeals. In 2013, Judge Alex Kozinski, writing for the same Ninth Circuit panel that overturned the initial verdict in 2008, decided MGA could keep the $139 million in legal fees spent fighting the Mattel lawsuit, but he vacated the award from the counterclaims.[5] Judge Kozinski held that MGA's counterclaim did not rest on the same "aggregate core of facts" as Mattel's original claim. In other words, the economic espionage claims should have been tried in a separate lawsuit. So MGA's win on the counterclaims was vacated on a procedural technicality. Still, Kozinski offered advice to the two litigants at the end of his decision, reminiscent of the advice "to chill" he had long before given Mattel, "While this may not be the last word on the subject, perhaps Mattel and MGA can take a lesson from their target demographic: Play nice."

It was Larian's turn to ignore Kozinski's advice—he neither wanted "to chill" nor to "play nice." He had come too far in his defense against the toy giant. His attorneys immediately refiled the suit claiming corporate espionage by Mattel in federal court as a stand-alone lawsuit, but Judge Carter viewed the mandate of the Ninth Circuit as denying the procession of those claims. So MGA turned to state court and currently the trial is in a holding pattern, awaiting a new trial date. MGA believes Mattel will finally settle, hoping that "Mattel is tired of torturing us." After all, as MGA sees it, Eckert was forced to resign from Mattel because he made so many bad choices in relentlessly attacking MGA. The year he lost the litigation battle against MGA, and after eleven years of service at Mattel, Eckert quietly exited the fraternity of professional CEOs and joined the private equity firm Friedman Fleischer & Lowe, calling the move a "logical next step." Perhaps worn down after the woes at Mattel and the pressures that led to his questionable behavior, Eckert said that after running a large public company, he was attracted to the prospect of working with private companies: "I think the governance model of private equity makes a lot of sense these days. Public companies oftentimes are unnecessarily focused on short-term results."[6] Otherwise, he refuses to speak about his time at Mattel, writing me in a polite but succinct e-mail: "Dear Professor Lobel: I received your kind invitation to be interviewed about my experience at Mattel. Unfortunately, I no longer work there, and I don't comment about the company. Thanks, however, for finding me. Warmest regards, Bob."

Larian told me he bought some McDonald's shares as a preemptive strike, based on a market buzz that Eckert aspired for the top job there. He then sent a letter to McDonald's CEO notifying him about "Eckert's lying on the stand." He says that if McDonald's had actually hired Eckert, he would have filed a shareholder class action suit. Eckert has been on McDonald's board of directors since 2003 and, even after moving to a private equity fund, remains in his position on the board.

In January 2012, Mattel filled the vacant CEO position with another Kraft Foods former board member, Bryan Stockton.[7] When Mattel's profits continued to drop under his leadership, Stockton explained "another disappointing quarter" simply: "The reality is we just didn't sell enough Barbie dolls." His time at Mattel was short-lived. He was fired in 2015.[8] In Mattel's 2015 Quarterly Report to the SEC, the theme was about a "turnaround of the business."[9] The report revealed that Barbie's consolidated gross sales fell 19 percent. In 2015, a new CEO, Christopher Sinclair, former CEO of PepsiCo, announced that he would be able to halt the company's free-fall decline by revitalizing the management team and bringing in outside talent.[10] As a part of this turnaround, in 2016, now in her late fifties, Barbie got a brand-new body.[11]

Mattel unveiled Barbie's transformation: a wide array of body types as well as varying skin tones, eye colors, and even facial structures in its new Fashionistas line. Finally departing from her single cast, Mattel's new line gives girls a choice in Barbie doll body shapes: curvy, petite, tall, and original.[12] The plans, which were kept top secret, were referred to as "Project Dawn."[13] Mattel announced that Barbie's dramatic shift is intended to promote healthy body images and to reflect the diversity of modern consumers. The full-bodied doll even received a cover spread on *Time* magazine. Mattel issued a statement: "We are excited to literally be changing the face of the brand—these new dolls represent a line that is more reflective of the world girls see around them—the variety in body type, skin tones and style allows girls to find a doll that speaks to them. We believe we have a responsibility to girls and parents to reflect a broader view of beauty."

Barbie sales continue to fluctuate, and Mattel's new leadership has finally brought innovation to its leading doll line. But while Mattel attempted to save Barbie, the company lost another major brand. Mattel had produced princess dolls for Disney since 1996, and as Barbie began her steady decline, Disney dolls became a hugely important revenue stream. On January 1, 2016, in what was described as "the greatest coup that Hasbro has had in the last three decades," Hasbro, which had survived a takeover attempt by Mattel in the late 1990s, received the deal to license Disney dolls, instead of Mattel. CEO Christopher Sinclair admitted, "We took Disney for granted. We weren't focusing on them. Shame on us." Following the Disney blunder, in another huge attempt to turn leadership around, two-thirds of Mattel's senior executives were forced out.

Despite the eventual victory, MGA has had a tough time recovering. Recent Bratz sales have been significantly lower than the near one-billion-dollar annual sales mark hit at the dolls' height of popularity in 2005. The line has seen a marked decline, bringing in only around forty million dollars a year in sales. Like Barbie, Bratz got a lot of heat owing to the dolls' over-sexualization, some of the bad press possibly covertly driven by Mattel's public relations arm.[14] Larian decided to develop a new generation of Bratz girls to be "more demure" in an attempt to acknowledge the complaints. Boldness carries high risk and Larian sadly admits that retailers had a lukewarm greeting for the new girls. In 2013, postvictory, after nearly a decade of exhausting court battles with Mattel, Larian actually decided to pull the Bratz dolls out of Toys "R" Us, Walmart, Target, and other stores. He waited nearly two years to relaunch Bratz in hopes of bringing back the original four sassy girls who captured the hearts of young girls in 2001. Larian explained that the company had lost the DNA of the product: "Barbie kept us in court for many years. We took our eye off the company and brand which is unfortunate."[15] Behind closed doors, he tells me he believes that "Bratz is over," that Mattel managed to "kill" her by suing MGA because "retailers don't like to get involved with competitors' disputes. I don't blame them." Still, despite his wife's advice about the wisdom of walking away even from righteous battles, he remains willing to fight Mattel and any other competitor in the courtroom until the bitter end.

EPILOGUE:
INNOVATION BEYOND
TOYLAND

WE, AS A SOCIETY, have a choice. We can choose to promote market dynamism or to permit a market of concentrated power. We can create shared spaces for creativity or allow a handful of companies to hoard cultural imagery. It takes a market actor as belligerent as Mattel to force society to examine itself and honestly consider the state of intellectual property law. The toy industry, once composed of mavericks, rule breakers, and rebellious artists, has become an oligarchy of rigid rulers ready to massacre newcomers with vexatious litigation. This has been the trajectory of many other industries as well. Intellectual property litigation continues to grow, barring new companies from competing. Now, even the most ingenious companies risk shifting from being great innovators to great gatekeepers as the goal of creativity and invention is supplanted by visions of rising share value. Corporate leaders are all too willing to litigate as a means of seizing and controlling knowledge. Smart leaders realize that a litigate-to-death strategy can backfire. But most of the time, small competitors with shallower pockets choose to walk away. And even when bold competitors, like Isaac Larian, prove worthy opponents, their victories are pyrrhic.

Like too many industries today, toy manufacturing has become remarkably concentrated. Individual competitors, like Fisher-Price, are swallowed by giant conglomerates in lucrative acquisitions. Retail has also shrunk to a handful of dominant players—Walmart, Target, Toys "R" Us, Amazon. Both manufacturing and retail titans are driven by a singular goal: profit.

In and of itself, that isn't a problem; corporations should strive to make money, as long as they operate within the boundaries of the law. But this concentration of market power, combined with increasingly corporate ownership over intellectual property, effectively ended the days of the lone inventor, the Geppettos of our world, building toys in their workshop, eyes gleaming with the spark of innovation. Instead, assembly lines mechanically pump out unimaginative and redundant toys in bulk. Many of today's toys are like fast food: low in nutrition, quickly consumed, and highly addictive. The toy industry's core business model is the constant expansion of accessories. In many cases, play is scripted, and there is, ironically, very little room to use one's imagination with modern playthings.

Mattel perfected these ideas early on: imitate the grown-up world, down to the exact detail—be it a woman, her convertible, her shoes, her purse, or her boyfriend—leaving little to the child's imagination but the desire for more of the same. And as we've seen, in stark contrast to the sweet appearance of their products, toy corporations are at least as ruthless as Silicon Valley tech companies and Wall Street moneymakers. Mattel's pink floors and cuddly stuffed-animal-covered walls are deceptive. Just like Apple up north, Mattel doesn't manufacture its products. That happens far away, usually in Asia. Mattel is in the business of owning brands, images, designs, and technology. In other words, it deals in intellectual property. Just as Steve Jobs transitioned from an innovative visionary and industry rebel to a militant enforcer of intellectual property rights, so too did Mattel begin as a creative enterprise that became an intellectual property shark. Early in Apple's meteoric rise, Jobs said, "Picasso had a saying—'good artists copy; great artists steal'—and we have always been shameless about stealing great ideas."

Toward the end of his life, dying from cancer, Jobs showed a very different side of himself, telling his biographer Walter Isaacson, "I will spend my last dying breath if I need to, and I will spend every penny of Apple's $40 billion in the bank, to right this wrong. I'm going to destroy Android, because it's a stolen product. I'm willing to go thermonuclear war on this." Apple began spending more money on litigation and protecting its existing intellectual property than on investment in new innovation. Down in Southern California, we've tracked Mattel's spiral down a similar trajectory.

Intellectual property is the workhorse of twenty-first century markets. Legal protections for knowledge and creativity were originally developed to add, as Lincoln hoped, the fuel of interest to the fire of genius. But intellectual property protection has expanded beyond its original goals. Today, every company that reaches the top is tempted to use the law in ways that block competition. Creative ventures, too often and too quickly, lock themselves in vexatious legal battles that assure nothing but their mutual destruction. Mattel still leads the toy industry in this regard, though other toy giants are adopting that mindset. Lego, which recently took Mattel's title of the world's largest toy company, patented its titular toy bricks in 1958, and since then the Danish company's revenues have grown to five billion dollars per year. When Mega Bloks began competing with Lego in 1991, Lego transformed the market dispute into a legal one, and it has been gripped in litigation with Mega Bloks ever since.

The last of Lego's patents actually expired in 1989, so Lego began relying on copyright and trademark protection to shield its market dominance, arguing the visual appearance of its standard, eight-stud brick is worthy of a trademark. Lego lost this argument in 2005 in a suit brought against Mega Bloks in Canada, and again in a similar suit brought in Europe. The Canadian Supreme Court sounded a warning to Lego similar to Judge Kozinski's warning to Mattel: "The fact is, though, that the monopoly on the bricks is over, and Mega Bloks and Lego bricks may be interchangeable in the bins of the playrooms of the nation—dragons, castles and knights may be designed with them, without any distinction . . . The appellant is no longer entitled to protection against competition in respect of its product. It must now face the rigors of a free market and its process of creative destruction."[1]

Now Lego has started suing competitors for introducing products that allegedly rip off Lego's "Friends" and pink-shelf products. However, these lines are not particularly novel or innovative, and are likely signs of the same intellectual and creative stagnation that prefaced Mattel's downfall. Critics have railed against these toys, as they are often designed around dated stereotypes of what a corporate board must think young girls are interested in. SPARK, a women's equality task force, collected over 55,000 signatures for a petition brought against the Lego Friends line, chastising the company for making 90 percent of its mainstream Lego characters male, while stereotyping the activities of the few female characters.

I believe the best toys transcend gender and even age. Think yo-yos, Legos (until they were separated out into traditional and pink), blocks, and board games like Scrabble and Monopoly. Mattel, it would seem, has set the tone on the dual fronts of competition and consumer marketing in the toy industry. When my friends and I made our film debuts, starring in those experimental psychology video clips in the 1990s, we understood that these experiments compared society's perceptions of "boy toys" and "girl toys." Overwhelmingly, the research showed that, at every age and around the world, kids think highly of girls who play with boy toys but denigrate boys who "cross over." I grew up knowing that, as consumers, our choices have consequences that go far beyond the immediate joy of play. So too the choices businesses make have consequences beyond immediate profit.

Law and markets, as they currently stand, offer businesses a dualistic perspective: either sell better products or demolish the competition with a sledge hammer. The intellectual property wars are hot. They pervade industries from pharmaceuticals to software, entertainment to food. Both patent and copyright law aim to induce innovation, but how, and even whether, they achieve this goal is intensely debated. At times these laws encourage creativity and progress, but, ever more often, they are used by litigants to impede and suppress innovation. There are admirable exceptions, of course, of courageous business leaders who base their decisions on something beyond the instant gratification felt after razing the competition. Elon Musk, the visionary founder of Tesla, stands out as one such leader. In 2014, Musk announced in an unusual move that it would not sue anyone who wants to use the company's patented technology. In other words, Tesla invited anyone to use its patents for free. Musk has a greater mission in building his company—expanding the overall market for electric vehicles to better our environment, protect our climate, and reduce our oil consumption. Tesla therefore welcomes competition.

Still, most companies, given the opportunity, will rely on their entire arsenal to launch attacks on competitors. Mattel has become a prime example of a conglomerate that does not allow others to do unto it what it had done unto others. The success of the largest owners of intellectual property in America is built on borrowed and remixed images and stories, and now those same content holders are blocking anyone else from continuing that remix. In the race to innovate or die, we find companies like the seemingly unflappable Mattel using litigation as an extension of the boardroom to prevent new entry into the markets they dominate, while at the same time engaging in problematic, and at times illegal behavior, to beat the competition.

Meanwhile, young inventors fight personal battles to reclaim their innovative energy, as well as their voice, within an entrenched, crushing corporate environment. These newcomers may dive into the metaphorical trash to find freedom, pawing through discarded ideas shelved by their mammoth corporate employer to reclaim their careers and independence. Their acts of subversion and entrepreneurship regenerate an industry that has become ossified, much to consumers' detriment. Just like rotten food and waste makes the best fertilizer for next season's crop, Mattel's failures provide opportunity for competitors to learn and grow. And yet our current policies have fueled a reality that makes it nearly impossible to enter markets without fear. The current reality is that corporations, not people, own most inventions, creations, and talent. Battles against corporate ownership of patents, copyrights, clients, and know-how are regularly fought, and lost, by writers, artists, designers, scientists, inventors, and aspiring entrepreneurs in every industry. These days, unless you are sitting in your attic pursuing your passion, your employer probably owns your talent. The law has expanded too far in enforcing corporate ownership over the world of ideas. Companies too easily weave their tentacles around every creative concept thought up by their employees: ideas explored outside the four walls of a company; ideas whose owner's creativity was rewarded with nothing more than a meager salary; ideas developed during weekends and nights; ideas that were merely related to the business but not commissioned or part of the employee's job description; ideas that have never left their creators' minds.

In a study I published with my collaborator (and husband) On Amir, a leading behavioral economist, in the *Harvard Business Review*, we examine how a person's ownership over his or her own skills and creative ventures impacts that person's motivation.[2] We find that when creators do not receive some stake over their talent, their motivation and performance are significantly depressed. As a society, we all lose when knowledge is fenced in and talent is locked up. In the end, we can't stop the flow of creativity. Digital technology is set to revolutionize the world of intellectual property, as three-dimensional printing threatens to tear down the walls separating consumer and producer. As the cost of these printers decreases, producing toys may become as easy as sharing files. The law must align itself with these realities and the interests of consumers at large. But to do so, as a society we must remember the original goals of intellectual property: developing creative communities, encouraging diverse content, and sustaining an ecosystem of ongoing innovation.

CHRONOLOGY

1945   Ruth and Elliot Handler found Mattel with their friend Harold Matson.

1952   Bild Lilli is born as a cartoon in the German daily newspaper *Bild Zeitung.*

1955   Greiner & Hausser introduces Bild Lilli in Europe as a plastic toy doll.

1956   Ruth Handler sees Bild Lilli in Switzerland.

1959   Mattel introduces Barbie to the world.

1960   Greiner & Hausser patents Bild Lilli's hip joint and exclusively licenses her to Louis Marx.

1961   Louis Marx and Greiner & Hausser sue Mattel for intellectual property theft.

1964   Mattel and Greiner & Hausser settle, and Mattel purchases G&H's Bild Lilli copyright.

1978   Ruth Handler is convicted of securities fraud and resigns from Mattel.

1980   Marx declares bankruptcy.

1983   Greiner & Hausser declares bankruptcy.

1987   Isaac and Fred Larian found MGA.

1993   Mattel buys Fisher-Price.

1994   Carter Bryant is hired at Mattel as a Barbie designer.

1997   Mattel buys Tyco Toys.

1998   Aqua releases the song "Barbie Girl."

1998   Carter Bryant takes time off from Mattel to go to Missouri.

1999   Carter Bryant returns to Mattel.

2000   Robert Eckert takes the reins at Mattel.

2000   August: Carter Bryant is introduced to MGA executives.

2000   September 18: Carter Bryant signs the Bratz agreement with MGA.

2000   September 28: Isaac Larian buys out his brother without mention of the impending Bratz deal.

2000   October 19: Carter Bryant resigns from Mattel.

2001   Bratz is released.

2001   Rolf Hausser's wife files suit against Mattel.

2002   Bratz wins the People's Choice award for Toy of the Year.

2002   Mattel releases MyScene.

2002   An anonymous letter arrives at Mattel, identifying Carter Bryant as Bratz's inventor.

2003   Mattel releases Flavas, shortly thereafter discontinuing the line.

2003   The Carter-Bratz nexus is first mentioned in public.

2003   Mattel introduces a new policy against using "misleading means" to spy on competitors.

2004   Kohl's ceases business with MGA.

2004   Greiner & Hausser loses its renewed case against Mattel.

2004   Mattel sues Carter Bryant alleging breach of contract; MGA intervenes as a defendant.

2004   Ken and Barbie split.

2005   Mattel sues Carter Bryant and MGA in federal court for intellectual property infringement.

2005   Bratz dethrones Barbie in holiday season sales.

2006   Ken attempts to rekindle his romance with Barbie in a marketing campaign.

2007   Carter Bryant settles his lawsuit with Mattel.

2008   MGA loses in trial and is ordered to pay one hundred million dollars to Mattel, pull Bratz from the market, and stop production.

2009   Judge Kozinski suspends the order transferring ownership of Bratz to Mattel.

2010   Judge Kozinski voids the lower court's ruling and orders a retrial.

2011   A new trial results in a verdict in favor of MGA.

2011   After seven years apart, Mattel announces that Ken and Barbie are again a couple.

2012   Mattel moves to throw out MGA's trade secret counterclaims victory.

2012   Mattel announces that Robert Eckert is stepping down.

2013   Judge Kozinski finds that the court should not have been allowed to consider MGA's counterclaims.

2014   MGA relaunches its one-billion-dollar trade secret allegation in California Superior Court.

2015   MGA puts Bratz back on the market.

2016   Barbie gets a new body.

2016   Mattel loses its licensing deal of Disney dolls to Hasbro.

2017   Comedian Amy Schumer drops out of Sony and Mattel's live action Barbie movie planned to be released in 2018.

ACKNOWLEDGMENTS

NO ONE CAN CLAIM complete, sole ownership over an idea, and the ideas for *You Don't Own Me* are the fruits of many. John Steinbeck once said ideas are like rabbits—put a couple together and you soon have a dozen. Creativity too is contagious in that way. Put a few creative people together and soon inspiration follows. I am incredibly fortunate to be surrounded by friends and colleagues who constantly bubble and buzz with intelligence and vision. The story of the contemporary battles over creativity, ownership, and entrepreneurship needed to be told, and the people who have helped me tell it are too numerous to recount here. Nonetheless, I will try to convey my greatest thanks to at least a few.

My first thanks goes to everyone at Norton who made this book a reality. Amy Cherry, my superb editor at Norton, offered brilliant guidance and creative direction. She is exactly the editor I dreamed of for this book, and it is so much stronger thanks to her. Remy Cawley was diligent and focused and kept me ahead of the deadlines and steps on the road to publication. My agent Lindsay Edgecombe is truly a wonder. She has the patience and faith to realize my vision and bring it to light.

My personal journey from Tel-Aviv, to Paris, to Chicago, to Massachusetts, to Connecticut, and finally to Southern California has helped reveal the significance of places and networks in cultivating a creative environment. *You Don't Own Me* is the product of years of research, practice, and teaching in law, business, and psychology. My writing has benefited greatly from numerous workshops I have given in the United States, Canada, Australia, China, Japan, Korea, Taiwan, Israel, Greece, Italy, Sweden, England, France, and Germany. I am grateful to all the organizers and participants who have provided invaluable input. The University of San Diego boasts an energetic academic community, and my colleagues surround me with support. I can always count on Larry Alexander, Jordan Barry, Laurie Claus, Don Dripps, Miranda Fleischer, Vic Fleischer, Dov Fox, Miranda McGowan, Frank Partnoy, Maimon Schwarzschild, Mila Sohoni, and Lisa Ramsey when I need encouragement during middle-of-the-semester madness. Ted Sichelman and David McGowan help me think about the intricacies of patent and copyright law. Rich Paul is a friend and mentor, and this semester my coteacher, who continues to share with me his wealth of litigation experience. Our Legal Research Center is terrific, and I thank our reference librarians, Judith Lihosit, Michele Knapp, Ruth Levor, Anna Russell, Melissa Abernathy, and especially Jane Larrington, who helped me, often on very tight deadlines, to collect materials and citations. Karin Spidel, my executive assistant, worked tirelessly and with great care in preparing documents and keeping our office suite organized and friendly. My students are smart, driven, and conscientious. Many of them have helped me to compile research for the manuscript, comb through court records, and contact attorneys, executives, and jurors, as well as to read through this book's many drafts. Lauren Titchbourne has a sparkle in her eye, and she doesn't even know yet how witty and insightful she is. She will soon be an amazing lawyer, and I can't wait to see all the good she does in her career. James DeHaan is a gifted writer and deep thinker. He tirelessly read through draft after draft and provided invaluable edits. He too will go on to do great things in the legal world; I am lucky to have had both Lauren and James as students and research assistants. Other research assistants who generously offered their time and insight in preparing this book include Keia Atkinson, Lisa Brevard, Ryan Davis, Karina Grawet, Courtney Jakofsky, Ben Kagel, Shelly Loakes, Beth Loter, and Haylee Saathoff.

Every spring a group of brilliant women law professors rents a house at Stinson Beach, just north of San Francisco, for a writers' collaborative. We eat, drink, and scheme about our next books and articles. Thank you to Rachel Arnow-Richman, Camille Rich, Leticia Saucedo, Michelle Travis, and Deborah Widiss. Who would believe that we do some of our best work exchanging research notes and brainstorming our next steps while sipping wine in a hot tub? I am particularly indebted to our retreat leader, Tristin Green, who sent me elaborate notes about the first iterations of the manuscript and encouraged me every step of the way.

Above all, my family makes everything else meaningful and worthwhile. My parents are, among many other things, writers. My mother, Thalma Lobel, is in truth a character in this book; needless to say, she has had a profound impact on my own story. My father, David Lobel, is a scientist, doctor, inventor, poet, and artist. He taught me that you don't need to choose between science and art, and indeed you must practice both with compassion. My brother Dory is a gifted musician and quite the talker. His life and work in the Los Angeles entertainment industry provided me plenty of windows into this world I now write about. Both Dory and his wife, Keren, a gifted designer, are my go-to advisors when I need to consider anything related to the aesthetic. Together, Dory and Keren are raising my most beloved nieces, Dean and Libby. My uncles Raffi and Rick are also Los Angeles–based fun-loving designers who are always supportive and encouraging.

As always, my writing is in memory of my brother Dani.

Living in sunny La Jolla means that I get to run, hike, swim, handstand by the sea, and bike year-round. It also means I am far away from my first home, Tel-Aviv. My closest friends on both sides of the Atlantic are always there for me, rain or shine. You know who you are.

My ultimate gratitude goes to On Amir—thank you for pushing me to work hard and play hard, and then letting me rest in your arms when the day is over. Our daughters Danielle, Elinor, and Natalie are pure joy and love, and I learn from them every day.

NOTES

Chapter 1: Inspired

1. Eric Clark, *The Real Toy Story: Inside the Ruthless Battle for America's Youngest Consumers* (New York: Free Press, 2007).

Chapter 2: Basura

1. Abraham Lincoln, "Second Lecture on Discoveries and Inventions," in vol. 3 of *The Collected Works of Abraham Lincoln*, ed. Roy P. Basler (New Brunswick, NJ: Rutgers University Press, 1955).
2. Abram Brown, "The Toy Mogul Who Became a Billionaire through His Fight to the Death with Barbie," *Forbes*, November 18, 2013.
3. Mitchell Sunderland, "Meet the Designers behind the Controversial Bratz Dolls," *Broadly*, January 26, 2016.
4. Ibid.

Chapter 3: Sugar Daddy

1. Christopher Palmeri, "Hair-Pulling in The Dollhouse," *BloombergBusinessweek*, May 1, 2005.
2. Ibid.
3. Karmel Melamed, "Bratz Toymaker Isaac Larian Living the American Dream," *Jewish Journal*, December 6, 2007.
4. Abram Brown, "The Toy Mogul Who Became a Billionaire through His Fight to the Death with Barbie," *Forbes*, November 18, 2013.
5. Ibid.
6. Melinda Fulmer, "Bratz Dolls' Maker Plays to Win in Battle with Barbie," *Los Angeles Times*, August 1, 2005.

7. Andrea Chang, "Bratz Doll Maker MGA Wins Court Battle with Mattel," *Los Angeles Times*, April 22, 2011.

8. "Are Kids Exposed to Sex too Soon?" BBC, February 21, 2007. http://www .bbc.co.uk/worldservice/programmes/worldtoday/news/story/2007/ 02/070221_child_sexualisation.shtml.

9. Karmel Melamed, "Bratz Toymaker Isaac Larian Living the American Dream," *Jewish Journal*, December 6, 2007.

10. Chelsea Greenwood, "From the Corner Office: Neil Friedman," *Success*, June 28, 2009.

Chapter 4: Once Upon a Time, Barbie Was a German Hooker

1. Alan D. Abbey, "The Eulogizer: Elliot Handler, Barbie's 'Dad,' and More on Alleged Mobster Francois Abutbul," *Jewish Telegraphic Agency*, August 9, 2011.

2. Richard Warren Lewis, "Jack Ryan and Zsa Zsa: A Millionaire Inventor and his Hungarian Barbie Doll," *People*, July 14, 1975.

3. Louis Marx and Co., Inc., and Greiner & Hausser G.m.b.H. v. Mattel, Inc., No. 341-61-WB, (S.D. Cal. Mar. 24, 1961).

4. Virginia G. Drachman, *Enterprising Women: 250 Years of American Business* (Chapel Hill: University of North Carolina Press, 2002), 143.

5. Sarah Kershaw, "Ruth Handler, Whose Barbie Gave Dolls Curves, Dies at 85," *New York Times*, April 29, 2002.

6. Stacey Handler, *The Body Burden: Living in the Shadow of Barbie* (Cape Canaveral, FL: Blue Note Publications, 2000).

Chapter 5: The Psychologist Who Sold Sex

1. William K. Zinsser, "Barbie is a Million-Dollar Doll," *Saturday Evening Post*, December 12, 1964.

2. Sonya M. Kahlenberg and Richard W. Wrangham, "Sex Differences in Chimpanzees' Use of Sticks as Play Objects Resemble Those of Children," *Current Biology* 20 (2010): R1067–R1068, doi:http:// dx.doi.org/10.1016/j.cub.2010.11.024.

3. Ernst Jentsch, "On the Psychology of the Uncanny (1906)," trans. Roy Sellars, *Angelaki: Journal of the Theoretical Humanities* 2 (1997), 7–16.

4. Masahiro Mori, "The Uncanny Valley," *Energy* 7 (1970): 33–35.

5. Olivia Waring, "This Couple Spent £209K Morphing into the Real-Life Barbie and Ken," *Metro*, October 20, 2015.

6. Christopher Turner, "The Hidden Persuader," *Cabinet* 44: 30–32; Ernest Dichter, *The Psychology of Everyday Living* (New York: Barnes & Noble, 1947).

7. Ernest Dichter, *Getting Motivated: The Secret behind Individual Motivations by the Man Who Was Not Afraid to Ask Why?* (New York: Pergamon, 2013).

8. "How Ernest Dichter, an Acolyte of Sigmund Freud, Revolutionised Marketing," *The Economist*, December 17, 2011.

9. Ibid.

10. Vance Packard, *The Hidden Persuaders* (New York: D. McKay, 1956).

11. Box 163, Ernest Dichter papers (Accession 2407), Hagley Museum and Library, Wilmington, DE 19807.

12. Jaclyn S. Wong and Andrew M. Penner, "Gender and the Returns to Attractiveness," *Research in Social Stratification and Mobility* 44 (2016): 113–123.

13. Rosalind Gill, *Gender and the Media* (Malden, MA: Polity, 2007), 117.

14. Brandy Zadrozny, "Happy Bday Barbie! You're Over," *Daily Beast*, March 8, 2014.

15. Cynthia Robins, *Barbie: Thirty Years of America's Doll* (Chicago: Contemporary Books, 1989), 121.

16. Sarah Kershaw, "Ruth Handler, Whose Barbie Gave Dolls Curves, Dies at 85," *New York Times*, April 29, 2002.

17. Ibid.

18. Emma Rush and Andrea La Nauze, *Corporate Paedophilia: Sexualisation of Children in Australia*, Australia Institute, October 2006, http://www.tai.org.au/documents/downloads/DP90.pdf.

19. Rebecca Haines, "5 Reasons NOT to Buy Barbie for Little Girls (It's Not Just Body Image!)," *Dr. Rebecca Hains* (blog), December 15, 2014, https://rebeccahains.com/2014/12/15/5-reasons-not-to-buy-barbie/.

20. Marci Warhaft-Nadler, *The Body Image Survival Guide for Parents: Helping Toddlers, Tweens, and Teens Thrive* (Lemont, PA: Eifrig, 2012).

Chapter 6: The Coldest Men in the Room

1. Michael Barbaro, "A Makeover of a Romance," *New York Times*, February 9, 2006.

2. Mattel 1999 Quarterly Report: Q-10 Form, filed November 12, 1999, http://www.sec.gov/Archives/edgar/data/63276/0000898430-99-004172-index.html.

3. Benjamin Levisohn, "Mastering the Universe: He-Man and the Rise and Fall of a Billion Dollar Idea by Roger Sweet and Dav," *PopMatters*, September 26, 2005.

4. Kenneth J. Arrow, "Economic Welfare and the Allocation of Resources for Invention," in *The Rate and Direction of Inventive Activity: Economic and Social Factors*, National Bureau of Economic Research (Princeton, NJ: Princeton University Press, 1962), 609, 620.

5. "Executive Profile: Robert A. Eckhert," *Bloomberg*, http://www.bloomberg.com/research/stocks/people/person.asp?personId=437523&ticker=MAT.

6. Mae Anderson, "Mattel CEO 2011 Compensation Even with 2010," *Seattle Times*, March 28, 2012.

7. Adam Bryant, "The Résumé? No, Let's Talk about You," *New York Times*, December 25, 2010.

8. Lisa Bannon, "Mattel's Project Platypus Aims to Inspire Creative Thinking," *Wall Street Journal*, June 6, 2002.

9. Ibid.

10. Mitchell Sunderland, "Meet the Designers behind the Controversial Bratz Dolls," *Broadly*, January 26, 2016.

11. Maureen Tkacik, "Dolled Up: To Lure Older Girls, Mattel Brings in Hip Hop Crowd; It Sees Stalwart Barbie Lose Market Share, So 'Flavas' Will Take on the 'Bratz,'" *Wall Street Journal*, July 18, 2003.

12. Jacqui Goddard, "Barbie Takes On the Bratz for $500M," *Telegraph*, December 10, 2006.

13. Marco della Cava, "New Google Glass Chief Ivy Ross Not Your Typical Techie," *USA Today*, June 24, 2014.

Chapter 7: Fantasy, Meet Parody

1. Mattel, Inc. v. MCA Records, Inc., 296 F.3d 894 (9th Cir. 2002).

2. Jada Toys, Inc. v. Mattel, Inc., 518 F.3d 628 (9th Cir. 2007).

3. Dr. Seuss Enterprises, L.P. v. Penguin Books USA, Inc., 109 F.3d 1394, 1400 (9th Cir. 1997).

4. Lucasfilm Ltd. v. High Frontier, 622 F. Supp. 931 (D.C. 1985).

5. Lucasfilm Ltd. v. Media Market Group, Ltd., 182 F. Supp. 2d 897 (N.D. Cal. 2002).

6. "Star Wars Porn Re-Makers Take the Fight to Lucas," *Guardian*, April 4, 2002.

7. Shaun Spalding, "Let the Wookie Win: A Short History of Star Wars Litigation," *New Media Rights*, July 20, 2010.

8. *MCA Records, Inc.*, 296 F.3d at 898.

9. Denise Gellene, "Barbie Protesters Aren't Playing Around," *Los Angeles Times*, May 10, 1997.

10. *MCA Records, Inc.*, 296 F.3d at 908.

11. Australia Day 2012, "Barbie Girl," *YouTube*, https://www.youtube.com/watch?v=C1cA2lBfYuc.

12. Ibid.

13. Stuart Elliott, "Years Later, Mattel Embraces 'Barbie Girl,'" *New York Times*, August 26, 2009.

14. Mattel, Inc. v. Walking Mountain Productions, 353 F.3d 792, 796 (9th Cir. 2003).

15. "Court Backs Barbie Artist in Doll of a Case," *Fox News*, August 16, 2001,

http://www.foxnews.com/story/2001/08/16/court-backs-barbie-artist-in-doll-case.html.

16. Walking Mountain Productions, 353 F.3d at 796.

17. Dan Collins, " 'Bondage Barbie' Gets a Boost," *CBS News*, November 8, 2002, http://www.cbsnews.com/stories/2002/11/08/national/main528639.shtml.

18. Mattel, Inc. v. Pitt, 229 F. Supp. 2d 315, 319 (S.D.N.Y. 2002).

19. Pitt, 229 F.Supp.2d at 322.

20. Vicki Haddock, "Hansen Sees Bright Future in Alternative 11-inch Generic Dolls," *San Francisco Examiner*, January 16, 1997.

21. P. Aufderheide and P. Jaszi, *Reclaiming Fair Use: How to Put Balance Back in Copyright* (Chicago: University of Chicago Press, 2011).

22. Jennifer Baumgardner and Amy Richards, *Manifesta: Young Women, Feminism, and the Future* (New York: Macmillan, 2000), 198.

23. Tara Kelly, "Sarah Haney, Photographer, Captures the Darker Side of Barbie," *Huffington Post*, March 19, 2012.

24. Sarah Haney, "21 Questions with Sarah Haney," September 12, 2010, http://www.thenervousbreakdown.com/shaney/2010/09/21-questions-with-sarah-haney/.

25. Cynthia Robins, *Barbie: Thirty Years of America's Doll* (Chicago: Contemporary Books, 1989), 32.

Chapter 8: Round I: Titans, Ideas, and Ownership

1. Graham School and Dance Foundation, Inc., et al. v. Martha Graham Center of Contemporary Dance, Inc., et al., Case No. 02-9451, 2004 U.S. App. LEXIS 17452 (2d Cir. Aug. 18, 2004).

2. Sony Corp. of Am v. Universal City Studios, 464 U.S. 417, 477 (1984).

3. Mattel, Inc. v. MGA Entertainment, Inc., 616 F.3d 904, 909 (9th Cir. 2010).

4. Andrew Hargadon and Robert Sutton, "Building an Innovation Factory," *Harvard Business Review* (May–June 2001), 55.

5. Gary Groth, "House of No Shame," *The Comics Journal*, no. 105 (February 1986).

6. Gay Toys, Inc. v. Buddy L Corp., 703 F.2d 970, 973 (6th Cir. 1983).

7. Baby Buddies, Inc. v. Toys R Us, Inc., 611 F.3d 1308, 1316 (11th Cir. 2010).

8. Aliotti v. R. Dakin & Co., 831 F.2d 898, 901 (9th Cir. 1987).

9. Ideal Toy Corp. v. Fab-Lu Ltd., 360 F.2d 1021, 1022 (2d Cir. 1966).

10. Durham Indus., Inc. v. Tomy Corp., 630 F.2d 905, 916-18 (2d Cir. 1980).

11. Mattel, Inc. v. Goldberger Doll Manufacturer Co. 365 F.3d 133, 133–134 (2d Cir. 2004).

12. Feist Publications, Inc. v. Rural Tel. Serv. Co., 499 U.S. 340 (1991).

Chapter 9: Taming Barbie: Starring Judge Alex Kozinski as Speechzilla

1. Scott Glover, "9th Circuit's Chief Judge Posted Sexually Explicit Matter on His Website," *Los Angeles Times,* June 11, 2008.

2. Alex Kozinski, "Trademarks Unplugged," *New York University Law Review* 68 (October 1993): 975.

3. White v. Samsung Electronics America, Inc., 989 F.2d 1512, 1519 (9th Cir. 1993).

4. *White,* 989 F.2d at 1513.

5. Google Inc., At-Will Employment, Confidential Information, Invention Assignment and Arbitration Agreement, on file with author, effective date March 2014, California Version.

6. Mattel, Inc. v. MGA Entertainment, Inc., 616 F.3d 904, 913 (9th Cir. 2010).

7. *Id.* at 911 (citing Dan Dobbs, Dobbs Law of Remedies: Damages-Equity-Restitution § 6.6(3) (2d ed. 1993).

8. Belair v. MGA Entertainment, Inc., 831 F. Supp. 2d 687, 690 (S.D.N.Y. 2011).

Chapter 10: Round 2: The Playground Bullies

1. Complaint at 2, MGA Entertainment, Inc. v. Mattel, Inc., No. BC532708 (Cal. Super. Ct. Jan. 13, 2014).

2. Jury Trial Proceedings, Day 3, Vol. 2, Testimony of Sal Villasenor, at 81, Mattel, Inc. v. MGA Entertainment, Inc., No. 04-9049 (C.D. Cal. Jan. 18, 2011).

3. MGA Entertainment, Inc.'s Reply to Fourth Amended Answer and Counterclaims at 4, Carter Bryant v. Mattel, Inc., No. 04-0949 (C.D. Cal. Aug. 16, 2010).

4. Answering Brief for Review, Mattel, Inc. v. MGA Entertainment, Inc. at 9, No. 11-56357 (9th Cir. Aug. 12, 2011).

5. Jury Trial Proceedings, Day 37, Vol. 2 at 51, Mattel, Inc. v. MGA Entertainment, Inc., No. 04- 09049 (C.D. Cal. Mar. 22, 2011).

6. "FBI Announces Economic Espionage Awareness Campaign," *FBI,* July 23, 2015, https://www.fbi.gov/news/pressrel/press-releases/fbi-announces-economic-espionage-awareness-campaign.

7. Rochelle Dreyfuss and Orly Lobel, "Economic Espionage as Reality or Rhetoric: Equating Trade Secrecy with National Security," *Lewis & Clark Law Review* 20, no. 2 (2016): 419.

8. Jury Trial Proceedings, Day, 37, Vol. 1, Testimony of Matthew Turetzky, at 30, Mattel, Inc. v. MGA Entertainment, Inc., No. 04-9049 (C.D. Cal. Mar. 22, 2011).

9. Jury Trial Proceedings, Day, 42, Vol. 1, Testimony of Jill Thomas, at 44, Mattel, Inc. v. MGA Entertainment, Inc., No. 04-9049 (C.D. Cal. Mar. 30, 2011).

10. Jury Trial Proceedings, Day 37, Vol. 2, Testimony of Sal Villasenor, at 72, Mattel, Inc. v. MGA Entertainment, Inc., No. 04-9049 (C.D. Cal. Mar. 22, 2011).

11. *Id*. at 118–119.

12. Jury Trial Proceedings, Day, 37, Vol. 1, Testimony of Matthew Turetzky, at 160, Mattel, Inc. v. MGA Entertainment, Inc., No. 04-9049 (C.D. Cal. Mar. 22, 2011).

13. Civil Complaint for Trade Secret Misappropriation, MGA Entertainment, Inc. v. Mattel, Inc., BC532708 (Cal. Super. Ct. January 13, 2014), Court Docket.

14. Jury Trial Proceedings, Day, 42, Vol. 1, Testimony of Jill Thomas, at 44, Mattel, Inc. v. MGA Entertainment, Inc., No. 04-9049 (C.D. Cal. Mar. 30, 2011).

15. Jury Trial Proceedings, Day 41, Vol. 2, Testimony of Robert Normile, at 76, Mattel, Inc. v. MGA Entertainment, Inc., No. 04-9049 (C.D. Cal. Mar. 29, 2011).

16. Julian E. Barnes, "P.&G. Said to Agree to Pay Unilever $10 Million in Spying Case," *New York Times*, September 7, 2001.

17. MGA Parties' Motion for Exemplary Damages and Fees, at 1, Bryant v. Mattel, Inc., No. 04-9049 (C.D. Cal. May 5, 2011).

18. Yuval Feldman and Orly Lobel, "Whistleblowers and Social Enforcement," in *Explaining Compliance: Business Responses to Regulation*, ed. C. Parker and V. Lehmann Nielsen (Northampton, MA: Edward Elgar, 2011); Yuval Feldman and Orly Lobel, "The Incentives Matrix: A Study of the Comparative Effectiveness of Monetary Rewards as Compliance Systems," *Texas Law Review* 88, no. 6 (2010): 1151–1212; Yuval Feldman and Orly Lobel, "Behavioral Versus Institutional Antecedents of Decentralized Enforcement: An Experimental Approach," *Regulation & Governance* 2, no. 2 (2008): 165–192.

19. Abigail Goldman, "Ex-Executive to Receive $6.9 Million from Mattel," *Los Angeles Times*, December 29, 2005.

20. Complaint at 28-29, MGA Entertainment, Inc. v. Mattel, Inc., No. 05-02727 (C.D. Cal. 2005).

21. Margaret Talbot, "Little Hotties: Barbie's New Rivals," *The New Yorker*, December 5, 2006.

22. Bridget Freeland, "Barbie v Bratz War Goes Nuclear," *Courthouse News Service*, February 7, 2011, http://www.courthousenews.com/2011/02/07/33951.htm.

23. Michael Barbaro, "A Makeover of a Romance," *New York Times*, February 9, 2006.

Chapter 11: The Jury Deliberation Room That Looked Like a Toys "R" Us

1. Complaint at 14, MGA Entertainment, Inc. v. Mattel, Inc., No. 11-01063 (C.D. Cal. Feb. 3, 2011).

2. Jonathan Stempel and Dan Levine, "Mattel Accused in Bratz Battle of Spying on Rivals," *Reuters*, August 17, 2010.

3. Edvard Pettersson, "Mattel Asks Appeals Court to Toss $310 Million MGA Loss," *Bloomberg*, February 29, 2012.

4. Abram Brown, "The Toy Mogul Who Became a Billionaire through His Fight to the Death with Barbie," *Forbes*, November 18, 2013.

5. Associated Press, "Judges Cut Back Damages Owed by Mattel in Doll Case," *New York Times*, January 24, 2013.

6. William Alden, "Former Mattel Chief Robert Eckert Joins Friedman Fleischer & Lowe," *New York Times*, September 25, 2014.

7. "Executive Profile: Bryan G. Stockton," *Bloomberg*, http://www .bloomberg.com/research/stocks/people/person.asp?personId=77997 83&ticker=MAT.

8. Phil Wahba, "So Much for Mattel Ex-CEO Resigning. He Was Fired," *Fortune*, April 9, 2015.

9. Mattel 2015 Quarterly Report: Q-10 Form, filed July 28, 2015, https:// www.sec.gov/Archives/edgar/data/63276/000162828016020388/ mat9301610-q.htm.

10. "Mattel Names Sinclair as Chief Executive Officer," *Mattel*, April 2, 2015, http://news.mattel.com/news/mattel-names-christopher-sinclair -as-chief-executive-officer.

11. For photos, see "See All the New Barbies from Curvy to Tall and Petite," *Time*, January 28, 2016.

12. Mattel, http://shop.mattel.com/family/index.jsp?categoryId=45063936.

13. Hannah Ellis-Peterson, "Barbie Finally Becomes a Real Woman—with a More Realistic Figure," *Guardian*, January 28, 2016.

14. Allie Townsend, "Barbie vs. Bratz: It's a Doll-Eat-Doll World," *Time*, April 22, 2011.

15. Clare O'Connor, "Barbie, Beware? Bratz Back on Shelves amid Billion-Dollar Mattel Battle," *Forbes*, July 21, 2015.

Epilogue: Innovation Beyond Toyland

1. *Kirkbi AG v. Ritvik Holdings Inc.*, 2005 SCC 65, paras. 61, 69 (Nov. 17, 2005).

2. On Amir and Orly Lobel, "How Noncompetes Stifle Performance," *Harvard Business Review* (January–February 2014): 26.

INDEX